TEACHING JEWISH LIFE CYCLE

TRADITIONS AND ACTIVITIES

BARBARA BINDER KADDEN
AND BRUCE KADDEN

D1716291

A.R.E. Publishing, Inc.
Denver, Colorado

Published by:
A.R.E. Publishing, Inc.
Denver, Colorado

Library of Congress Catalog Number 97-71022
ISBN 0-86705-040-3

Printed in the United States of America
10   9   8   7   6   5   4   3   2   1

DEDICATION

To those whose life cycle observances we have been privileged to share.

ACKNOWLEDGEMENTS

"Make for yourself a teacher, acquire for yourself a friend."
(*Pirke Avot* 1:6)

We would like to thank these friends and teachers who have supported us:

Randee Freedman of Sounds Write Productions, Inc., for her suggestions of
appropriate Jewish music.

Rabbi Richard Litvak, for inspiring thoughts and warm friendship.

Rabbi Jeffrey K. Salkin, Rabbi Patricia Karlin-Neumann, Stan Beiner, and
Rabbi Raymond A. Zwerin, for contributing material for the book.

Our children, Alana and Micah, for their understanding and love.

Audrey Friedman Marcus and Rabbi Raymond A. Zwerin of A.R.E. Publishing, Inc.,
for their patience, encouragement, and constructive comments which have
helped us immeasurably.

CONTENTS

FOREWORD

by Rabbi Jeffrey K. Salkin

I HAVE TWO CALENDARS ON MY DESK. THE first one is Day Timers, a thick, loose-leaf volume that details my existence into the foreseeable future. The second, sitting next to its leather-bound colleague, is a Jewish calendar, detailing Hebrew dates, dates of festivals, candle lighting times, and Torah portions. I travel back and forth between those two calendars. One tells me about my life, and the other tells me how to live that life — the story and meaning that makes the days that are detailed in Day Timers into days of value and substance.

Truth be told, Judaism also has two calendars — the *public* and the personal. The public Jewish calendar is the festival cycle. It chronicles the story of the Jewish people, our encounter with God, with nature, with history, and with ourselves. It contains moments of joy, of introspection, of gratitude, of serious contemplation of the Jewish past and future, of anger, and of sorrow. We celebrate those moments both in the privacy of our homes and in the public realm of the synagogue and the community.

The *private* Jewish calendar is the life cycle — birth, maturity, marriage, and death. We celebrate those moments in the public realm and in the private realm — both in family contexts and with other Jews in community (which deepens and enriches and contextualizes those celebrations).

But note: There has been an interesting and significant shift in the way that Jews live their lives. With the exception of Rosh HaShanah and Yom Kippur (which remind us of the patterns of life and our own fragility), the spirituality of most modern Jews has usually shifted from the festival calendar to the life cycle — from the public to the private.

When Jews tell the stories of their lives, when they talk about the moments of holiness and transcendence, the stories they tell, invariably, are of *Brit Milah,* baby namings, Bar and Bat Mitzvah celebrations, weddings, and funerals. Those are the times when we awaken from our spiritual slumber and realize that there is a God in the world.

There are all sorts of reasons why this has happened. We live in a very self-oriented time. People tend to think less in terms of group and more in terms of self. We live in a time that has seen the triumph of individualism. Sometimes, the only community that we know well is our family. The synagogue may be a public space, with publicly owned ritual items such as prayer books and *tallitot* and *yarmulkes,* but the meanings that we bring to it are often very private — and often take precedence over the public meanings.

I have always believed that the reclamation of the life cycle is a suitable spiritual project for modern Jews. At their best, when the poetry works and the magic does its stuff, life cycle celebrations keep Jews connected to the Jews people, to God, and to Torah. There are so many moments when we might feel personally adrift — when a new baby enters our lives, when we struggle with the meaning of adolescence, when we are going from being a non-Jew to being a Jew, when we are going from single existence to married existence, when we look into the abyss and confront the meaning of death. In each of those cases, Judaism and its wisdom is there for us, with all its potential anchoring and healing power.

Ideally, how does life cycle do its magic? *By helping us feel the unseen presences.* We feel the presences of our beloved departed (there is no life cycle ceremony without those presences). But there are historical and even *mythical* presences as well. And those presences have much potential power.

At a *Brit Milah* ceremony, the *mohel* recites the words that God spoke to Abraham: *"Hithalaych Lifanai Veheyay Tamim"* (Walk before Me and be perfect). Pointing to an empty chair, the *mohel* says, *"Zeh Kisay Shel Eliyahu HaNavi"* (This is the chair of Elijah, the prophet). Abraham is "there" as the first covenanted Jew. Elijah is "there" to ensure that the covenant lives. Abraham is the first Jew. Elijah, the harbinger of the Messiah, is the last Jew. Who knows? The newborn infant may be the Messiah, or may help usher in the Messianic Age. What potential this child has!

The same thing is true at Bar and Bat Mitzvah. The no-longer child/newly emerging adult is not alone. Yes, he/she is surrounded by clergy and friends and family. But in a powerful sense, every Jew who has ever lived and will ever live is there as well. The covenant is re-affirmed. The sanctuary may be *visibly* half full. It is *invisibly* very full. That's what parents understand as well: *I am not the last Jew in the world.*

The same thing is true at conversion. At that moment, the new Jew feels the presence of Abraham, the first Jew and the first convert; and Ruth, the classic Jew-by-Choice; and all the departed and living teachers of our tradition.

The same thing is true at the wedding. The Jewish wedding is more than two people celebrating and confirming their love. it is the reprise of the covenant between God and Israel. The bride and groom are no longer themselves. The seven wedding blessings urge the couple to imagine themselves as Adam and Eve, back in the Garden of Eden.

And the same thing is true at death. The service ends with the community saying to the mourners: *"HaMakom Y'nachaym Etchem B'toch Sh'ar Avaylay Tzion ViYerushalayim"* (May God comfort you among those who are mourners for Zion and Jerusalem). The message is clear: You are not alone. The entire Jewish people is with you.

I heartily welcome you to this wonderful volume. Written by my two old friends, Barbara and Bruce Kadden, it will open you and your students to the world of the Jewish life cycle. This book not only contains material about ancient life cycle rituals (*Brit Milah* is, in fact, the oldest ritual in the Western world!), but modern rituals as well. As the Jewish people grows and evolves, we sense that there are all sorts of moments — getting a driver's licence, aging, etc. — that need sacred reminders, that could use the ancient and new poetry of our experience to bring meaning to our lives. And there are other, sadder times in life which have always had rituals associated with them, e.g., divorce. Those rituals can be reconsidered, redrawn, re-imagined — and they, too, can have their healing power.

May God bless all your moments of passage with holiness, with depth, and with joy.

Rabbi Jeffrey K. Salkin is the Senior Rabbi of The Community Synagogue in Port Washington, New York; the Co-chair of the UAHC Commission on Reform Jewish Outreach; and the author of *Putting God on the Guest List: How to Reclaim the Spiritual Meaning of Your Child's Bar or Bat Mitzvah* (Jewish Lights Publishing).

INTRODUCTION

H E [RABBI JUDAH BEN TEMA] USED TO say: At five years of age [one begins to study] Scripture. At ten years of age [one begins to study] Mishnah. At thirteen years of age [one is ready to observe] the *mitzvot*. At fifteen years of age [one begins to study] Talmud. At eighteen years of age [one is ready] for marriage. At twenty years of age [one is ready] to pursue [a livelihood]. At thirty years of age [one is ready] for strength. At forty years of age [one is ready] for understanding. At fifty years of age [one is ready to give] advice. At sixty years of age [one is ready] for old age. At seventy years of age [one reaches] fullness of age. At eighty years of age [one reaches] strong old age. At ninety years of age [one becomes] bent. At 100 years of age it is as if one had died and left the world.

(*Pirke Avot* 5:24)

While most contemporary Jews might challenge many of Rabbi Judah's claims about what activity was appropriate at a particular age, the fact that this second century scholar laid out such a detailed view of the Jewish life cycle indicates just how deep its roots go. Rituals have been an important part of Jewish life from our beginnings as a people in the wilderness and continued through the centuries to enhance the life of the people. Indeed, even as we enter upon the twenty-first century, we still resonate to many of the same insights and still attempt to enhance life cycle events by creating rituals that respond to significant transitions from birth to death.

Life cycle rituals have a mystique that transcends the life passages they celebrate or commemorate. They connect us across space and time to generations of the Jewish people who have come before us, they connect us to the One Who enables us to live from age to age, and they connect us to our inmost self.

Debra Orenstein has noted that "Traditional religious ritual was designed, and continues, to meet a variety of needs that relate to life passages: The need for the individual to be acknowledged by community, the need for the community/tribe to read itself into the passages of each member, the need for binding, which serves both individual and community, the need to (re-) enact dramatically the great stories and messages of the tradition, for the sake of individuals and of the tradition" (*Lifecycles: Jewish Women on Life Passages & Personal Milestones*, Vol. 1, p. xx).

But the life cycle is much more than the rituals that have developed to celebrate and observe birth, Bar/Bat Mitzvah, Conversion, marriage, divorce, death, and other significant moments. The life cycle is also the more subtle, but no less important, change that transpires as we live and grow, experience life, and learn from it. Even when we do not undergo elaborate rituals, we still grow older and make the transition from childhood to adolescence and from adolescence to adulthood. Throughout our life, we change physically, emotionally, and spiritually. Acknowledgment of such changes lies at the core of many of our life cycle rituals.

Teaching Jewish Life Cycle: Traditions and Activities addresses both the important rituals we experience and the changes that occur as we grow older. The reader will find herein significant material about every stage of the life cycle. Each chapter begins with a detailed Overview featuring the issues, rituals, and concerns which are addressed by Jewish tradition. This background material will help the teacher prepare a lesson that reflects Jewish tradition and will prepare the teacher to answer students' questions.

Sources from the Tradition consists of a variety of quotations which shed important insights on the topic. Many of these are incorporated into the activities for that chapter. Teachers may choose to create posters of the sayings to display in the classroom.

Activities round out each chapter. These activities are divided into the following categories:

Primary (Grades K-3)

Intermediate (Grades 4-6)

Secondary (Grades 7-12)

Hebrew

Adult

Family

All-School

While the activities have been placed in what the authors felt to be the most appropriate category, creative teachers will often adapt activities to another age group or setting. Family activities are sometimes designed for families with children of all ages and sometimes for a particular age group of children and their parents.

Each activity is designed so that it may be done independent of any other activity or it may be combined with other activities as part of a unit which covers a particular life cycle ritual or the entire life cycle.

Each chapter also contains a Glossary of relevant terms for quick reference. At the end of every chapter is list of resources of books, articles, and audiovisual material referred to in the chapter and pertinent to the topic. The books and magazines are divided between those primarily for the teacher/adult learner and those appropriate for student use.

At the end of the book are: an annotated Bibliography of all books and audiovisual materials cited and a list of addresses for obtaining audiovisual material, an Appendix which contains three dramatic presentations cited in the text, and an Appendix which contains two articles about ritual in Jewish life. Resources in the Bibliography which cover the entire life cycle, and which therefore would be especially useful for the teacher, are marked with an asterisk.

USING THIS BOOK

Teaching Jewish Life Cycle may be used in virtually every Jewish educational setting. Religious School teachers will be able to select activities appropriate for their curriculum or design a life cycle unit of their own. Day School teachers will find many appropriate activities to enhance their lessons.

Hebrew teachers looking for something different will discover creative ways to teach Hebrew words, phrases, and blessings related to the life cycle. Family educators, adults education teachers, principals responsible for all-school programs, camp counselors, and unit heads will all find a variety of activities appropriate to their settings.

Anyone who wants a better understanding of the Jewish life cycle and how to teach it will greatly benefit from reading and using this book.

Our schools always teach the Jewish holidays, and usually also teach rituals related to the home, such as *kashrut* (dietary laws) and *mezuzah*. Less often do we focus on the rituals of the life cycle even though they are as important a part of Jewish life as any other rituals. Our students need to be introduced to these rituals and to the important issues that relate to each stage of the life cycle.

Due in part to changes in Jewish communities — especially the privatization of so many transitional events — students are exposed to fewer of these celebrations and observances than might have been the case in previous generations. They generally do not have the opportunity to attend *Brit Milah* celebrations or weddings, which once were open to and celebrated by the entire community. They rarely would have occasion to attend a funeral. And while they probably do attend the B'nai Mitzvah of their contemporaries, such participations are usually limited to early adolescence. Even if they are fortunate enough to attend life cycle ceremonies, they often do not come away with an understanding of the background and meaning of many of the rituals. Fostering such understanding becomes the challenge of teachers of the life cycle.

Through the background material and activities in this book, students will come to understand the significance of these rituals and observances. They will then be able to anticipate and incorporate them into their lives, and find meaning and connectedness through their usage.

STRATEGIES FOR LIFE CYCLE CURRICULA

Teachers who are faced with the challenge of designing a life cycle curriculum over the course of a number of weeks or a year might consider one of the following strategies to tie the lessons together:

1. Create a life cycle line around your classroom, using a simple clothes line. As you study each life cycle event, attach a symbol of the ritual to the line with a clothes pin.
2. Invent a family that you will follow as they experience the life cycle. Consider beginning with a young couple who falls in love and gets married, and then experiences the birth of children and the rituals pertaining to birth, adolescence, etc. As the couple ages, they face the challenges of adulthood, grandparenthood, and eventually death.

   Depending on the ages of the students, you might use dolls for family members or, select students to role play different family members on a rotating basis or make life-sized stuffed figures.
3. Create a mural depicting each stage of the life cycle to help put each activity into the context of the whole.
4. Play *The Jewish Life Cycle Game* (A.R.E. Publishing). This game is a good introduction for students, enabling them to understand the concept of the life cycle and the relationship of the various Jewish rituals to each stage of life.

   The teacher should also be aware of opportunities for students to attend or participate in life cycle rituals in the congregation or community. Ask Rabbis and/or Cantors to keep you informed as to ceremonies that will be public observances or as to families who may be willing to include a class in their *simchah*.

Teaching about the life cycle requires a special sensitivity on the part of the teacher. Many of the issues relating to the life cycle can be emotionally charged. If, for example, a student has recently had a death in the family, that student might be especially affected by a lesson pertaining to death or mourning.

Similarly, for children whose parents are divorced or separated, a unit about divorce or marriage (e.g., asking students to bring in their parents' wedding album) might be painful. It is therefore especially important that the teacher be aware of any situations in the personal lives of the students which might affect their reaction to the material.

It might be appropriate to write a letter to the parents before beginning to teach about the life cycle, outlining the planned curriculum and asking them to share with you any concerns they might have.

Emotions sometimes run high with regard to such life cycle topics as intermarriage, divorce, and death. It is important that the teacher be aware of the institutional position on these and other issues, if any. Teachers should consider discussing these issues with the Rabbi or Director of Education to clarify any uncertainties or concerns prior to teaching about any of these issues.

Despite these concerns, teaching about the Jewish life cycle should be a rewarding experience for both the teacher and the students. As students study the life cycle, the rituals and transitions, we hope they will identify how these experiences can play a role in their lives and that they will discover the beauty and meaning in Jewish life.

CHAPTER ONE
BEGINNINGS
BIRTH • BRIT MILAH • NAMING

OVERVIEW

THE BIRTH OF A CHILD IS WELCOMED WITH great joy and celebration in Judaism. Not only is childbirth recognized as a participation in the ongoing process of creation, but also as a fulfillment of the first *mitzvah* in the Torah, to "be fruitful and multiply" (Genesis 1:28). This *mitzvah,* according to tradition, is only incumbent on the male, and is fulfilled when one has fathered two children, at least one of whom is male.

The traditional ceremonies for the birth of a child include *Brit Milah,* the covenant of circumcision; naming; and *Pidyon HaBen,* the redemption of the firstborn. In recent years, a variety of other rituals have been developed to recognize and sanctify the beginning of life.

Pregnancy and Childbirth

Traditional Judaism developed virtually no rituals for the process of childbirth. Anita Diamant notes that "Judaism, which sanctifies so many of life's passages with *brachot* (blessings) and *mitzvot* (sacred obligations) is comparatively silent about the awe-inspiring experiences of conception, pregnancy, and birth" (*The New Jewish Baby Book,* p. 3).

Rabbi Debra Orenstein, in her book *Lifecycles: Jewish Women on Life Passages & Personal Milestones,* points out that "the failure to take ritual notice of childbirth seems especially incongruous, given the traditional Jewish emphasis on family, procreation, teaching the next generation, and national/religious continuity" (p. 1). She suggests two reasons for the lack of childbirth rituals: (1) the sensitivity of Jewish tradition toward the precariousness of mother and baby following childbirth.

This sensitivity is reflected in the customs of not naming a boy until his circumcision and not buying any item for the baby until after birth; and (2) the fact that childbirth "is women's domain at its most mysterious, powerful, and frightening" (p. 2).

In recent years, however, a variety of Jewish rituals have been created and developed for virtually every significant stage of the childbirth process, reflecting the desire to mark all important life cycle moments with appropriate prayers and rituals. These include:

Acknowledging the decision to become parents by going to the *mikvah* (ritual bath) (Diamant, pp. 4-5).

Petitionary prayers for conception.

Prayers for learning one is pregnant (*On the Doorposts of Your House,* Chaim Stern, ed., pp. 105-108).

Prayers said during pregnancy (Diamant, p. 7; Stern, p. 108).

Rosh Chodesh rituals for pregnancy (*Miriam's Well: Rituals for Jewish Women Around the Year,* Penina Adelman, pp. 55-56).

Brachot to be said at birth, such as the *"Shehecheyanu"* and *"HaTov V'haMaytiv"* (the One who is good and Who makes good).

A prayer to be said at a Caesarean birth (Orenstein, pp. 20-21).

A prayer for the parents of babies with disabilities (Orenstein, pp. 22-24).

A prayer to be said when holding one's child for the first time (Diamant, p. 11).

A prayer for bringing a child home for the first time (Stern, p. 110).

A post partum celebration based on a Yemenite custom called *al-wafaa* ("*Al Wafaa: A Post-Partum Celebration,*" Dina Dahbany-Miraglia, in *Ceremonies Sampler,* Elizabeth Resnick Levine, ed., pp. 9-11).

An afterbirth ritual for planting the placenta ("New Afterbirth Ritual Takes Root in Berkeley," Eve Kessler Jacobson, in *Forward,* October 22, 1993, p. 12).

A Jewish weaning ritual (Orenstein, pp. 272-275).

New rituals have also been developed for women who experience difficulty conceiving a child (Orenstein, pp. 44-45) and for women and couples who are not able to have children and must come to terms with their infertility (Orenstein, pp. 41-44; "Prayers on Infertility," Rabbi Nina Beth Cardin, unpublished).

In addition, ceremonies have been created to help expectant parents grieve following a miscarriage, stillbirth, or abortion. Traditionally, there was no mourning required for a baby who died before it was 30 days old. At a time of high infant mortality, this practice served to reduce communal involvement in mourning. However, in recent years, the need to grieve over such losses has been recognized and appropriate rituals, some based on traditional Jewish mourning customs, have been developed.

Sh'lom Zachar

Sh'lom Zachar, the well-being of the son, is a traditional ritual observed on the first *erev* Shabbat following birth. (In recent years, some families have observed a similar ceremony for girls called *Sh'lom N'kayvah.*)

According to Anita Diamant, "Guests assembled in the new baby's home to recite psalms, sing songs, and discuss Torah. Little children were invited to recite the *Shema . . . near* the cradle" (p. 210).

Guests would often bring gifts of amulets to ward off evil spirits. Lilith, who according to tradition was Adam's first wife and who is attracted to infants, was especially worrisome. Yemenite Jews, for example, would hang a *hamsikah,* an amulet shaped like outstretched hands, over the crib to protect the child. It often contained Psalm 121, because of the verse, "The sun will not strike you by day, nor the moon by night" (Psalm 121:6). Another Yemenite custom was to place sweets under the bed in order to occupy the evil spirits who would eat them (*The Second Jewish Catalog,* Sharon Strassfeld and Michael Strassfeld, eds., p. 15).

Other customs which were believed to protect the child include:

Hanging garlic in the baby's room.

Tying a red thread onto the crib.

Undoing all knots on the mother's clothes and keeping doors and windows of the house open.

Drawing a circle with chalk around the bed.

Sounding the shofar (since demons are driven away by loud noises).

The evening before a boy's *Brit Milah* was considered a night of particular danger from Lilith or other demons. It was therefore customary among some to hold a *Layl Shimurim* or *Vach Nacht* (Yiddish), a Night of Watching. A *minyan* would often be held, with the participants standing around the crib. A similar observance in the Sephardic community is called *Zocher HaBrit,* "Remembering the Covenant." It sometimes includes a festive meal with singing and dancing.

Brit Milah

Circumcision is not unique to the Jewish people. However, though common in the ancient Near East, dating back to the earliest days of civilization, it was not universally practiced.

Some ancient peoples performed circumcision on adolescents, as a puberty rite marking the passage from childhood to adulthood. Jews perform the rite on infants, interpreting it as a symbol of the covenant between God and the Jewish people. According to Stanley Gevirtz, "Making the removal of the foreskin an indispensable component of a covenant between deity and man, rather than merely an elimination of a social stigma or a superstitious taboo, imbued it with a religious significance it seems never to have had before" ("Circumcision in the Biblical Period," in *Berit Mila in the Reform Context,* Lewis M. Barth, ed., p. 93).

Brit Milah, the covenant of circumcision, is the first life cycle ritual mentioned in the Torah. God, in establishing the covenant with Abraham, commands that every male child be circumcised. "You shall circumcise the flesh of your foreskin, and that shall be the sign of the covenant between Me and you" (Genesis 17:11). God further specifies that all males (including slaves who are part of the household) be circumcised at the age of eight days.

Abraham, who was already 99 years old, circumcised himself, his son Ishmael, and every male of his household in response to God's command. Later, when Abraham and Sarah's son Isaac is born, Abraham circumcises him on the eighth day (Genesis 21:4).

Circumcision plays a significant role in a number of biblical stories. When Shechem rapes Dinah, and then wants to marry her, Jacob's sons insist that only after Shechem and his people are circumcised can marriages to take place between the two peoples (Genesis 34:15-17). However, three days after Shechem and the other males are circumcised, Simeon and Levi, two of Dinah's brothers, kill them all in revenge for Shechem's act.

When Moses is returning to Egypt from Midian, God seeks to kill him, apparently for failing to circumcise his son (Exodus 4:24-26). Only when Moses' wife, Zipporah, performs the circumcision, is Moses spared.

The Torah states that a resident alien may eat of the Passover offering only if he and all males of his household are circumcised. Slaves belonging to Israelites must also be circumcised before partaking of the Pascal lamb. Those who are uncircumcised are proscribed from eating the offering (Exodus 12:43-48).

While circumcision has been a significant act throughout Jewish history, it has not been practiced at all times. None of the Jews born in the wilderness of Sinai were circumcised until Joshua was commanded to circumcise them before entering the land of Israel (Joshua 5:5-8).

Circumcision was also apparently abandoned in the Northern Kingdom of Israel during the reign of King Ahab and his Phoenician wife Jezebel (I Kings 19:14). It is said to have been reinstated by the prophets of the time, Elijah and Elisha.

As Hellenism, which eschewed circumcision, spread throughout the Middle East, many Jews abandoned the practice (Jubilees 15:33-34). Some Jews, who wanted to participate nude in Greek athletic events, underwent surgery in order to restore their foreskin.

The first ruler to prohibit circumcision was Antiochus IV, the Syrian ruler at the time of the Chanukah story. Some women, nevertheless, had their sons circumcised, often at the cost of the lives of both mother and child (II Maccabees 6:10).

Later, under Roman rule, Hadrian prohibited circumcision. In more recent times, the practice was largely abandoned by Jews in the Soviet Union.

Reform Judaism's attitude toward *Brit Milah* has varied. In 1842, lay leaders in Frankfurt, Germany claimed that circumcision was not a required religious act. Rabbinic leaders meeting in Germany in 1844, 1845, and 1846 considered the issue too controversial to deal with. Only in 1871 were the German Rabbis able to pass a resolution which both endorsed "the highly important meaningfulness of circumcision" and declared that "a boy born to a Jewish mother, and for whatever reason not circumcised, is . . . to be regarded as a Jew and treated as such in all matters of ritual practice" ("Berit Mila Within the History of the Reform Movement," Michael A. Meyer, in Barth, p. 146). A similar resolution had been passed by American Reform Rabbis two years earlier.

Dr. Michael Meyer sums up Reform Judaism's attitude toward circumcision and *Brit Milah* thusly: "While it was never officially rejected by the Movement, a few individual Reformers were ready to abandon it. Others found it problematic either as such or in the way in which it was carried out. Even though it continued to be generally practiced as an operation, it lost its meaningfulness as a religious rite. Only recently have Reform Jews sought to make circumcision once more into *berit mila*" (Meyer, in Barth, p. 142).

Brit Milah is traditionally performed at home on the morning of the eighth day — the day of birth counting as the first day. Even if the eighth day falls on Shabbat or any other holiday, the circumcision is performed. The only justification for delaying the procedure is concern for the health of the child.

According to tradition, a father is responsible for circumcising his son. However, it is common practice for the father to delegate a *mohel* to act for him. A *mohel* (in Yiddish pronounced *moyel*) is a ritual circumciser who is trained in the medical procedure and is familiar with the Jewish ritual. In the traditional community, a mohel must be *"Shomer Shabbat"* and ritually observant in all respects. In the liberal community, a physician may be called upon to do the circumcision while a Rabbi conducts the ritual. Recently, the Reform movement has instituted a program for the training of *mohelim* and *mohelot*.

The *Brit Milah* ceremony includes a welcome, specific *brachot* and statements, the circumcision, and the naming of the child. The ceremony is followed by a *Seudat Mitzvah*, a festive meal celebrating the *mitzvah*.

Three friends or relatives play specific roles in the ritual. The *kvatter* (godfather) and *kvatterin* (godmother) bring the child into the room where the circumcision will take place. The *sandak*, usually one of the child's grandfathers, holds the child during the circumcision on a pillow placed on a table or on his lap.

During the ceremony, the *sandak* will often sit in a special chair, called the *Kisay Eliyahu*, the chair of Elijah. Elijah is considered the guardian of the child during and after the circumcision, and is spiritually present at the *Brit Milah* much as he is said to be present at the Passover *Seder*. Since it is thought that Elijah will ultimately announce the crowning of a messiah or anointed one to redeem humankind, he is symbolically present at every *Brit Milah* as if to see if this child will be the awaited one.

When the baby is brought into the room by the *kvatter* and *kvatterin*, all present rise and welcome him with the phrase *"Baruch HaBa"* (Blessed be he who comes). The numeric value of the word *HaBa* is eight. Therefore, the phrase might be translated "Blessed be the eight-day-old."

Next, the father recites the formula which begins *"Hineni Muchan Um'zuman* — I am ready to fulfill the *mitzvah* of circumcising my son, as God commanded in the Torah: 'Every male throughout your generation shall be circumcised at the age of eight days'" (Genesis 17:12). In some communities, both parents bring their son into the covenant by reciting the blessing together.

The *mohel* then recites the blessing for circumcision and performs the act:

בָּרוּךְ אַתָּה יְיָ אֱלֹהֵינוּ מֶלֶךְ הָעוֹלָם,
אֲשֶׁר קִדְּשָׁנוּ בְּמִצְוֹתָיו וְצִוָּנוּ עַל הַמִּילָה.

Baruch Atah Adonai Elohaynu Melech HaOlam,
Asher Kidshanu B'mitzvotav V'tzivanu al HaMilah.

Blessed are You, Adonai our God, Sovereign of the universe, Who has made us holy with *mitzvot* and commanded us concerning circumcision.

The father (or both parents) then recites the following *brachah*, entering the child into the covenant:

בָּרוּךְ אַתָּה יְיָ אֱלֹהֵינוּ מֶלֶךְ הָעוֹלָם, אֲשֶׁר קִדְּשָׁנוּ
בְּמִצְוֹתָיו וְצִוָּנוּ לְהַכְנִיסוֹ בִּבְרִיתוֹ שֶׁל אַבְרָהָם אָבִינוּ.

Baruch Atah Adonai Elohaynu Melech HaOlam
Asher Kidshanu B'mitzvotav V'tzivanu L'hachneeso
Bivreeto Shel Avraham Avinu.

Blessed are you, Adonai our God, Sovereign of the Universe, Who has made us holy with mitzvot and commanded us to enter him into the covenant of Abraham our father.

Next all present respond:

כְּשֵׁם שֶׁנִּכְנַס לַבְּרִית כֵּן יִכָּנֵס לְתוֹרָה וּלְחֻפָּה
וּלְמַעֲשִׂים טוֹבִים.

K'Shem Shenichnas LaBrit Kayn Yikanays L'Torah,
L'Chupah, Ul'Ma'aseem Toveem.

As he has entered the covenant, so may he be brought to the study of Torah, to the marriage canopy, and to the practice of good deeds.

The *mohel* recites the blessing over the wine, followed by a prayer for the well-being of the child and his family, and a prayer in which the child's Hebrew name is announced. The *mohel* or parents then drink the wine, with drops given to the child. Sometimes, the priestly benediction (Numbers 6:24-26) concludes the ritual.

Psalm 119 is an alphabetical acrostic with eight verses beginning with each letter of the Hebrew alphabet. It is customary to select a verse for each letter of the child's name and read these during the *Brit Milah*.

Pidyon HaBen

Rabbi Eugene Cohen has observed that "The first fruit that one realizes after great effort must be offered as a gift to the Eternal. This is true of agriculture, the birth of a domestic animal, and the first son who opens the mother's womb" (*Guide to Ritual Circumcision and Redemption of the First-born Son*, p. 76).

Pidyon HaBen, the redemption of the (firstborn) son, is a ritual which allows a firstborn male to be exempt from certain traditional responsibilities. These responsibilities derive from the story of the Exodus. "For every firstborn is Mine: at the time that I smote every firstborn in the land of Egypt, I consecrated every firstborn in Israel, human and animal, to Me, to be Mine . . ." (Numbers 3:13).

However, God exempts firstborn males from service. When the people enter the land of Israel "you shall set apart for the Lord every first issue of the womb: every male firstling that your cattle drop shall be the Lord's. But every firstling ass you shall redeem with a sheep; if you do not redeem it, you must break its neck. And you must redeem every firstborn male among your children" (Exodus 13:12-13).

In place of the firstborn males, God selects the Levites to serve as priests in the *Mishkan* — the Tabernacle in the wilderness (Numbers 3:12). They qualified for this special privilege, according to Jewish tradition, because they stepped forward when Moses — angered by the Golden Calf — says "Whoever is for the Lord, come here" (Exodus 32:26).

Although the firstborn have been officially relieved of their responsibilities, they must still be redeemed from such service. This is done by way of the *Pidyon HaBen* ritual.

Since Judaism considers a child viable only after 30 days, *Pidyon HaBen* takes place on the thirty-first day. If that day is Shabbat or a festival, the ceremony is postponed a day. The ceremony may take place in the synagogue or at home.

The ceremony takes place between the father of the child (or the mother or another adult if the father is not able to fulfill his responsibility) and a *Kohen,* a descendent of biblical priests who once had the primary responsibility for conducting the Temple sacrifices. If no *Kohen* is available, another Jew may act as the *shaliach* (messenger) for the *Kohen;* or, the daughter of a *Kohen* may accept the redemption.

The father officially presents his son, usually on a special tray, to the *Kohen,* who then asks if the father wants to redeem the child or leave him with the *Kohen.* The father responds that he wants to redeem him, and does so by giving the *Kohen* five coins, originally *shekels,* but most often five silver dollars (or coins of the country).

The father then recites the blessing for performing the *mitzvah* of *Pidyon HaBen* and the *"Shehecheyanu."* After the *Kohen* confirms that the child has been redeemed and returns him to his father, the ritual ends with the blessing over the wine and the priestly benediction. It is traditional to celebrate with a *Seudat Mitzvah.*

Pidyon HaBen is performed only if the firstborn son "is the first to open the mother's womb" and neither mother nor father is a *Kohen* or *Levi.* Thus, if the child was delivered by Caesarean section (and therefore did not open the womb), the ritual is not performed. If the mother had previously miscarried or had an abortion of a fetus which existed more than 40 days in utero, *Pidyon HaBen* is not performed. The firstborn male must be the first opening of the womb.

Pidyon HaBen is usually practiced by Orthodox and Conservative Jews; it is usually not observed by Reform or Reconstructionist Jews, who do not recognize priestly status in modern times. *Pidyon HaBen* has inspired new ceremonies called by various names including *Pidyon HaBat* (redemption of the daughter), *Kiddush Petter Rechem* (sanctification of the one who opens the womb), and *Seder Kedushat Chayay HaMishpachah* (order of the holiness of family life). In these ceremonies, which celebrate becoming parents for the first time, "the focus is not on redeeming a child from obligation but on sanctifying and dedicating the child for a life of service" (Diamant, p. 206).

Hebrew Names

Traditionally, a boy was given his Hebrew name at his *Brit Milah* and a girl was given hers when her father was honored with an *aliyah* in the synagogue shortly after her birth. Names have always been important in Judaism. As Rinna Samuel has written,

"For Jews, naming has always been a way of narrating history, demonstrating continuity, preserving the memory of those who have died, and celebrating significant events." ("The Game of the Name," in *Keeping Posted,* October, 1972).

While there are no laws pertaining to the choosing of a Hebrew name, there are important customs. Ashkenazic Jews (those whose ancestors come from Central or Eastern Europe) often name a child for a deceased relative, as a way of perpetuating the person's memory. Sephardic Jews (those whose ancestors come from Spain or Portugal) often name a child in honor of a living relative.

While the practice of giving two names, one civil and one Jewish, originated in Europe in the thirteenth century, there are many examples in the Talmud of Jews with Greek and Roman names. Even some biblical names such as Moses (Egyptian) and Esther (Persian) are not of Hebrew origin.

A person's complete Hebrew name is his or her first name (and middle name), then *"ben"* (son of) or *"bat"* (daughter of), then the person's father's and mother's first (and middle) names. If the father is a *Kohen* or *Levi* then the name ends with the word *"HaKohen"* or *"HaLevi"* respectively.

For the Birth of a Daughter

In recent years, creative rituals have been developed to celebrate the birth of a daughter, to welcome her into the covenant, and to announce her Hebrew name. These rituals are known by a variety of names: *Simchat Bat* (Rejoicing of the Daughter), *Brit HaChayim* (The Covenant of Life), *Brit Kedushah* (Covenant of Holiness), *Brit Sarah* (Covenant of Sarah), *Brit Banot* (Covenant of the Daughters), *Brit HaNayrot* (Covenant of the Candles), *Brit Rehitzah* (Covenant of Washing), and *Brit Kidush Levanah* (Covenant of the Sanctification of the Moon).

Rabbi Laura Geller has observed that while early ceremonies for girls "tended to be closely modeled after *Brit Milah* in that they were set on the eighth day after birth and used much of the traditional imagery and blessings . . . more recent ceremonies forsake *Brit Milah* as the model" (*"Brit Milah and Brit Banot,"* in Orenstein, p. 63). She points out that two symbols that have become popular in such ceremonies are water/*mikvah* and lunar celebrations. Both of these symbols are related to female spirituality.

Although ceremonies for girls vary widely, many include the lighting of candles (to symbolize Shabbat and festival candle lighting, one of the few positive *mitzvot* traditionally incumbent upon women), a blessing over wine, a blessing for entering the covenant, and a prayer announcing the girl's name. While these ceremonies are sometimes held on the eighth day, parallel to the timing of the *Brit Milah,* they are often held at other times.

The Sephardic community has a special ceremony following the birth of a girl called *Zeved HaBat,* the gift of the daughter. It includes singing, dancing, and a festive meal.

The Mitzvah of Procreation

After creating the first man and woman, "God blessed them and said to them: Be fruitful and multiply. . ." (Genesis 1:28). This charge is repeated to Noah after the flood (Genesis 9:1,7) and to Jacob immediately after God changes his name to Israel (Genesis 35:11).

Many commentators consider this *mitzvah* not only first in order, but in importance. "This is an important *mitzvah,* by virtue of which all the *mitzvoth* in the world are fulfilled" (*Sefer haHinnuch: The Book of [Mitzvah] Education,* Aaron HaLevi, vol. 1, p. 83). The Talmud warns that "One who does not engage in procreation is as if the person committed murder" (*Yevamot* 63b).

As stated previously, this *mitzvah* is only incumbent on Jewish males, according to the Talmud (*Yevamot* 65b). In order to fulfill one's obligation a man must father two sons, according to the School of Shammai, or a son and a daughter, according to the School of Hillel (*Yevamot* 6:6), whose ruling is followed by Jewish law.

However, Jewish tradition strongly favored bearing more than two children. Maimonides, for example, taught that "Although a man has fulfilled the *mitzvah* to be fruitful and multiply, he is commanded by the Rabbis not to desist from procreation while he still has strength" (*Mishneh Torah, Ishut,* 15, 16).

In contemporary times, Orthodox, particularly Chasidic families, tend to have many children. Some

Jews, on the other hand, have chosen to bear two or fewer children because of concerns for world population. For other couples, the devastating loss of Jewish population because of the Holocaust and recent Jewish population trends are important factors in deciding to have more than two children.

Adoption

Judaism teaches that those who raise a child are called mother and father, rather than those who are responsible for the birth (*Exodus Rabbah* 46:5). Michael Gold, in his book *and Hannah wept: Infertility, Adoption, and the Jewish Couple,* notes that while "Judaism has a long history of adoption de facto . . . adoption as a judicial act does not exist" (p. 157). A major reason for this is a concern with a child's biological identity, which cannot be changed.

Nevertheless, adoption is widely practiced in the contemporary Jewish community. When the biological mother is non-Jewish, the child must undergo a formal conversion to become a Jew. For a boy, the conversion process includes circumcision (or *Hatafat Dam Brit,* taking a drop of blood if he has already been circumcised) and immersion in a *mikvah.* For a girl, only immersion in a *mikvah* is required. The child receives a Hebrew name and is welcomed into the Jewish community.

Many Reform Rabbis and some Reconstructionist Rabbis do not require immersion in a *mikvah,* but consider the naming of the child and raising the child as Jew to be sufficient. However, such a child is not recognized as being Jewish by Conservative and Orthodox Judaism.

Due to several factors, including the small number of Caucasian babies available for adoption in the United States, some Jewish couples consider interracial (also called transracial) adoption. Jewish families have adopted African-American babies, as well as babies from China, South America, Korea, Vietnam, and other countries.

Michael Gold observes that "Interracial adoption is one area in which Jewish law is far more liberal than Jewish social values. The Jewish community, and particularly Jewish relatives, may not be as quick to accept the child as a Jew" (p. 198).

Interracial adoption has been the subject of much controversy, particularly regarding the adoption of black babies by white families. While agencies will usually try to match the racial and ethnic backgrounds of a baby and its adoptive parents, this is not always possible. Many Jewish couples seriously consider and successfully complete an interracial adoption. Other Jewish couples prefer not to adopt a child of a different race because of the added challenges it presents.

Mamzerut

According to Jewish tradition, a child is a *mamzer* (usually translated "bastard"), i.e., illegitimate, if he or she is born to parents whose sexual relationship is forbidden in Torah to the extent that such behavior is punishable by death or being cut off from the community. The two most common examples of such relationships are between a man and a woman who is already married to another man (but not between an unmarried woman and a man married to another woman), or between a brother and sister or any other incestuous unions forbidden by the Torah.

Most significantly, a child whose parents are not married is not a *mamzer,* but is fully legitimate. Because the Torah says, "A *mamzer* shall not enter the congregation of *Adonai*" (Deuteronomy 23:3), marriages between *mamzerim* and other Jews are not permissible. *Mamzerim* are only permitted to marry other *mamzerim.*

All children of *mamzerim* are also considered to be *mamzerim,* including the children of a *mamzer* and a legitimate Jew. In all other ways, a *mamzer* is considered equal to other Jews. In fact, the Mishnah teaches that "a *mamzer* who is a scholar takes precedence over a high priest who is unlearned" (*Horayot* 3:8).

Reform and Reconstructionist Judaism do not recognize the status of *mamzerut,* so as not to penalize children for the actions of their parents (or other ancestors). Conservative Judaism and many in Orthodox Judaism follow the practice of not inquiring about one's status.

When One Parent Is Not Jewish

In Orthodox and Conservative Judaism, a child is Jewish if his or her mother is Jewish, regardless of the father's religion. If the father is Jewish, and the mother is not, then the child is not Jewish unless it is converted.

This tradition emerged during the Rabbinic period. In the Torah, descent appears to follow the male line, since the children of Jacob and Moses are considered Jewish, despite their mothers' background.

The reasons that Jewish descent traditionally follows the matrilineal line is apparently because the identity of the mother is always known.

Reform and Reconstructionist Judaism have embraced Patrilineal Descent, which recognizes the child of a Jewish father and a non-Jewish mother as being Jewish if that child is raised solely as a Jew. Formal conversion is not required.

Birth Control

Despite Judaism's teachings on the *mitzvah* of bearing children, certain forms of birth control are permitted according to *halachah*. In part, the willingness to allow birth control is based on Judaism's view that marital sex is not only for the purpose of bearing children, but also for the pleasure derived from intercourse. Indeed, a husband is obligated to have regular sexual relations with his wife. According to the Talmud, if a husband wanted to change occupations and his new occupation would take him away from home for longer periods of time, he must receive his wife's permission (*Ketubot* 62b).

David Feldman observes that Judaism views "marital relations as the duty of the husband and the privilege of the wife" (*Marital Relations, Birth Control and Abortion in Jewish Law,* p. 64). There is therefore no objection to intercourse in which the participants consciously avoid procreation, including the use of certain types of birth control.

However, some forms of birth control are forbidden by traditional Jewish law, based primarily on the prohibition against wasting or destroying seed. This prohibition is based in part on the biblical story of Er and Onan (Genesis 38). Onan is supposed to cohabit with the wife of his deceased brother, Er, fulfilling the responsibility of providing a child to assume Er's name and inheritance. However, Onan, knowing that the seed would not count as his, let it spill on the ground when he joined with his

brother's wife (Genesis 38:9). God takes Onan's life for this offense. Later legal literature forbids destroying seed (*Mishneh Torah, Issurei Bi'ah* 21:18). According to the *Zohar,* it is "a sin more serious than all the sins of the Torah" *(Vayeshev).*

Dr. Fred Rosner sums up the traditional approach as follows: "The Jewish attitude toward contraception by any method is a non-permissive one if no medical or psychiatric threat to the mother or child exists. The duty of procreation, which is primarily a commandment on man, coupled with the wife's conjugal rights in Jewish law, mitigates against the use of the condom, coitus interruptus or abstinence under any circumstances. Where pregnancy hazard exists, and where Rabbinic sanction for the use of birth control is obtained, a hierarchy of acceptability emerges from the Talmudic and Rabbinic sources. Most acceptable are contraceptive means that least interfere with the natural sex act and least interfere with the full mobility of the sperm and its natural course. Oral contraception by pill enjoys preferred status as the least objectionable method of birth control" ("Contraception in Jewish Law," in *Jewish Bioethics,* Fred Rosner and J. David Bleich, eds., p. 95).

Liberal Judaism takes a more permissive attitude toward the use of birth control, recognizing the right of parents to determine family size, as well as the timing of bearing children. At the same time, parents are exhorted to consider seriously the survival and future of Judaism and the "tragic decimation of our people during the Holocaust" (*Gates of Mitzvah,* Simeon J. Maslin, ed., p. 11) when making decisions about birth control and family size.

Artificial Insemination

Artificial insemination, by which semen is placed in the woman's genital tract by instruments rather than through intercourse, is one method of treating infertility. The semen may be from the woman's husband, from a donor, or be a mixture of the two.

Although artificial insemination is a relatively modern technique, the Talmud mentions the possibility of a woman becoming pregnant from a bath that contained semen (*Hagigah* 14b).

The majority of Rabbinic authorities oppose artificial insemination using a donor's sperm (or a mixture of donor's and husband's sperm) primarily because of a concern regarding incest, since the child that is born from such a procedure could grow up and unknowingly marry a biological relative.

Other Rabbinic reasons for opposing this procedure are because the child's genealogy is not known and because of concerns about inheritance. Some Rabbis even consider artificial insemination using donor's sperm to be adultery, although most do not, since no intercourse has taken place. Furthermore, most authorities consider any child born by such means to be legitimate.

Artificial insemination using the husband's semen is permitted according to Jewish law, but Rabbis insist that it be used only if the wife had been unable to become pregnant naturally. A period of time (ranging from two to ten years according to various Rabbinic opinions) must pass following the wedding to establish that the woman cannot become pregnant by natural intercourse before a couple may pursue artificial insemination.

According to Reform Jewish *Responsa,* artificial insemination using either the husband's semen, or a donor's, or a mixture of the two is permitted.

In Vitro Fertilization (Test Tube Babies)

In vitro fertilization is a medical procedure in which fertilization of an egg takes place in a petri dish, rather than in a woman's fallopian tubes. The fertilized egg incubates in the petri dish, as it would in the fallopian tube, and is then placed into the woman's uterus, where it develops until birth. Unlike certain other infertility procedures, both the egg and the sperm belong to the couple, rather than to donors.

In vitro fertilization is utilized by couples when infertility problems are due primarily to difficulties with the fallopian tubes or to low sperm count.

While Jewish law raises many concerns about in vitro fertilization, particularly the method for obtaining sperm (since masturbation is forbidden according to Jewish law), most authorities agree that there is no legal impediment to this procedure. J. David Bleich, a leading authority on Jewish bioethics, concludes that "if properly controlled and not permitted to become a substitute for normal human procreation, this revolutionary technique can

be a welcome means of bestowing the happiness and fulfillment of parenthood upon otherwise childless couples" (*Judaism and Healing,* p. 91).

Surrogate Motherhood (Host Mothers)

Surrogate motherhood is another contemporary medical strategy for dealing with infertility. In this procedure, a naturally fertilized egg is removed from the womb of a pregnant woman and implanted in the uterus of another woman, where it remains and develops until birth, at which time it becomes the child of the biological parents. Many legal issues have been raised about surrogate motherhood, particularly in well publicized cases in which the surrogate (host) mother has wanted to keep the child, despite having contracted to turn it over to its biological parents upon birth.

Surrogate motherhood is normally used when the egg can be fertilized naturally, but is not able to continue its normal development in the womb. In some cases, artificial insemination is used to fertilize the egg, after which it is transplanted to the host womb.

Jewish law permits such a procedure "only in the absence of an alternative" (*Compendium on Medical Ethics,* David M. Feldman and Fred Rosner, eds., p. 51). Furthermore, *halachic* authorities insist that surrogate motherhood be used only in cases of inability to carry full term, and not by someone seeking to avoid the inconvenience of pregnancy. Rabbi Immanuel Jakobovits, former Chief Rabbi of Great Britain, argues that "to use another person as an 'incubator' and then take from her the child she carried and delivered for a fee is a revolting degradation of maternity and an affront to human dignity" (*Judaism and Healing,* p. 92).

Abortion

The traditional Jewish attitude toward abortion cannot be characterized as either "pro-choice" or "pro-life." Rather, Judaism permits (in some cases even mandates) abortion of a fetus if the mother's life is in danger. According to the Mishnah, "If a woman is in difficult labor, one cuts up the fetus in her womb and removes it limb by limb, because her life comes before its life. But if the head has emerged, one may not touch it, for one may not set aside one person's life for another" (*Oholot* 7:6).

The tradition concludes that the only justification for abortion would be a threat to the life of the mother. While this threat is usually physical, it may also be psychological, according to some authorities. Immanuel Jakobovits has written, "If it is genuinely feared that a continued pregnancy and eventual birth . . . might have such debilitating effects on the mother as to present a danger to her own life or the life of another by suicidal or violent tendencies, however remote this danger may be, a therapeutic abortion may be indicated with the same justification as for other medical reasons" (*Jewish Bioethics,* p. 124).

Nevertheless, Rabbinic authorities condemn abortion of a deformed or crippled fetus, or when prenatal tests indicate the presence of a deadly disease. For example, amniocentesis can determine if a fetus contains two genes of the fatal disease Tay Sachs, a congenital disorder that disproportionately occurs in Jews of Eastern European background.

Carriers of one Tay Sachs gene are unaffected by the disease. However, the offspring of two carriers have a 25 per cent chance of inheriting two Tay Sachs genes and therefore the disease. Although normal at birth, a Tay Sachs infant begins exhibiting symptoms at six months and almost always dies by age three. There is currently no cure for the disease. While authorities such as Rabbi Moshe Feinstein favor pre-marital screening to determine if one is a carrier of the gene, most oppose amniocentesis "whose natural and logical consequence is abortion" (*Jewish Bioethics,* p. 185).

Most non-Orthodox Rabbis take a more liberal approach to abortion, recognizing the right of a woman to make decisions pertaining to her body. At the same time, these Rabbis argue that abortion should not be used as a form of birth control, and that any decision to terminate a pregnancy should be made with careful consideration of all factors and with input from the father.

A pagan philosopher asked Rabbi Hoshai: "If circumcision is so dear to God, why was the mark of circumcision not given to Adam at his creation?" He replied: "According to your reasoning, why should you shave the hair of your head, but leave the hair of your beard intact?" The pagan answered: "Because the hair of your head grew in the days of foolish childhood." Rabbi Hoshai then said: "If so, he should blind his eyes, lop off his hands, and break his legs, which also grew along with him since the days of foolish childhood." The philosopher exclaimed: "Have we come to such foolishness?" R. Hoshai said: "I cannot let you go without a proper answer. Observe that everything that was created during the six days of creation needs finishing: mustard needs sweetening, vetches need sweetening, wheat needs grinding, and even man needs finishing."

(*Genesis Rabbah* 11:6)

When Hezekiah was ill, the prophet Isaiah visited him. "And Isaiah . . . came to him and said to him: 'you shall die and not live'" (2 Kings 20:1). Hezekiah asked why he was receiving such a severe punishment. Isaiah answered, "Because you did not try to have children." Hezekiah said, "It was because the holy spirit showed me that children issuing from me will not be worthy." Isaiah responded: "What have you to do with the secrets of the Holy One? What you have been commanded, you should have done, and let God do whatever God wishes."

(*Berachot* 10a)

R. Eliezer said, "One who does not engage in being fruitful and multiplying is as though the person shed blood . . . ." R. Akiva said, "It is as though the person diminished God's image." Ben Azzai said, "It is as though the person both sheds blood and diminishes God's image."

(*Yevamot* 63b)

R. Ishmael said, "Great is circumcision, for the word 'covenant' is mentioned 13 times in relationship to it [in Genesis 17]." R. Yosi said, "Great is circumcision, for it even sets aside the law of Shabbat." R. Meir said, "Great is circumcision, for despite everything that Abraham had done, he was not called 'perfect' until he circumcised himself . . . . " Rabbi [Judah] said, "Great is circumcision, for it is equal in importance to all precepts in the Torah."

(*Nedarim* 31b-32a)

The custom of not naming after a living relative is based on Ashkenazic folklore in which God sends the angel of death to bring the souls of the deceased to heaven. The angel descends to earth and calls the person's name. If the infant had the same name as an older relative, there was fear that the wrong person would die, a fear which intensified at times of high infant mortality.

One medieval commentator suggests that when Abraham was circumcised, his wife, Sarah, went to the *mikvah* as her ritual of entering the covenant (*Me'irir* to *Yevamot* 46a). This tradition is the basis for the use of water or ritual immersion in ceremonies for girls.

A Talmudic tradition states that a cedar tree was planted at the birth of a boy and a cypress tree at the birth of a girl. The children would tend to their trees, and when they were to marry, branches from the trees were used to hold up the wedding *chupah*.

(*Gittin* 57a)

There is a tradition that while in the womb, a fetus learns the entire Torah. However, before birth, an angel touches the infant on the upper lip and causes the infant to forget all that he or she knows. This explains the indentation on the upper lip.

ACTIVITIES

Primary

1. Ask each student to bring in a baby picture and a current picture. Mix them up and display them. Ask the students to pair them. After all the pictures have been correctly paired, discuss how the students have changed since they were babies. Also discuss how people change throughout their lives. Explain how rituals help to make certain changes in one's life special. Then focus on rituals related to birth.

2. Read to your students *Did My First Mother Love Me?* by Kathryn Ann Miller, *Through Moon and Stars and Night Skies* by Ann Turner, *Tell Me a Real Adoption Story* by Betty Jean Lifton, or another appropriate story about adoption. Discuss the reasons why some adults adopt children. How is being adopted similar and different from not being adopted?

3. To help the students learn their Hebrew names, write each student's name on a small pre-made jigsaw puzzle. Give each student his/her puzzle pieces and ask them to assemble the puzzle. Students can then trade with a partner, and after assembling the puzzle, explain Hebrew names to each other.

4. Make cookie or pretzel dough names. Write out each student's Hebrew name. Give a portion of pre-made dough to each student to form his or her name. Bake and eat.

   Recipe for pretzel dough:
   Add 1 tablespoon yeast to ½ cup warm water. Add 1 teaspoon honey and then 1⅛ cups flour. Knead. Take small portions of dough and roll into long pieces. Shape these into the letters. Beat an egg and brush on the letters. Sprinkle with kosher salt. Bake for 10 minutes at 425 degrees. Makes enough for 3-4 students.

   Recipe for cookie dough:
   Mix 2 eggs, ⅓ cup honey and 1 tablespoon oil in a bowl. Add 1 tablespoon orange or lemon rind, ½ teaspoon salt, and 1½ cups oatmeal. Mix well. Take small portions of dough and roll into long pieces. Shape these into the letters. Bake for 8-10 minutes at 400 degrees. Makes enough for 3-4 students.

5. Play two or three Jewish lullabies for the students. Ask the students how it makes them feel to hear lullabies. How do the Jewish ones compare with others they might remember? Invite the Cantor or music specialist to teach the students a lullaby.
   Resources: *A Legacy of Lullabies* and *Lullabies and Love Songs* by Tanja Solnik; *Lullabies & Quiet Time* by Myrna Cohen; *Sleep My Child: A Collection of Jewish Lullabies Sung in Yiddish, Hebrew, Ladino, and English.*

6. Ask each student to bring a doll or stuffed animal. Explain the traditions associated with choosing Hebrew names. Help each student choose a Hebrew name for his/her doll and hold a mock naming ceremony. Prepare certificates for each student. During the ceremony explain the importance of Hebrew names and when they are used.

7. Introduce the word *brit* to your students, with its English translation — covenant. Explain the word *brit* as a type of promise. Discuss making promises with your students. Why is it important to keep promises? What happens when someone does not keep a promise? Create a class *brit,* with promises that the students and teacher make to each other.

8. Make "A Special Person" poster for each student. The poster should say: "A special person was born on . . ." with both the secular and Hebrew date of birth. The poster should also include a picture, the student's Hebrew name, favorite Jewish holiday, favorite Jewish food, Jewish hero, etc.

9. Read to the class *Sophie's Name* by Phyllis Agins Grode. Questions to discuss: Why is Sophie unhappy about her name? What changes

her mind? Who was she named after? Ask the students who they were named after.

10. Enable your class to be part of a caring community and reach out to a family that has just given birth to or adopted a new baby. Contact the Rabbi or educator to identify such a family. Brainstorm a list of ideas for helping a family with a new child, such as preparing a meal, running errands, or inviting older siblings to play. Implement one or more of the ideas.

11. Read to the students Genesis 2:19, the account of the naming of each of the creatures by the first human being. Bring to class pictures of a variety of animals. Ask the students to pretend that they were the first human being and had the opportunity to name the animals. Show the pictures of the animals to the students one at a time (without mentioning their names) and ask them to come up with an appropriate name for each animal. Write the suggestions on the board and have the students vote on their favorite name for each animal.

12. With your class, do the dance *midrash* "Naming the Creatures" from *Torah in Motion: Creating Dance Midrash* by JoAnne Tucker and Susan Freeman, pp. 8-9.

Intermediate

1. Ask students to bring in and share pictures, certificates, and videotapes of their naming or *Brit Milah* ceremonies. List on the board important facts about these ceremonies that the students learn from looking at this material. Discuss the similarities and differences between the ceremonies. Hold a class naming ceremony for those who never received a Hebrew name.

2. Discuss what Hebrew name students would choose for a new baby brother or sister. Allow students to browse through Hebrew name books for ideas and then present the name to the class, explaining why they like it.
Resource: *The Complete Dictionary of English and Hebrew First Names* by Alfred J. Kolatch.

3. Psalm 119 is written as an alphabetic acrostic with seven verses beginning with each letter. It is often used at baby namings, with one verse read for each letter of the child's name. Allow each student to select one verse for each letter of his or her name, writing out the translation. Students take turns reading them and explain why they chose the particular verses.

4. Discuss with the class the symbolic importance of the presence of Elijah at a *Brit Milah*. With the class make a *Kisay Eliyahu*, a chair of Elijah, which is traditionally used during a *Brit Milah*. Use an unfinished chair, or a chair that may be painted over. Present the finished product to the synagogue or school to be used by families during a *Brit Milah*.

5. Gather children's books which include the theme of adoption (see Primary activity #2 for suggestions). Each child reads one of the books and writes a short report with an illustration. The report should include: title, author, a brief description of each character in the story, summary of the story, and the reader's response to the idea of adoption. Place the reports on a bulletin board with the caption: "Judaism teaches that those who raise a child are called mother and father" (*Exodus Rabbah* 46:5).

6. There are a number of Jewish customs designed to protect a young child. Present these to the students (see Overview, p. 2). Discuss why parents might do these things even if they think that they are superstitions. In groups, have the students choose one custom and make a diorama to illustrate it.

7. View the videocassette *The Eighth Day: Circumcision/Hanukah*, which focuses on the issue of whether a couple in the days of the Maccabees will circumcise their son, in defiance of Greek law. Ask the students to pretend they were the couple and to decide what they would do.

8. Share with the class the tradition of planting trees for the birth of male and female babies

and then using branches of the trees for their *chupah*. Ask the students to write a short story on this theme.

9. In the book of Exodus, we learn that Moses was adopted by Pharaoh's daughter. Read to the class Exodus 2:1-10. Have students write newspaper headlines reporting this event. Encourage the students to be creative and funny. (Was this a scandal in the eyes of the Egyptians? What are the rumors about the true identity of the child?) Extend the activity by having students write short articles to go with the headlines and by making a newspaper.

10. If your congregation has public naming ceremonies, arrange for your class to attend. At the following class session, discuss the ceremony. Who participated in the ceremony? What did each of the people do? Did the students recognize any of the prayers? If possible, invite to class the parents of the child who was named so that students can ask questions such as why they chose the name.

11. Ask students to create their own birth announcements. Students should include their given name and Hebrew name, date of birth according to the Gregorian and Jewish calendar, and an appropriate saying or drawing reflecting their names. They could also add some humor by including an area of interest, favorite sport or hobby such as: "A future Little League first baseman was born . . ."
Resources: For examples of announcements, see *The New Jewish Baby Book* by Anita Diamant, pp. 194-202; to find one's Hebrew birth date, see *The Standard Guide to the Jewish and Civil Calendar* by Fred Reiss.

12. Distribute to the students the words in the Glossary and direct them to create a word search using those words. Have students trade with each other and try to find the words in the word search.

13. Perform a reader's theater of the skit "The

Birth of a Jewish Child — An Epic Tale" in *Class Acts: Plays & Skits for Jewish Settings* by Stan J. Beiner, pp. 65-73. Make a list of all the Jewish traditions the students learned from the skit.

14. When Sarah learns that she is going to have a baby, she laughs. Introduce this story to your students with the dance *midrash* "Sarah Laughed" from *Torah in Motion: Creating Dance Midrash* by JoAnne Tucker and Susan Freeman, pp. 20-21.

15. Complete the mini-course *Circumcision* by Raymond A. Zwerin, Audrey Friedman Marcus, and Leonard Kramish with your students.

Secondary

1. Invite a *mohel* to speak to the students about *Brit Milah*. Brainstorm with the class a list of questions ahead of time.

2. Divide the class into three groups and assign each group one of the following biblical selections pertaining to *brit*: Genesis 9:9-17; Genesis 17:1-14; Exodus 24. Each group should read and discuss the passage and prepare a presentation of the section, which should include a visual representation using a medium of choice and a dramatic presentation.

3. Provide the students with a variety of *brit* and naming ceremonies. Direct the students to compare them to each other. What do they have in common? How are they different from each other? From this comparison, what can the students conclude are the essential parts of a *brit* or naming ceremony?

4. Invite a priest or a minister and a Rabbi to compare baptism with *Brit Milah*. In what ways are they similar? How are they different? How does baptism compare to Judaism's use of the *mikvah*?

5. With the students, create a questionnaire for their parents about *Brit Milah* and naming. Among the questions to ask are: Did you have

a *Brit Milah* for your sons? Why or why not? Was it done by a *mohel* or doctor? Was it held on the eighth day? If there was no *Brit Milah,* was there any other ceremony? What type of a ceremony was held for daughters? Compile the results after surveying the parents and discuss.

6. Introduce the following ethical dilemma to your students: A couple who is not able to have a child naturally finds a woman to be a surrogate mother. The couple's egg is implanted in the woman, where it will develop until birth. A few week's before the child is due to be born, the surrogate mother announces that the baby is hers and that she intends to keep it. Should she be allowed to keep the baby? Why or why not? Read the story *Horton Hatches the Egg* by Dr. Seuss to the students. Ask the students: Who deserves to have the baby, the bird or the elephant? Why? How does this story compare to the moral dilemma of the surrogate mother?

7. Assign students to research circumcision in other cultures. When is it done? What are the reasons for doing it? Compare with Judaism's reasons for circumcision.

8. Invite a local Jewish artist to speak to the class about amulets in the Jewish tradition. Pay particular attention to the symbols used on Jewish amulets. The artist may also be able to make simple amulets with the students.

9. Read Genesis 21:1-8, about the birth of Isaac, to the students. Briefly discuss this passage, reminding the students how long Abraham and Sarah had waited for a child. Recreate the feast to celebrate Isaac's weaning that is mentioned in verse 8. Assign roles of: Abraham, Sarah, Hagar, Ishmael, Isaac, and others. Each person should say what the ceremony means to him/her and offer a blessing for Isaac.

10. Choose a specific bioethical issue pertaining to birth, such as artificial insemination or surrogate motherhood. Examine *Responsa* that have been written about the issue. What are the basic

Jewish principles used to determine a position on the issue? Do the students agree or disagree with the position of the *Responsa*? You may wish to stage a debate on a particular issue using the *Responsa* and other resources.
Resources: *American Reform Responsa* edited by Walter Jacob; *Contemporary American Reform Responsa* by Walter Jacob; *Kitzur Shulchan Aruch* by A. Ganzfried.

11. Invite a folklorist to present traditions and customs from a variety of cultures pertaining to ceremonies celebrating the birth of a child and welcoming that child to the community. Compare these rituals with Judaism's traditions.

12. With the students, create a fictional family going through the end of pregnancy, childbirth, and the first weeks of a baby's life. Divide the students into groups and assign each group one of the time periods to write a short script for a radio play. Encourage students to be humorous, but also to include references to Jewish tradition whenever possible. Present the play at an assembly or service.

13. Complete the instant lesson *LifeChoices* by Ira J. Wise, which focuses on abortion.

Hebrew

1. Teach the song *"Eliyahu HaNavi"* to the students. Explain the relationship between Elijah and the ceremony of *Brit Milah.*
Resource: *Manginot: 201 Songs for Jewish Schools,* edited by Stephen Richards, p. 150.

2. Create a banner with the phrase:

כְּשֵׁם שֶׁנִּכְנַס לַבְּרִית כֵּן יִכָּנֵס לְתוֹרָה וּלְחֻפָּה וּלְמַעֲשִׂים טוֹבִים.

K'Shaym Shenichnas (Shenichnasah) LaBrit, Kayn Yichanays (Tikanays) L'Torah, L'Chupah, Ul'Ma'aseem Toveem.

"As he (she) has entered the covenant, so may he (she) be brought to Torah, to the marriage canopy, and to good deeds."

Teach the phrase to the students and explain its use at a *Brit Milah* or naming ceremony.

3. Create a matching game for students to learn the meaning of certain Hebrew names. Choose names such as Ari (lion); Dov (bear); Yonah (dove); Malkah (queen), Shoshanah (lily), etc. Cut pictures from magazines or draw pictures on separate cards. Students try to match the name to its meaning. Students may help to create the game if you wish.
Resources: *The Complete Dictionary of English and Hebrew First Names* by Alfred J. Kolatch; *The New Jewish Baby Book* by Anita Diamant.

4. Hebrew names are used when called to the Torah. Students can learn how to call each other up to the Torah. Each student will need to know his or her full Hebrew name, which includes one's first and middle names, one's parents names, and whether one is a *Kohen* or *Levi*. In pairs, students can call each other to the Torah.
Resource: *This Is the Torah* by Alfred J. Kolatch, p. 151.

5. Play "To Tell the Truth" using each person's Hebrew name. To prepare for the game, each student must know his or her full Hebrew name (example, *Yitzchak ben Avraham v'Sarah*), its meaning, and who he or she was named after (if anyone). Divide the students into groups of three boys or three girls. Each student writes a short script such as: "My name is *Yitzchak ben Avraham v'Sarah*. The name *Yitzchak* means 'he will laugh,' but it is not a very funny name. I was named after my mother's grandfather Irving, whose Hebrew name was also *Yitzchak*." The two other students in the group each write a short script beginning the same way, "My name is *Yitzchak ben Avraham v'Sarah*," but making up the rest of their presentation. (Each student therefore prepares three scripts: his or her own and two pretend ones.) Invite another class to observe the presentations and to guess who is telling the truth.

Adult

1. In recent years there has been some controversy about circumcision. Some physicians, among others, have expressed opposition to the procedure. Invite a physician, a Rabbi, a *mohel,* and other experts to serve on a panel to discuss circumcision.

2. Resolve, Inc. is a national organization which helps couples with infertility problems. Invite a member of this organization to speak about infertility. You may also find a couple who is willing to share their struggle with infertility.
Resource: Resolve, Inc., 1310 Broadway, Somerville, MA 02144, or a regional chapter.

3. Reform and Reconstructionist Judaism have in recent years endorsed Patrilineal Descent, which recognizes the child of a Jewish father and non-Jewish mother as being Jewish if the child is raised solely as a Jew. Conservative and Orthodox Judaism oppose this measure, insisting that such a child must undergo conversion to be considered Jewish. Hold a panel discussion with representatives of both positions. Try to include intermarried couples who are directly affected by this issue.

4. The Jewish obligation to be fruitful and multiply may conflict with the concerns about over-population which have been expressed in recent years. Because of the Holocaust and assimilation, some Jewish leaders believe that Jews have a greater obligation to bear children to assure the future of Judaism. Hold a discussion on the topic: "Jews and Fertility: We Are Obligated to Be Fruitful and Multiply."

5. A beautiful *midrash* says that when the Jewish people had gathered at Mount Sinai to receive the Torah, God said to them: "I will give you my Torah if you prove to me that you deserve it." The people answered: "Our ancestors are our proof." God said: "Your ancestors are not sufficient. Bring me better proof, and I will give you My Torah." They responded: "Our prophets are our proof." God said: "Your prophets are not

sufficient. Bring me better proof, and I will give you My Torah." They responded: Our children are our proof." God said: "They are certainly sufficient proof. For their sake I give My Torah to you." Use this *midrash* as a theme for an adult program on the importance of children for the future of Judaism. Present a variety of workshops on such themes as: Being Jewish in a Non-Jewish World, Celebrating Shabbat at Home, Raising Your Child to be a Mensch, Family Tzedakah Projects, etc.

6. View the videocassette *A Question of Authority,* which examines the moral dilemma of a pregnant woman who suffers a fall and is declared brain dead. Who has the authority to decide if the child should be delivered? Invite a doctor and a Rabbi to comment on the film.

7. Ask each participant or couple to list one time during the childbirth process when they felt especially significant. It could be: finding out one was pregnant, first time feeling the fetus kicking, moment of childbirth, first time feeding the child, etc. In small groups, discuss the feelings, emotions, and thoughts that one had at that time. Encourage each person or couple to write a prayer for that moment. Compile these prayers into a booklet and distribute to interested parties.

8. View the video *Intimate Story,* an Israeli film in Hebrew with English subtitles, about a childless couple who lives on a *kibbutz* and their struggles with infertility. Invite couples who have overcome problems with infertility to comment on the film.

9. With a Rosh Chodesh group or other women's group, create a ritual for Rosh Chodesh which celebrates pregnancy. Include prayers, poems, and songs.

Resources: *Miriam's Well* by Penina V. Adelman; *Lifecycles: Jewish Women on Life Passages & Personal Milestones,* Vol. 1, edited by Debra Orenstein.

10. Establish a Women's Study Group to learn about, reclaim, and create new rituals for pregnancy and childbirth.
Resources: *A Ceremonies Sampler* by Elizabeth Resnick Levine; *Lifecycles: Jewish Women on Life Passages & Personal Milestones,* Vol. 1, edited by Debra Orenstein; *Miriam's Well* by Penina V. Adelman.

11. Offer an adult education class for expectant parents and parents in the adoption process to help them create a *Brit Milah* or naming ceremony for their child. Invite the Rabbi, Cantor, and a *mohel* to speak to the group and offer suggestions. Provide samples of services and other appropriate material.

12. Present to a group of new and expectant parents the guided fantasy "A New Baby" in *Jewish Guided Imagery* by Dov Peretz Elkins, pp. 120-121. Discuss the feelings that this experience evoked. Ask parents to create a list of things they can do so that the fantasy becomes a reality in their lives.

13. Offer an adult education program about Tay-Sachs and other Jewish genetic diseases to educate prospective parents, teenagers, and other interested members of the community. Invite a doctor or nurse with expertise to present information about these diseases, including how one can be tested to determine if one is a carrier. If possible, create a committee which will bring this information to the attention of newlyweds and prospective parents on a regular basis.
Resources: The National Tay-Sachs and Allied Diseases Association, 2001 Beacon Street, Brookline, MA 02146; National Gaucher Foundation, 11140 Rockville Pike, Suite 350, Rockville, MD 20852.

14. Show the video *Losing Isaiah,* which is the story of an abandoned African-American crack baby and his adoption by a white family. When the birth mother attempts to regain custody of the child, a court battle ensues. Break into groups of 8-10 people to discuss the issues generated by the film such as: What role would race play in the adoption process? How does one determine who is a fit parent? Should a biological parent always have rights to a child? Invite a representative from an adoption agency to help facilitate the discussions and offer comments to the entire group about interracial adoption.

Family

1. A *wimpel* is a Torah binder made of fabric which has been used to swaddle an infant at birth. Each family can make its own *wimpel* to use at special occasions in the family's life such as Bar Mitzvah, Bat Mitzvah, or *aufruf* (*aliyah* before one's wedding). To make a *wimpel:* Cut a piece of cotton fabric (preferably muslin or a light color) 4" to 6" wide by at least 54" long. Decorate it with fabric markers, applique, embroidery, fabric paint, or a combination of these media. The traditional phrase includes the child's Hebrew name, birthdate, and the blessing (see page 15 for the Hebrew):

   "As he was brought to the *brit,* so may he be brought to study Torah, to the *chupah,* and to a life of good deeds. Amen. *Selah.*"

   Families may use this phrase for a particular child or choose a biblical quote that has particular meaning for the family, or create their own phrase. Finish off the edges in one of the following ways: a rolled hem on a serger sewing machine, a turned-under hem by hand or machine, or with a facing fabric which is sewn with right sides facing, leaving a 5"-6" space unsewn. Turn wimpel right side out and hand stitch the opening closed.

2. Hold a family celebration of Hebrew names. Prior to the program, ask each family to bring the Hebrew names of each of its family members. Those who do not have a Hebrew name will be able to choose one. In family groups discuss each family member's name, the meaning, and who each person was named for. Name books should be available to help find the meaning of names or for those who need to choose names. Each child then makes a name plaque. Use square or rectangular ceramic tiles. Write the name and appropriate designs on the tile with pencil and then use acrylic craft paint in a variety of colors to create the design. Parents can help young children or make their own plaque. Conclude the program with a naming ceremony for those who have just chosen a Hebrew name.
   Resource: *The Complete Dictionary of English and Hebrew First Names* by Alfred J. Kolatch.

3. Divide families into groups of 4-5 families each. Each group should be seated in a circle. One adult/teacher should be appointed discussion facilitator for each group. Group members are given the following statements:

   "My covenant/commitment to Judaism began with _____." I continue this covenant/commitment by _____."

   The discussion facilitator should allow a few minutes for each group member to fill in the blanks. Then, as a group, share responses.
   Break the group up into family units. Ask families to brainstorm ideas to complete the following statement:

   "As a family we can strengthen our covenant/commitment to Judaism by _____."

   Bring the families together to share their ideas. Conclude the program by asking families to choose one or two ideas and to implement them in their families. One month later, have a follow-up group discussion to share the results.

4. Ask families to bring information about their family tree, particularly about the first names of

family members. The goal of this program is to trace back as many generations as possible, making the connection between generations. Beginning with the children, families should discuss the names and who the person is named after. Parents should explain why the name was chosen and share stories about the ancestor, or qualities about the person's life that were particularly important. Continue by examining the parents' names in a similar manner. Each family member should create a linked chain beginning with his/her name. Add a link for the person or persons that one is named after, including information about the people. Add links for each previous generation to which one can trace a name. If one is named for a biblical, Talmudic, or other historical ancestor, add a link for that person and include his or her important characteristics.

5. Hold a workshop for families that are expecting a child. Invite a speaker from Jewish Family Service or a similar agency to talk to the adults about what to expect from their other children when a new sibling arrives, how to create a welcoming atmosphere, how to balance the needs of a newborn with the needs of older children. At the same time, offer a session for the children to help them prepare for the arrival of a sibling. Activities to include: reading a story about a family that is expecting a baby, teaching how to hold a baby, making a banner or sign to welcome the baby, listing ways they can help their family after the baby is born. Conclude by bringing each family together to share what they learned.

All-School

1. Ask each student, teacher, Rabbi and educator to bring a baby picture with his/her name on the back. Create a bulletin board entitled: "Who in the world is this kid?" with the pictures displayed and numbered. Distribute sheets of paper with numbers to the students so that they can guess the identity of each baby. Give creative prizes (diaper pin, baby rattle, etc.) to those who identify the most babies correctly.

2. As a school, make "Tzedakah Opportunity Quilts" to be distributed to hospitals, shelters, and family crisis centers. For younger children, the quilts should be prepared ahead of time. Older students can help prepare the quilts. Supplies: Two 1¼ yard by 44"-45" pieces of cotton fabric, 1¼ yard quilt batting. Pre-wash fabrics. Place the two 1¼ yard fabrics right sides together. Place the batting against one wrong side of the fabric. You have created a "quilt sandwich." Machine stitch all the way around this quilt sandwich, leaving an 8" inch opening to turn the quilt right side out. Fold in this 8" opening and machine or hand stitch it closed. Supplies for finishing: Embroidery thread or yarn with appropriate sewing needles, scissors, fabric marking pencil, or disappearing ink marker. Evenly mark one side of the quilt every 4"-5" with the fabric pencil or marker. With the needle threaded with embroidery thread or yarn, push the needle through the quilt at a mark and pull it back through to the front. Make sure your needle goes through the quilt sandwich and comes back up to the front of the quilt. Remove the needle and make a square knot with the thread.

3. Ask each student to bring his or her baby album to school or to bring a sheet of paper with the information for this activity. Set up stations around a large room or in each classroom. In small groups students proceed to each station and record the appropriate information.

Station 1: *What I weighed when I was born.* Create a large calibrated scale on poster board and each student records his or her weight at birth.

Station 2: *How long I was at birth.* Create a giant yard stick on poster board and each student records his or her length at birth.

Station 3: *Where I was born.* Post a map of the world and each student uses a push-pin to indicate his or her birthplace.

Station 4: *How I was welcomed.* Each student creates a picture of the ceremony (*Brit Milah,* naming, welcoming home, etc.) with which they were welcomed into their family and community.

Station 5: *When I got my first tooth.* On a large calendar, students mark how old they were when they got their first tooth.

Station 6: *My first word.* On large poster board students write their first word.

Create other stations as desired. Bring everyone together at the end to view each display and give funny prizes in selected categories.

4. A representative of each class (or group with students of mixed classes), called a family, draws out of a brown paper bag a slip of paper describing the "family's" new arrival. Examples: girl, boy, twins, triplets, baby kangaroo or other animal, new car. Each group is to: choose a name or names (including a family name), create a birth/arrival announcement, write a newspaper announcement, create and act out a welcoming ritual, make a birth certificate with vital statistics, write a cheer or song to welcome the arrival. Each family presents their completed work to the others.

For more activities on *Brit Milah,* see *Teaching Mitzvot: Concepts, Values, and Activities* by Barbara Binder Kadden and Bruce Kadden, Unit 7.

For activities on *Pidyon HaBen,* see *Teaching Mitzvot: Concepts, Values, and Activities* by Barbara Binder Kadden and Bruce Kadden, Unit 8.

GLOSSARY

Brit Milah – Covenant of circumcision ceremony.

Hamsikah – Yemenite amulet shaped like an out-stretched hand.

Hatafat Dam Brit – Ritual of taking a drop of blood from the penis as a symbolic circumcision.

Kisay Eliyahu – Chair of Elijah on which the *sandak* sits during the *Brit Milah*.

Kohen – Member of the priestly tribe who descends from the High Priest Aaron. A father redeems his son from a *Kohen* in a *Pidyon HaBen*.

Kvatter – Godfather.

Kvatterin – Godmother.

Layl Shimurim – Night of watching. The evening before a boy's *Brit Milah* when special rituals to protect the child are performed. Also called *Vach Nacht* in Yiddish.

Lilith – Adam's first wife (according to folklore), who is believed to endanger the life of newborns.

Mamzer/Mamzeret – Literally, bastard. A child born of a relationship which is illegal according to Jewish law.

Mikvah – Ritual bath.

Mohel – One trained to perform ritual circumcision (pronounced *moyel* in Yiddish and *mo-hail* in Hebrew).

Patrilineal Descent – Recognizing the child of a Jewish father and non-Jewish mother as being Jewish so long as the child was raised solely as a Jew.

Pidyon HaBat – Ceremony celebrating the redemption of a firstborn daughter.

Pidyon HaBen – Ceremony celebrating the redemption of a firstborn son.

Sandak– Person who holds the baby during a *Brit Milah,* usually a grandparent.

Shehecheyanu – Blessing said on the first day of holidays, at joyous life cycle events, and to celebrate something new.

Sh'lom Zachar – Ritual to welcome the birth of a son on the first Friday evening after his birth.

Seudat Mitzvah – Meal celebrating a life cycle event such as *Brit Milah* or wedding.

Tay-Sachs – Genetic disease disproportionately affecting Jews of Eastern European ancestry.

Wimpel – Cloth Torah binder.

Zeved HaBat – Sephardic ceremony for celebrating the birth of a daughter.

Zocher HaBrit – Literally, remembering the covenant. Ceremony held on the night before *Brit Milah* to protect the child.

RESOURCES

For the Teacher

Adelman, Penina V. *Miriam's Well: Rituals for Jewish Women around the Year.* 2d ed. New York: Biblio Press, 1990.

Barth, Lewis M., ed. *Berit Mila in the Reform Context.* Los Angeles: Berit Mila Board of Reform Judaism, 1990.

Bleich, J. David. *Judaism and Healing: Halakhic Perspectives.* New York: KTAV Publishing House, Inc., 1981.

Cohen, Eugene J. *Guide to Ritual Circumcision and Redemption of the First-Born Son.* New York: KTAV Publishing House, Inc., 1984, o.p.

Diamant, Anita. *The New Jewish Baby Book: Names, Ceremonies & Customs, A Guide for Today's Families.* Woodstock, VT: Jewish Lights Publishing, 1993.

Elkins, Dov Peretz. *Jewish Guided Imagery: A How-To Book for Rabbis, Educators and Group Leaders.* Princeton, NJ: Growth Associates, 1996.

Feldman, David M. *Marital Relations, Birth Control and Abortion in Jewish Law.* New York: Schocken Books, 1974, o.p.

Feldman, David M., and Fred Rosner, eds. *Compendium on Medical Ethics: Jewish Moral, Ethical and Religious Principles in Medical Practice.* New York: Federation of Jewish Philanthropies of New York, Inc, 1984, o.p.

Gold, Michael. *and Hannah wept: Infertility, Adoption, and the Jewish Couple.* Philadelphia: Jewish Publication Society, 1988.

———. *Does God Belong in the Bedroom?* Philadelphia: Jewish Publication Society, 1992.

HaLevi, Aaron. *Sefer haHinnuch: The Book of [Mitzvah] Education,* vol. 1. New York: Feldheim Publishers, 1978.

Jacob, Walter, ed. *American Reform Responsa.* New York: Central Conference of American Rabbis, 1983.

Jacob, Walter. *Contemporary American Reform Responsa.* New York: Central Conference of American Rabbis, 1987.

Kadden, Barbara Binder, and Bruce Kadden. *Teaching Mitzvot: Concepts, Values, and Activities.* Rev. ed. Denver: A.R.E. Publishing, Inc., 1996.

Kessler, Eve Jacobson. "Jewish Magic: New Age Jews and Chasidim Discover Ancient Charms in Segullas and Amulets." In *Forward,* September 9, 1994, p. 11.

———. "New Afterbirth Ritual Takes Root in Berkeley." In *Forward,* October 22, 1993, p. 12.

Kohn, Ingrid; Perry-Lynn Moffit; with Isabelle A. Wilkins. *A Silent Sorrow: Pregnancy Loss: Guidance and Support for You and Your Family.* New York: Dell Publishing Co. Inc, 1993.

Kolatch, Alfred J. *The Complete Dictionary of English and Hebrew First Names.* New York: Jonathan David Publishers, Inc., 1984.

———. *This Is the Torah.* Middle Village, NY: Jonathan David Publishers, Inc., 1988.

Levine, Elizabeth Resnick, ed. *A Ceremonies Sampler: New Rites, Celebrations, and Observances of Jewish Women.* San Diego: Woman's Institute for Continuing Jewish Education, 1991.

Lieberman, Dale. *Witness to the Covenant of Circumcision: Bris Milah.* Northvale, NJ: Jason Aronson Inc., 1997.

Maslin, Simeon J., ed. *Gates of Mitzvah: A Guide to the Jewish Life Cycle.* New York: Central Conference of American Rabbis, 1979.

Orenstein, Debra, ed. *Lifecycles: Jewish Women on Life Passages & Personal Milestones,* Vol. 1. Woodstock, VT: Jewish Lights Publishing, 1994.

Reiss, Fred. *The Standard Guide to the Jewish and Civil Calendar.* West Orange, NJ: Behrman House, Inc., 1986.

Richards, Stephen, ed. *Manginot: 201 Songs for Jewish Schools.* New York: Transcontinental Music Publications and New Jewish Music Press, 1992.

Rosenkrantz, Linda, and Pamela Satran. *Beyond Sarah & Sam: An Enlightened Guide to Jewish Baby Naming.* New York: St. Martin's Press, 1992.

Rosner, Fred, and J. David Bleich, eds. *Jewish Bioethics.* Brooklyn, NY: Hebrew Publishing Company, 1979, o.p.

Samuel, Rinna. "the game of the name." In *Keeping Posted.* Vol. XVIII, No. 1. October, 1972.

Stern, Chaim, ed. *On the Doorposts of Your House: Prayers and Ceremonies for the Jewish Home.* New York: Central Conference of American Rabbis, 1994.

Strassfeld, Sharon, and Michael Strassfeld, eds. *The Second Jewish Catalog: Sources and Resources.* Philadelphia: Jewish Publication Society, 1976.

Tucker, JoAnne, and Susan Freeman. *Torah in Motion: Creating Dance Midrash.* Denver: A.R.E. Publishing, Inc., 1990.

For the Students

Beiner, Stan J. *Class Acts: Plays & Skits for Jewish Settings.* Denver: A.R.E. Publishing, Inc., 1992.

Gersh, Harry. *When a Jew Celebrates.* West Orange, NJ: Behrman House, Inc., 1971, pp. 17- 34.

Grishaver, Joel Lurie. *The Life Cycle Workbook.* Denver: A.R.E. Publishing Inc., 1983, pp. 14-25.

Grode, Phyllis Agins. *Sophie's Name.* Rockville, MD: Kar-Ben Copies, Inc., 1990.

Lifton, Betty Jean. *Tell Me a Real Adoption Story.* New York: Alfred A. Knopf, 1993.

Miller, Kathryn Ann. *Did My First Mother Love Me? A Story for an Adopted Child.* Buena Park, CA: Morning Glory Press, 1994.

Pasachoff, Naomi. *Basic Judaism for Young People: God.* West Orange, NJ: Behrman House, Inc., 1987, pp. 35-42.

Shekel, Michal. *The Jewish Lifecycle Book.* Hoboken, NJ: KTAV Publishing House, Inc., 1989.

Seuss, Dr. *Horton Hatches the Egg.* New York: Random House Books, 1966.

Turner, Ann. *Through Moon and Stars and Night Skies.* New York: HarperCollins Publishers, 1990.

Wise, Ira J. *LifeChoices: An Instant Lesson on Abortion.* Los Angeles: Torah Aura Productions, 1993.

Zwerin, Raymond A., and Richard J. Shapiro. *Judaism & Abortion.* Washington, DC: Religious Coalition for Reproductive Choice, n.d.

Zwerin, Raymond A.; Audrey Friedman Marcus; and Leonard Kramish. *Circumcision.* Denver: A.R.E. Publishing, Inc., 1983.

Audiovisual

Cohen, Myrna. *Lullabies & Quiet Time.* Sounds Write Productions, Inc. Audiocassette.

The Eighth Day: Circumcision/Hanukah. Ergo Media, Inc. Videocassette.

Intimate Story. Ergo Media Inc. Videocassette.

Losing Isaiah. Videocassette available at video stores.

A Question of Authority. Ergo Media Inc. Videocassette.

Sleep My Child: A Collection of Jewish Lullabies Sung in Yiddish, Hebrew, Ladino and English. Sounds Write Productions, Inc. Audiocassette/CD.

Solnik, Tanja. *A Legacy of Lullabies.* Sounds Write Productions, Inc. Audiocassette/CD.

———. *Lullabies and Love Songs.* Sounds Write Productions, Inc. Audiocassette/CD.

CHAPTER TWO
GROWING UP
CHILDHOOD • ADOLESCENCE • B'NAI MITZVAH

OVERVIEW

I F THE JEWISH FAMILY HAS BEEN PRAISED and envied, it is in no small measure due to its attitude toward children. It is virtually impossible to exaggerate the importance of children in Judaism. It can be said that God's first commandment is to be fruitful and multiply (see Chapter 1), to which Jews have added . . . and give to your offspring a good Jewish education.

"A religion that relies so strongly on the continuation of generation after generation to transmit its message will naturally value children and what they learn and do, to a great extent" (*Jewish Parenting*, Judith Z. Abrams and Steven A. Abrams, p. 35).

Indeed, the passing down of the Jewish heritage from generation to generation informs most of the rituals and celebrations concerning the young. This chapter will explore Judaism's teachings about childhood and adolescence, and the life cycle ceremonies that mark this period of time.

JEWISH EDUCATION

Throughout most of Jewish history, the family was the primary institution for educating children. Growing up in a home in which Judaism was as integral to life as breathing, children quickly developed an abiding knowledge of and commitment to Judaism. "It is the duty of parents to train their children in the practice of all the *mitzvot*, whether biblical or Rabbinic. Each child should be trained in accordance with his or her intelligence. It is also required for parents to guard their children against any forbidden act" (*Shulchan Aruch, Choshen Mishpat* 165:1).

When it comes to child rearing, Jewish sources go beyond the specifically Jewish; all areas and aspects of child development become their purview. Here is just one example of such teaching: "Abaye said: My mother said that the proper treatment for a child consists of [bathing it in] warm water and [rubbing it with] oil. If [the child] has grown a little, [give the child] an egg with *kutah* [a preservative]. If [the child] grows up more [one should expect] the breaking of clay vessels. Therefore Rabbah bought clay vessels in damaged condition so that his children could break them" (*Yoma* 78b).

Many suggestions focus on Jewish practice. While a young person was not required to observe any *mitzvot* until becoming a Bar or Bat Mitzvah, the Rabbis recognized that teaching them to do *mitzvot* at an early age was greatly beneficial. For example: "Our Rabbis taught: a minor who knows how to shake [the *lulav*] is required to shake the *lulav*. [One who knows how] to wrap himself [in a *tallit*] is required to perform the *mitzvah* of *tzitzit* . . . *one who is able to speak, his father teaches him Torah and the recitation of the Sh'ma*" (*Sukkah* 42b). Early childhood educators affirm the value of learning at a young age.

Formal opportunities for early childhood learning abound in the Jewish community. Large synagogues often have parenting centers which offer classes and programs for parents and young children. Most Jewish communities have one or more Jewish preschools, some of which provide extended day care during which learning takes place.

Some congregations offer "Cradle Roll" or other parent-child programs to introduce young children to the holidays and other Jewish observances. And many synagogues offer Tot Shabbat services especially designed for preschool aged children. All of these programs are based upon the shared belief that exposing a child to Judaism at a young age will help create the foundation for a strong Jewish identity.

Supplementing what is learned in the home, a young child's Jewish education was continued in school. For centuries, that school took the form of a small room — a *cheder* — which was usually connected to the synagogue. The *cheder* was a rudimentary school for the teaching of Jewish subjects to the very young. Usually it was a private school, with the teacher being paid by the parents. Children began *cheder* at age three and studied there until age 13. The focus of the curriculum was the *Siddur*, Torah with Rashi's commentary, and — for the older students — Talmud.

According to tradition the first day of *cheder* was marked with a special celebration. The letters of the Hebrew *aleph bet* were written on a child's slate and smeared with honey. As children pronounced a letter, their reward was to lick off its honey. Thus, from the outset, Jewish learning was connected with sweetness.

In contemporary Jewish communities, families have a choice between day schools and supplementary schools to provide formal Jewish education. Until the last third of the twentieth century, day schools were the virtual domain of the Orthodox community. The vast majority of American Jews were solidly committed to public school education — because it offered a popular education seen as the key to "getting ahead" in the word, and because it enabled children to mix and integrate with non-Jews in a secular society. By the 1980s, a variety of factors conspired to change this reality, including school busing, the deterioration of inner city schools, renewed interest in Judaism, and recognition of the importance of Jewish education.

Virtually every major metropolitan area with a significant Jewish population has at least one Jewish day school. Many communities offer a variety of day schools including Reform, Conservative, Orthodox, and non-denominational or community day schools. Parents often opt to send their children to a Jewish day school not only to get a quality Jewish education and learn Hebrew, but also because of the excellent general education that such schools offer.

Some day schools divide the curriculum by teaching general subjects in the morning and Judaica in the afternoon, or vice versa. Others offer an integrated approach in which Judaica is integrated into all aspects of the curriculum, including general studies.

While the number of students receiving a day school education has increased significantly in recent years, a vast majority of Jewish children receiving any Jewish education attend a supplementary school. These include synagogue schools as well as community based Talmud Torah schools. Such schools face the challenge of providing a quality Jewish education for Jewish children after they have attended a full day of school and/or on weekend mornings.

Complementing formal Jewish education are the informal Jewish educational experiences of camp and youth group. Camping may be the most successful Jewish educational endeavor. By providing an environment in which Jewish youth live a Jewish life 24 hours a day, camps have been able to instill pride and knowledge and social connections while also putting the children into contact with older counselors and adults who model an enthusiasm for Jewish life. Even Jewish camps which do not offer explicit Jewish programming offer the opportunity for Jews to spend significant amounts of time with other Jews. This in itself is of no small benefit.

Both the Reform and Conservative movements have an extensive system of camps (UAHC and Ramah) throughout North America. In addition, some large congregations sponsor their own camps. Jewish Community Centers and other organizations and agencies offer both day camping and overnight camping experiences.

While most camping experiences take place during summer months, youth grouping provides informal educational experiences the year round. Youth groups serve to bring together Jewish children and teenagers for social, religious, and educational programs. The Reform (National Federation of Temple Youth/NFTY), Conservative (United Synagogue Youth/USY) and Orthodox (National Conference of Synagogue Youth/NCSY) movements each sponsor youth programming. In addition, organizations such as B'nai B'rith (B'nai B'rith

Youth Organization/BBYO – AZA/BBG) and Hadassah (Young Judea) sponsor youth groups for all denominations and for the unaffiliated.

The recent concern for Jewish continuity has triggered the creation of a variety of other programs directed at strengthening the Jewish identity of our youth. The most significant of these programs is the Israel Experience — a summer trip to Israel for Jewish teenagers. Since it is these youngsters who will be the future members and leaders of the Jewish community, it is to them that such programs are directed. The Israel Experience and other Israel programs seek to instill a love for the land of Israel, as well as a commitment to Judaism.

Upsherin

A relatively obscure ritual observed by Hasidic and some other Orthodox Jews is *upsherin*, a Yiddish word meaning "to shear off." It is the celebration of a Jewish boy's first haircut, usually held on *Lag B'Omer* after the child's third birthday.

Upsherin (also called *hachlakah* — Hebrew for "to make smooth") dates back at least as far as sixteenth century Poland. At this communal event, family and friends cut the child's hair, leaving the side curls called *payot* (Hebrew) or *payes* (Yiddish). There is a tradition that the hair is weighed and the boy's family donates a comparable amount of money to *tzedakah*.

The ceremony also serves to celebrate the child's beginning of Jewish education and the wearing of the *tallit katan*, a small *tallit* with *tzitzit* (ritual fringes) which is worn at all times by observant male Jews.

Consecration

The beginning of a child's formal Jewish education is celebrated in many schools with a ceremony called Consecration. Usually held on Simchat Torah, Consecration is observed with the new students in the school being called up to the *bimah*. They sometimes sing a song relating to education or recite the *Sh'ma* or another appropriate blessing. In turn they are blessed by the Rabbi and usually given a miniature Torah scroll. Sometimes they are honored by leading the first *hakafah* to celebrate Simchat Torah.

Bar/Bat Mitzvah

The most important life passage of Jewish childhood and adolescence is Bar Mitzvah for a boy and Bat Mitzvah for a girl. "Bar and Bat Mitzvah is about ritual maturity. It is about growing up as Jew. It is about becoming a fuller member of the Jewish community. But it is also about moral responsibility, about connecting to Torah, to community, to God" (*Putting God on the Guest List*, Jeffrey K. Salkin, p. 11.).

Bar Mitzvah refers to a young man who has reached age 13, when he is expected to follow the *mitzvot* and to take personal responsibility for his actions. A young woman becomes a Bat Mitzvah at age 12½, when she, too, is expected to observe the *mitzvot* incumbent upon women and take responsibility for her actions. One automatically becomes a Bat or Bar Mitzvah at age 12½ or 13 respectively, regardless if there is a worship ceremony to mark the occasion. In fact, for most of Jewish history, there was no formal ceremony; reaching the age of Jewish maturity was synonymous with being a Bat or Bar Mitzvah.

The terms Bar Mitzvah and Bat Mitzvah are not contained in the Tanach, and ages 12½ and 13 are not recognized as significant points in one's life. Rather, age 20, when a male was fit for military service, is the primary age of significance. When God tells Moses to take a census, God says, "All who are entered upon the records, from age 20 upward, shall give an offering to God" (Exodus 30:14). Later, when another census was needed, God says, "You and Aaron shall record them by their groups, from the age of 20 years up, all those in Israel who are able to bear arms" (Numbers 1:3). Twenty is also a key age for another reason. Those who were over twenty when the people left Egypt were to die in the wilderness. Those who had not reached that age at the time of the Exodus would be allowed to enter the Promised Land.

The earliest Rabbinic sources, however, indicate that age 13 had become an important milestone. Rabbi Judah ben Tema, presenting an overview of the development of one's life as a Jew wrote, ". . . at age 13 [one should observe] *mitzvot*" (*Pirke Avot* 5:24). In the Talmud and in *Midrashic* literature, age 13 is significant as a time of religious and legal maturity. For example, the Rabbis taught that Abraham looked into heaven at age 13 and recognized that there was a God. He rejected his father's idols at the same age (*Pirke deRabbi Eliezer* 26). A *midrash* also teaches that at age 13, Jacob went to study Torah, while his brother Esau went to worship idols (*Genesis Rabbah* 63:10).

A young man could serve on a *Bet Din* at age 13 and could purchase specified items; any vows he made were considered binding (*Niddarim* 5:6). The Rabbis understood that age 13 for boys and age 12½ for girls were significant because they were the ages of physical maturity (*Kiddushin* 16b). Whereas a person was born with a *Yetzer HaRa* (evil inclination), the Rabbis asserted that the *Yetzer HaTov* (good inclination) developed fully only at age 13. Therefore one could fully control one's desires only at this later age (*Avot deRabbi Natan* 16).

Becoming a Bar Mitzvah, and therefore responsible for one's actions, meant that one's parents were for the first time relieved of this obligation. In recognition of this transfer of moral responsibility, it became the practice for the father of a 13-year-old son to recite the following:

בָּרוּךְ שֶׁפְּטָרַנִי מֵעוֹנְשׁוֹ שֶׁל זֶה.

Baruch Shep'tarani May'onsho Shel Zeh.

Blessed is the One who has freed me from responsibility for this one.

It is clear that for much of Jewish history, becoming a Bar Mitzvah or Bat Mitzvah was an automatic development, not recognized in any formal way. During the Middle Ages, however, a ceremony developed to mark this important transition. In order to symbolize his participation in the community as an adult, accepting the responsibility for observing the *mitzvot*, the young boy would be given an *aliyah* (called to the Torah) to read *Maftir* (the last few verses of the *Parashah*). He would also chant the *Haftarah*, the weekly reading from *Nevi'im* (the Prophets) or *Ketuvim* (the Writings).

In some communities, the young man would also lead part or all of the worship service and deliver a *drashah*, a short discourse interpreting the Torah reading or pertaining to a matter of Jewish law.

Originally, the *drashah* was offered at the celebration after the worship service — often held in the family's home.

The Bat Mitzvah ceremony for young Jewish women did not begin until the twentieth century. Some nineteenth century families celebrated a girl's twelfth birthday with a special meal (*Seudat Mitzvah*) and other non-synagogue rituals. However, the first Bat Mitzvah to be celebrated in conjunction with a worship service occurred in 1922. It was celebrated by Judith Kaplan, the daughter of Rabbi Mordecai Kaplan, then a teacher at the Jewish Theological Seminary. He would go on to found Reconstructionist Judaism, and she to become a respected musicologist. During the service, Judith Kaplan read the Torah blessings and part of her Torah portion from a book, rather than from the Torah scroll, and did so only after her father had read the same portion. As the Bat Mitzvah ceremony has evolved, young women in some congregations are permitted to do all of the rituals that young men do.

Today, in Reform, Reconstructionist, and most Conservative congregations, there is no appreciable difference between the involvement of a Bar Mitzvah and Bat Mitzvah in the worship service. In some Conservative congregations, the Bat Mitzvah is limited to reading the *Haftarah*, or the like. In some Traditional congregations, Bat Mitzvah takes place on a Friday evening at a Kabbalat Shabbat Service, during which one or more young women present readings to those assembled. Orthodox Jews do not mark a girl's Bat Mitzvah with any religious ritual, but the rite of passage is usually recognized with a special observance or party.

Throughout much of contemporary Jewish history there has been concern about the meaning of Bar Mitzvah and Bat Mitzvah, and the overemphasis on the celebration, as opposed to the ceremony. In some European communities, sumptuary laws were established by the Rabbis to discourage excessive expenditures for such celebrations. Similar concerns have been raised by some Rabbis in the contemporary North American Jewish community.

In order to enhance the meaning of the experience for the young man or young woman, a variety of strategies has been tried in recent years. These include:

Bar/Bat Mitzvah Twinning: In the 1970s, when Jews in the Soviet Union were not allowed to practice their religion, a Bar/Bat Mitzvah would be "twinned" with a boy or girl in the Soviet Union who was not able to celebrate a Bar or Bat Mitzvah. The Bar/Bat Mitzvah was encouraged to write to his/her twin and to symbolize the twin's participation in the ceremony by placing a *tallit* and prayerbook in an empty chair on the *bimah,* or in some other manner. When the Soviet Union allowed more Jews to emigrate in the late 1980s, "twins" were often able to get together face to face in the United States or Israel. Some twinning still occurs with children in the former Soviet Union who did not emigrate. In recent years, twinning has also extended to Ethiopian Jewish children in Israel.

Mitzvah/Tzedakah projects: To emphasize the responsibility of becoming a Bar/Bat Mitzvah, some congregations require a *tzedakah* project or the completion of a number of *mitzvot* (often 13). These range from simple projects such as visiting residents of a nursing home or serving a meal at a local soup kitchen to long term projects. Sometimes, guests are asked to bring canned food or other items for a particular charity or to make a donation in lieu of a gift. Often, the Bar/Bat Mitzvah will contribute a percentage of the money received as a gift to *tzedakah.*

Bar/Bat Mitzvah in Israel: Some families choose to celebrate the Bar or Bat Mitzvah of their child in Israel rather than at one's congregation, thus strengthening the family's ties to the land of Israel. The ceremony is often held at the *Kotel* (Western Wall) or on Masada.

MAZON: A Jewish Response to Hunger offers grants to organizations in North America, Israel, and other countries which provide food to those in need. MAZON collects most of its funds by asking families that celebrate a *simchah* (such as a Bar/Bat Mitzvah or a wedding) to donate three percent of the cost of the food served at the reception. Many synagogues encourage families to participate in this *mitzvah.*

Confirmation

Confirmation was one of the most important religious innovations made by the early Reform Movement. The first Confirmation ceremony was held in 1810 in the synagogue in Kassel, Germany. It was an adaptation of the Confirmation ceremony then held in Christian churches in Germany, and was held as an alternative to Bar Mitzvah. Unlike Bar Mitzvah, Confirmation was done as a group ceremony; young women as well as young men were included. Most significantly, Confirmation was held usually at age 16, at the end of tenth grade, thus extending Jewish education by several years. Rather than focusing on the ability to read Hebrew and chant the Torah and *Haftarah,* Confirmation focuses on the commitment of the young people to Judaism.

The Confirmation ceremony is most often held on Shavuot, the holiday celebrating the receiving of the Torah at Mount Sinai. Confirmation students symbolically accept the Torah during the ceremony, and usually speak about the meaning of Judaism.

In some Reform congregations (especially in the nineteenth century and the first part of the twentieth century), Confirmation replaced Bar Mitzvah. In most, it was in addition to Bar Mitzvah. Today, most Reform, Conservative, and Reconstructionist congregations, and many Traditional congregations, celebrate Confirmation. The ceremony is sometimes called by another name, such as *Kabbalat Torah* (accepting the Torah).

ADOLESCENCE

Adolescence is one of the most challenging stages of life. Experiencing increased independence, teenagers often test parental limits and their own personal limits with drugs, alcohol, and sex. Real and perceived pressure sometimes leads to eating disorders, depression, and attempted suicide, among the many potentially serious problems. Jewish youth are not exempt from any of these challenges. Yet, because of the perception that the Jewish family is invariably strong and should therefore be impervious to problems of this sort, when such problems occur they are sometimes ignored or downplayed.

Many synagogues and Jewish institutions, however, provide a variety of programs that deal with these challenges. They are often addressed as part of the supplementary school and day school curriculum for teenagers. Frequently they are brought to the fore through parent-teen forums and discussions sponsored by the synagogue, the school, or some other communal agency.

Adolescence is a time of important transitions. Getting a driver's license is one of the most important rites of passage for a teenager. It represents a time of increased independence and responsibility. Registering and then voting in an election for the first time is another significant event in the life of a young person. Jews have taken the privilege to vote quite seriously and have tended to vote in numbers disproportionate to the population. Jewish organizations, such as the Religious Action Center of Reform Judaism, the National Council of Synagogues, and the National Jewish Community Relations Advisory Council have instituted voter registration drives prior to major elections to encourage Jews to register and vote.

Registering for military service is another impor-tant milestone. Although there is currently no draft and the military has become a profession, anyone who considers himself/herself to be a conscientious objector should indicate such at the time of register-ing. The status of conscientious objector is not an easy on for Jews to affirm, since it implies that one would have refused even to have fought against Hitler. Nevertheless, some Jews have claimed this status and have used Jewish texts to support their claim.

Perhaps the most significant rite of passage of the teenage years is leaving home, usually to enter college, but sometimes to enter the military or to take a job. Such a transition in the family often leads to a new type of relationship between child and parent(s). Some Rabbis and laypersons have experi-mented with creating rituals to mark a young person's leaving home. (For some suggestions regarding creating such rituals, see *The Second Jewish Catalog,* Sharon Strassfeld and Michael Strassfeld, p. 89.)

SOURCES FROM THE TRADITION

Rabbi Pinchas in the name of Rabbi Levi said: "Jacob and Esau were like a myrtle and a rose bush that were growing next to each other. When they grew up, this one [Jacob] gave its fragrance, but the other one [Esau] gave its thorns. For 13 years, each went to school and came home from school. Then Jacob went to the house of study, while Esau went to the houses of idol worship." Rabbi Eliezer ben Rabbi Simeon said, "Parents are responsible for their children until they reach age 13. Then a parent shall say, "Blessed is God who has freed me from the responsibility of this one."

(*Genesis Rabbah* 63:10)

He [Rabbi Judah ben Tema] used to say: "At five years of age [one should study] Bible; at ten [one should study] *Mishnah*; at thirteen [one should perform the] *mitzvot*; at fifteen [one should study] Talmud . . . ."

(*Pirke Avot* 5:24)

One should not make children fast at all on Yom Kippur. However, one should train them a year or two before [they are of age] so that they get used to religious practices . . . . Rav Huna said: "At eight and nine years one trains them by hours. At 10 and 11 years they must fast to the end of the day according to a Rabbinic ordinance. At 12 they must fast to the end of the day according to biblical law." This refers to girls. Rav. Nahman said: "At 9 and 10 one trains them by hours. At 11 and 12 they must fast to the end of the day according to a Rabbinic ordinance. At 13 they must fast to the end of the day according to a biblical law." This refers to boys.

(*Yoma* 82a)

The time for training a child in the performance of positive *mitzvot* depends upon the ability and the understanding of that child. Therefore, when the child understands the significance of Shabbat, it is the child's responsibility to hear the *Kiddush* and *Havdalah*, etc. The time to train a child to observe the negative commandments, whether biblical or Rabbinic, is when the child understands when told that we are forbidden to do a certain thing or that we are forbidden to eat certain food. One should train a child to respond "*Amen*" and other responses at synagogue. From the time that an infant begins to respond "*Amen*," the child has a share in the world to come.

(*Shulchan Aruch, Choshen Mishpat* 165:2)

ACTIVITIES

Primary

1. A major part of a Jewish child's education is learning how to perform Jewish rituals. To show students how various parts of their bodies perform different rituals do simple outline drawings of the mouth, nose, eyes, ears, head, hands, and feet (each body part should be on a separate piece of paper). The students volunteer several rituals for each body part while dictation is taken and added to the appropriate drawing. Note: Some rituals use multiple body parts. As a follow-up, outline the body of each of the students on butcher paper. The students decorate their outlines with facial features, clothes, shoes, etc. using crayons, markers, or construction paper. Each student chooses a Jewish ritual and adds it to their outlined bodies. The ritual is added as a label and the bodies can be cut out and used as a classroom display.

2. For Consecration or another significant occasion, obtain plain white *kipot*. Provide the students with a variety of fabric paints and markers. Have the students decorate *kipot* with their Hebrew names and Jewish symbols. (If it is not the custom for girls to wear *kipot* in your synagogue, have them decorate *kipot* for their father, brother, or other individual.)

3. To help celebrate Consecration or another rite of passage, bake loaves of *challah* in a special shape, such as a Torah or *Magen David*. To shape a Torah: provide each student 1 to 1½ cups of dough. Using ⅔ of this amount, mold with hands into a rectangle at least 1" thick. With the remainder of the dough, make the *Atzay Chaim* (the Torah rollers) which extend on both narrow ends of the rectangle. If desired, reserve additional dough and decorate the body of the Torah like a mantel. To shape a *Magen David*: provide each student with one cup of *challah* dough. Each student should divide his/her dough into two equal parts. The dough is then rolled into two long cylinders of equal length. Each length is then formed into an equilateral triangle. Place one triangle on top of the other to form a six-pointed star.

4. Read to the class *My Brother's Bar Mitzvah* by Janet Gallant. Ask the students to recall any experiences they had at the Bar/Bat Mitzvah of a sibling, cousin, or friend. As a class, write a story about a Bar/Bat Mitzvah, featuring the students' favorite storybook or television characters. Write the story on large sheets of paper, leaving room for student illustrations.

5. Each student creates a "Book of Firsts." Brainstorm with the class the important firsts in the students' lives. For example, first tooth, first step, first Chanukah, naming or *Brit Milah*, first day of school, first day of Jewish education, first haircut, etc. Create a book with one page for each first. Title each page and draw appropriate shapes on some pages (outline of a Torah on the first day of Jewish education, outline of a tooth for first tooth, a *dreidle* or *chanukiah* on the first day of Chanukah). Copy all pages for each student in the class. Collate into a book. Invite the parents to provide appropriate materials such as pictures and written descriptions and place them in the book.

6. Create a miniature Ark for the Torah scrolls each student will receive at Consecration. Visit the sanctuary for the students to see the Ark and the Torah scrolls it contains. Point out the doors, curtains, and other significant features. Tell the students they will receive a miniature Torah and that they will make an Ark to keep it in. Provide each student with a shoe box or other appropriately-sized carton, fabric to line the box and to make curtains, paper to cover the exterior, and markers, crayons, and paints to decorate the outside.

7. Organize a "reading picnic" for your students. Gather together a variety of Jewish storybooks and folktales about the life cycle, holidays, or other topics, and two or three large blankets that can be used outdoors. Find a comfortable spot and hold a reading picnic. This may be an

excellent opportunity to mix younger students (non-readers or beginning readers) with older students (readers).

8. To demonstrate to the students how they are growing and changing during their school years, create booklets which record their physical and mental development. Information to list includes: height, weight, shoe size, learned the *aleph bet*, recited the *Sh'ma*, Shabbat blessings, Four Questions, "*Shehecheyanu*," learned to read, read a chapter/book, counted to 100, add/subtract, multiply/divide.

9. Read *The Narrowest Bar Mitzvah* by Steven Schnur to the class. Together with the students, recount and list all the calamities that befell the family. Did they all think that the Bar Mitzvah would not take place? Also, ask the students to describe the grandfather's house. Help the students make an actual model of one of the rooms in the house. Block off a 6' wide space. Plot out where furniture, plants, and rugs would go. How many students can fit in the space. Is it comfortable? Could they imagine a Bar Mitzvah in such a small space? Have students write a story that includes challenges and problems. Include in the story creative solutions.

10. Make paper weights using a rock and a photo of each child. Choose various Jewish rituals that the children can demonstrate (e.g., holding a *Kiddush* cup, opening the doors to the Ark, holding and reading from a *Siddur*, lighting the Shabbat candles). Pose each child performing the ritual and take a snapshot. Choose appropriate sized rocks to hold the developed pictures (you may want to develop the photos in a small size format). Have the students paint the rocks with thinned white glue or decoupage glue (sold in craft stores). Mount the photos on the wet rocks. Allow to dry.

11. To greet students on their first day of Religious School, prepare a mystery picture for each of them. Use white construction paper and write a brief welcome message to each student using white crayon or a white wax candle. Distribute a mystery picture to each student along with a ¾" wide paintbrush and one color of tempera paint. Instruct students to paint over the mystery picture and a special message will appear.

12. Celebrate Hebrew birthdays in your class room. Use a perpetual Hebrew calendar to determine each child's Hebrew birthday. Have children decorate individual paper birthday cakes with their name, Gregorian birth date, and Hebrew birth date. Create a bulletin board display and place a Hebrew calendar with it. On each child's Hebrew birth date have a class celebration. Resource: *The Standard Guide to the Jewish and Civil Calendar* by Fred Reiss.

13. Complete the instant lesson *A Lifetime of Torah* by Joel Lurie Grishaver, which introduces the students to the importance of studying Torah at all stages of the life cycle.

Intermediate

1. B'nai Mitzvah students are able to share more about themselves and their thoughts or ideas about Judaism with a Bar/Bat Mitzvah poster. Using poster board or foam core, each student creates a display which includes the following: a photograph, a short autobiography, name and synopsis of their Torah portion, thoughts about Judaism and their relationship to it, a description of their Bar/Bat Mitzvah project, and any additional photos or illustrations. This poster is then placed right outside the sanctuary on the student's Bar/Bat Mitzvah day for worshipers to read.

2. Invite the parents to class and watch the video *The Mitzvah Machine*, a 10-minute trigger film about a boy who builds a robot to perform in his place at his Bar Mitzvah. Utilize the discussion guide which comes with the video to facilitate a conversation about the issues raised by the video.

3. Create a mock-up of a Western Union telegram or a format for an e-mail. Using one or more of the following words or phrases, have the student write congratulatory messages to someone who is celebrating a Bar/Bat Mitzvah: *mazal tov* (congratulations); *nachas* (pride); *simchah* (joyous occasion); *shalom u'vrachah* (peace and blessing).

4. Students will create mini-information booklets on one of the Jewish life cycle events associated with childhood. Allow students to choose between Consecration, Bar/Bat Mitzvah, or Confirmation. Provide resources for the students so that they may choose the facts they would like to include in their booklets. One fact should be written on each page. Students may add illustrations. Students share their completed projects with each other.
Resources: *Rites of Passage: A Guide to the Jewish Life Cycle* by Ronald H. Isaacs; *The Jewish Life-cycle Book* by Michal Shekel; *The Life Cycle Workbook* by Joel Lurie Grishaver; *When a Jew Celebrates* by Harry Gersh.

5. Introduce the Jewish art form of micrography. Micrography consists of tiny writing that takes a form, such as an outline of Jerusalem, a Torah scroll, a Jewish symbol, a famous Jewish personality, etc. Students should choose a symbolic shape that is associated with Bar/Bat Mitzvah such as Torah, *tallit*, *Magen David*, etc. Using a poem, prayer, or original writing, students write the words in the chosen shape.

6. View the video *The Journey*, the story of a 13-year-old Soviet boy who learns about Bar Mitzvah from an American while the two travel on a train. Discuss: How does the American try to teach the Soviet boy about Judaism? What is the Soviet boy's response? What does the American learn about the meaning of Judaism during the journey? In what way does the boy become a Bar Mitzvah? Ask the students to imagine that it is now ten years later and the boy, now a young man, is writing to the American. Each student writes a letter as the boy, reflecting on what the experience meant to him and how the experience changed his life.

7. Ask your students whether they have been to a Hall of Fame and to describe it in brief. Tell the students that you think it has been a great oversight that there is no B'nai Mitzvah Hall of Fame, but together the class will create one. Ask each student to make up a name for a B'nai Mitzvah and the reason for enshrining that person in the B'nai Mitzvah Hall of Fame. Give students examples to get them started such as: Oscar Meyerstein holds the record for receiving the most fountain pens: twelve. Hillary Handelmacher holds the record for quickest recitation of the *Haftarah*: 7.5 seconds. Encourage the students to be humorous. Give each student a large sheet of paper to draw a portrait and write the caption. Display on a bulletin board entitled B'nai Mitzvah Hall of Fame.

8. View *The Discovery*, about a 12-year-old boy struggling with his Jewish identity as he prepares for his Bar Mitzvah. After viewing the film, allow the students to express their reactions by creating a mural. Provide a long sheet of butcher paper, markers, glue sticks, crayons, scissors, and Jewish magazines. Upon completion of the mural, each student should explain his or her part and its relationship to the film.

9. Have each student design a Bar or Bat Mitzvah invitation which reflects the theme of a particular *parashah*. Assign each student a *parashah*. Students should read through the *parashah*, choose a phrase and image(s) for the invitation. For example, for *parashah* Balak the student might choose "How goodly are your tents O Jacob, your dwelling places O Israel" (Numbers 24:5) with a design of tents or the entrance to a synagogue. Use high quality art paper, chisel point markers, and other media, such as watercolors, pastels, and/or colored markers.

10. Make a silhouette of each student's head. Tape a large sheet of black construction paper on the wall. Seat the student on a chair and shine a

bright light. With white chalk, carefully draw around the shadow that has been created. Using the chalk line as the cutting line, have each student cut out his/her silhouette. Attach the silhouette to a poster board or bulletin board. Each student is to create a word bubble out of white construction paper. Each student completes the phrase, "When I think of my Bar/Bat Mitzvah I . . . ." Students copy their completed phrase inside the word bubble and mount it on the poster.

11. To help students express their Jewish identity, have each one prepare an "All about My Jewish Self" poster. Supplies needed for this activity are: a poster board for each student, glue sticks, scissors, magazines, and newspapers of Jewish and secular content. Students select pictures, illustrations, words, and phrases to assemble their posters. These items are placed crazy-quilt style at various angles to make the posters busy, full, and colorful.

12. Read *Emma Ansky-Levine and Her Mitzvah Machine* by Lawrence Bush to your class, one or two chapters per session. Choose one or more of the following activities:
   a. As Hebrew words and Jewish holidays or concepts are mentioned, have the students keep a list of the words with definitions.
   b. Make up crossword puzzles or word searches using the Jewish and Hebrew vocabulary contained in the chapters as they are read.
   c. As a class, or in small groups, write another chapter based on a Jewish teaching for Emma and her *mitzvah* machine.

13. Complete the instant lesson *Gabriel's Ark* by Sandra Curtis, the story of the Bar Mitzvah of a child with special needs.

Secondary

1. There are many (Jewish) steps taken before a student becomes a member of the Confirmation class. Have students trace back the steps which were taken to bring them to this time and place. Provide students with small size cut-outs of feet or shoes and have them record each Jewish step they remember. The students can ask their families to provide more information. Ask the students to predict future Jewish steps they plan to take and add those to the footprints.

2. Create a ritual for obtaining a driver's permit or license. Include the following: readings about responsibility and safety, a pledge not to drink and drive, and the "*Shehecheyanu.*" The ceremony could be done by an individual family or by a class of students with their parents.

3. With your class, create a video about Bar/Bat Mitzvah. Students will serve as producer, director, writers, actors, and will be responsible for costumes and props. Write an original script including preparation for the event, family reunion, the ceremony, and the celebration.

4. Create stained glass windows with your students reflecting the themes of Jewish education, Consecration, B'nai Mitzvah, or Confirmation. Use a stained glass kit such as Gallery Glass by the company Plaid, available at most hobby and craft stores. Follow the directions on the kit.

5. Use historical Confirmation pictures to trigger a study of the Jewish demographics of your community. Examine the pictures that are available and record the number of students in each class. Make a graph to chart the results. Based on the chart, create a number of hypotheses about the demographics of the community. For example: when was the community the largest, when was it smallest? Are there any significant trends? Use other available records such as membership directories, bulletins, and congregational records to collect more data and to test your hypotheses.

6. Have students make welcome badges for the entering preschool or Kindergarten class. Using several different colors of felt, have students cut out badges in the shape of their choice (large enough to contain words of wel-

come and the recipient's name). With smaller pieces of felt, embellish the badge. With fabric writers, print the child's name and the phrase for welcome: *Baruch HaBa* (for a boy) or *B'ruchah HaBa'ah* (for a girl).

7. Assemble a panel to speak about the importance of registering to vote. The panel might include a local politician, a representative of the registrar of voters, an immigrant who has recently become a citizen, and a longtime voter. Be sure to provide information and material about how one registers to vote. If the timing is appropriate, students can run a voter registration campaign in the synagogue or community.

8. Invite a speaker from a local suicide prevention hotline or organization. Ask the speaker to focus on issues of teenage suicide. If appropriate, include opportunities for students to role play situations in which they respond to a friend who appears to be depressed or suicidal.
   Resource: *When Living Hurts* by Sol Gordon.

9. Hold a debate on the topic: Should a synagogue require that B'nai Mitzvah students give a percentage of their gifts to *tzedakah*?

10. Introduce your class to the concept of sumptuary laws which were enacted by various communities to limit wedding and Bar Mitzvah celebrations. Also share concerns by contemporary Rabbis about certain Bar/Bat Mitzvah parties (i.e., renting the Orange Bowl or a cruise ship, staging a safari with the Bar/Bat Mitzvah riding in on an elephant). Divide the class into three groups, assigning each group a task as follows:

    Group One creates the most outrageous Bar/Bat Mitzvah party the students can imagine. They will be called upon to defend their celebration.

    Group Two, acting as Rabbis and community leaders, create posters with slogans in opposition to such celebrations. They will be called upon to explain the sumptuary laws and why they should be observed.

Group Three, the chorus, writes a song which parodies the situation. Use popular tunes, writing new words to create the parody, for example, "It's My Party and I'll Spend If I Want To" to the tune of "It's My Party and I'll Cry If I Want To," "Born to Be Spoiled" to the tune of "Born to Be Wild."

The first group presents its Bar or Bat Mitzvah. As the group is about to finish, the second group interrupts with its protest and speech. Then the third group sings its parody. Groups One and Two should continue debating the issue, with Group Three asking questions and voting at the end.

11. Distribute to the class copies of the reading "At My Bar Mitzvah — and His" by Howard Kahn, which powerfully contrasts the typical Bar Mitzvah with the "Bar Mitzvah" of a 13-year-old Holocaust Resistance fighter. Divide the class in half and read the selection responsively. Discuss: What was the Bar Mitzvah of the Resistance fighter? How did it compare to the typical Bar Mitzvah? Present the reading at a Yom HaShoah service.
    Resource: *Mahzor Hadash: The New Mahzor for Rosh Hashanah and Yom Kippur,* compiled and edited by Sidney Greenberg and Jonathan D. Levine.

12. Complete the instant lesson *Coming of Mitzvah: What the Jewish Tradition Has to Say about Coming of Age* by Emily Feigenson and Joel Lurie Grishaver. This instant lesson explains the concept of a rite of passage, the meaning of maturity and responsibility, and the significance of Bar and Bat Mitzvah.

13. With girls preparing for Bat Mitzvah, do the instant lesson *Changes Recognized, Changes Achieved: Bat Mitzvah* by Emily Feigenson. This instant lesson examines what is unique about becoming a Jewish woman and relates it to the celebration of Bat Mitzvah.

14. With boys preparing for Bar Mitzvah, do the instant lesson *The True Story of Bar Mitzvah* by Joel Lurie Grishaver, which explores the background of Bar Mitzvah and examines what Judaism says about becoming a male adult.

15. With high school students, complete the instant lesson *Prevention Is a Mitzvah,* which raises the issue of whether schools should provide students with condoms and information about safer sex.

Hebrew

1. Distribute a sheet of sandpaper to each student along with various lengths and colors of yarn. Have students practice forming Hebrew letters and words they have learned by laying the yarn on the sandpaper.

2. Make quick stitch *aleph bet* boards for your students. Using Styrofoam trays or thin cardboard, pre-punch Hebrew letter forms into the tray. Number the punched holes one through the total number of holes needed for the letter, with holes approximately 1" apart. Note: Styrofoam trays are available for purchase from the meat counter of most grocery stores or from craft shops. Use a Phillips head screw driver or other blunt tipped tool for punching holes. Use large needles and yarn to do the stitching.

3. Have each child make a Hebrew name plaque for his/her family. Purchase a wooden plaque and, if desired, a stick for putting the sign into the ground. Instruct the students to outline the Hebrew word *mishpachah* (family) followed by the family's last name in Hebrew letters. The lettering may be done free-hand or with stencils. Using acrylic paint or permanent markers, have students decorate their plaques. Additional wooden shapes may be glued on and painted. Attach the plaques to the wooden sticks with wood glue. Allow to dry. Spray with a finish to permanently seal the plaque. Each child will have a gift to present to his/her family. Note: wooden plaques, sticks, and cut-outs are available at craft stores.

4. Teach your students the songs *"La'asok B'divrei Torah"* and *"Aylu Devarim."* Perform at a service.
Resources: *Sparks of Torah* by Kol B'seder; *Lifeline* by Beged Kefet.

5. Teach your students that the plural of Bar Mitzvah is B'nai Mitzvah (not Bar Mitzvahs) and the plural of Bat Mitzvah is B'not Mitzvah. Use other examples of plurals such as B'nai Yisrael (children of Israel) and B'nai B'rith (children of the covenant). Ask students to complete sentences such as:
Joey became a _____.
Deborah became a _____.
Joey and Jason became _____.
Susan and Ellen became _____.

Adult

1. Create a support group for parents of adolescents. Find a facilitator through such resources as Jewish Family Service or another agency. The group should explore strategies for dealing with teenagers with relationship to such issues as: drug and alcohol use, interdating, and premarital sex. Be sure to include the Rabbi or other Jewish professionals to provide the Jewish perspective on these issues.

2. Hold a panel discussion of parents who have celebrated a Bar or Bat Mitzvah of a child, inviting parents whose children will be celebrating a Bar or Bat Mitzvah. The panelists should talk about the experience, what it meant for the family, and practical suggestions. If there is interest, plan further meetings to explore specific issues.

3. Parents are often confused about the Jewish educational options available for their children. Invite representatives of local day schools and other community schools, as well as the congregational Religious School to speak on a panel about what their institutions have to offer. Target parents of young children for the audience. Do the same with personnel from Jewish camps.

4. Children leaving home can be an emotional time for parents. Hold a discussion on the "Empty Nest Syndrome." Invite parents who have already experienced their children leaving home to share their experiences and coping strategies. Together, create a ritual that families can observe when a child leaves home.

Family

1. It was a Jewish custom in Eastern Europe for the father to carry the young son to his first day of *cheder*, where the child was presented with sweets. The teacher would also write Hebrew letters on the child's new slate with honey for him to lick off. Expand this tradition by including both parents and sons and daughters. On the first day of the child's Jewish education, the parents should carry the child into the classroom and the teacher should present the child with a bag of treats. Explain the significance of the "*Shehecheyanu*" and sing it with students and parents. Take photographs of the children with their parents. To extend the activity each child may be presented with a photo scrapbook to begin recording and keeping mementos of his/her Jewish education.

2. Invite pre-B'nai Mitzvah students and their parents to view the video *Bar Mitzvah in Israel*. Break up into groups and discuss the similarities and differences between celebrating a Bar/Bat Mitzvah in Israel and in one's synagogue. What would be the advantages and disadvantages of celebrating a Bar/Bat Mitzvah in Israel in the view of the students? the parents? Invite a family that has celebrated a Bar/Bat Mitzvah in Israel to address the group. Provide information for those families that might be interested in celebrating a child's Bar/Bat Mitzvah in Israel.

3. To help families prepare for Bar/Bat Mitzvah complete the mini-course *Bar and Bat Mitzvah: A Family Education Unit* by Audrey Friedman

Marcus, et. al. This unit will help families understand the history and significance of Bar/Bat Mitzvah and discuss what the event means to their family.

4. Play the *Bar/Bat Mitzvah Game* by Nachama Skolnik Moskowitz with Grade 6-8 students and their parents. This values clarification game helps families examine significant issues related to Bar and Bat Mitzvah.

5. Invite pre-B'nai Mitzvah students and their parents to complete the instant lesson *Maseket Bar/Bat Mitzvah* by Joel Lurie Grishaver, which enables participants to create a "Coming of Mitzvah Tractate."

All-School

1. Each class makes a large *tallit* to be used for special group blessings of the class. Use a large piece of plain muslin fabric (at least 40" x 72"). Students embellish the *tallit* with Jewish and Hebrew phrases, their names, the date the *tallit* was begun, and Jewish symbols, using fabric paints, fabric applique, decorative stitches, and ribbon. The class can add to the *tallit* each year as new students join the class and the group celebrates life cycle events together.

2. Hold a special service or assembly to honor the teachers in your school. The program should include readings and songs on the theme of Talmud Torah, remarks or presentations by students and members of the Education Committee and/or Rabbi, and a gift for each teacher. You may also wish to honor former teachers and administrators.

3. Culminate the year with a program in which each class offers a presentation on the theme "On the Path of Jewish Learning." Each presentation should reflect a major component of the year's study through song, interpretive dance, poems, skits, or art.

GLOSSARY

Bar Mitzvah (pl. B'nai Mitzvah) – A 13-year-old boy who is expected to observe the *mitzvot* and the ceremony to celebrate reaching this milestone.

Bat Mitzvah (pl. B'not Mitzvah) – A 12½-year-old girl who is expected to observe the *mitzvot* incumbent upon women and the ceremony to celebrate reaching this milestone.

Cheder – Traditional Jewish elementary school.

Confirmation – Ceremony, usually held for tenth graders on Shavuot, in which students reconfirm their commitment to Judaism.

Consecration – Ceremony, usually held on Simchat Torah, celebrating the beginning of a child's formal Jewish education.

Talmud Torah – The study of Torah or a school, usually supplementary, for this purpose.

Upsherin – Celebration of a Jewish boy's first haircut, usually held on Lag B'Omer after the child's third birthday.

RESOURCES

For the Teachers

Abrams, Judith Z., and Steven A. Abrams. *Jewish Parenting: Rabbinic Insights.* Northvale, NJ: Jason Aronson, Inc., 1994.

Bell, Roselyn, ed. *The Hadassah Magazine Jewish Parenting Book.* New York: The Free Press, 1989.

Diamond, Barbara. *Bat Mitzvah: A Jewish Girl's Coming of Age.* New York: Viking Press, 1995.

Geffen, Rela M. *Celebration & Renewal: Rites of Passage in Judaism.* Philadelphia: Jewish Publication Society, 1993.

Greenberg, Sidney, and Jonathan D. Levine, eds. *Mahzor Hadash: The New Mahzor for Rosh Hashanah and Yom Kippur.* Bridgeport, CT: The Prayer Book Press, 1978.

Isaacs, Ronald H. *Rites of Passage: A Guide to the Jewish Life Cycle.* Hoboken, NJ: KTAV Publishing House, Inc., 1992.

Kimmel, Eric A. *Bar Mitzvah: A Jewish Boy's Coming of Age.* New York: Penguin Books USA Inc., 1995.

Leneman, Helen, ed. *Bar/Bat Mitzvah Basics: A Practical Family Guide to Coming of Age Together.* Woodstock, VT: Jewish Lights Publishing, 1996.

———. *Bar/Bat Mitzvah Education: A Sourcebook.* Denver: A.R.E. Publishing Inc., 1993.

Reiss, Fred. *The Standard Guide to the Jewish and Civil Calendar.* West Orange, NJ: Behrman House, Inc., 1986.

Rossel, Seymour. *A Spiritual Journey: Bar Mitzvah and Bat Mitzvah Handbook.* West Orange, NJ: Behrman House, Inc., 1993.

Salkin, Jeffrey K. *Putting God on the Guest List: How to Reclaim the Spiritual Meaning of Your Child's Bar or Bat Mitzvah.* Woodstock, VT: Jewish Lights Publishing, 1992.

For the Students

Bush, Lawrence. *Emma Ansky-Levine and Her Mitzvah Machine.* New York: UAHC Press, 1991.

Curtis, Sandra. *Gabriel's Ark.* Los Angeles: Torah Aura Productions, 1996.

Feigenson, Emily. *Changes Recognized, Changes Achieved: Bat Mitzvah.* Los Angeles: Torah Aura Productions, 1993.

Feigenson, Emily, and Joel Lurie Grishaver. *Coming of Mitzvah: What the Jewish Tradition Has to Say About Coming of Age.* Los Angeles: Torah Aura Productions, 1993.

Gallant, Janet. *My Brother's Bar Mitzvah.* Rockville, MD: Kar-Ben Copies, Inc., 1990.

Gersh, Harry. *When a Jew Celebrates.* West Orange, NJ: Behrman House Inc., 1971.

Gordon, Sol. *When Living Hurts.* New York: UAHC Press, 1985.

Grishaver, Joel Lurie. *The Life Cycle Workbook.* Denver: A.R.E. Publishing, Inc., 1983.

———. *A Lifetime of Torah.* Los Angeles: Torah Aura Productions, 1991.

———. *Maseket Bar/Bat Mitzvah.* Los Angeles: Torah Aura Productions, 1996.

———. *The True Story of Bar Mitzvah.* Los Angeles: Torah Aura Productions, 1993.

Marcus, Audrey Friedman, et. al. *Bar and Bat Mitzvah: A Family Education Unit.* Denver: A.R.E. Publishing, Inc., 1983.

Moskowitz, Nachama Skolnik. *The Bar/Bat Mitzvah Game*. Los Angeles: Torah Aura Productions, 1986.

―――. *The Jewish Life Cycle Game*. Denver: A.R.E. Publishing, Inc., 1984.

Prevention Is a Mitzvah. Los Angeles: Torah Aura Productions, 1992.

Schnur, Steven. *The Narrowest Bar Mitzvah*. New York: UAHC Press, 1986.

Schulweis, Harold M. "Seek Converts!" In *Moment*. April 1997/Nissan 5757, pp. 43-45.

Shekel, Michal. *The Jewish Lifecycle Book*. Hoboken, NJ: KTAV Publishing House, Inc., 1989.

Wolff, Ferida. *Pink Slippers, Bat Mitzvah Blues*. Philadelphia: Jewish Publication Society, 1989.

Audiovisual

Bar Mitzvah in Israel. Ergo Media Inc. Videocassette.

Beged Kefet. *Lifeline*. Sounds Write Productions, Inc. Audiocassette/CD.

The Discovery. Ergo Media Inc. Videocassette.

The Journey. Ergo Media Inc. Videocassette.

Kol B'seder. *Sparks of Torah*. A.R.E. Publishing, Inc. Audiocassette.

CHAPTER THREE
CONVERSION
BECOMING A JEW-BY-CHOICE

OVERVIEW

THE FIRST JEWISH LIFE CYCLE EVENT experienced by those who choose to become Jewish is conversion. The conversion ceremony marks the culmination of a period of study and participation in the Jewish community. While Judaism has been open to accepting converts throughout its history, the extent to which conversions took place and the manner in which Jews-by-Choice were accepted and viewed by the community has varied significantly. This chapter examines the history of conversion to Judaism, the conversion process and rituals, and significant issues pertaining to conversion in contemporary Judaism.

Biblical Period

The Hebrew word for a male convert is *ger,* for a female, *gioret;* the plural is *gerim* and the word *gerut* refers to conversion. In biblical Hebrew, however, the word *ger* referred to a stranger or sojourner, i.e., one who lived in the land, but did not claim it as one's own. The Torah says that the Hebrews were *gerim* in Egypt, even though they lived there for 400 years. A related biblical term, *ger toshav* — usually translated as resident alien — refers to a stranger who has settled on the land on a permanent basis.

Throughout the *Tanach,* the term *ger* refers to a stranger or sojourner, and does not imply a change in religious status. In fact, conversion as we speak of it today is not known in the Torah. Abram is called an *Ivri,* a Hebrew (Genesis 14:13). While the origin of this term is unclear, many biblical scholars believe it is related to the Semitic words *habiru* or *hapiru,* which refer to a social class of people who resided in the Fertile Crescent from the nineteenth to the

fourteenth centuries B.C.E. Nomads, they kept their group identity while living as foreigners in many lands. The term *Ivri* is also said to be derived from Ayver, one of the descendants of Noah's son, Shem (Genesis 10:24). Some also relate it to the root עבר, meaning to cross or pass over, because Abram and his family crossed over the Euphrates River.

After the Exodus from Egypt, the most common term used to refer to Abraham's descendants is *B'nai Yisrael,* the children of Israel. This people is a tribal ethnic group, with shared laws, values, and religious ritual.

Maintaining group identity is a serious concern. Abraham, for example, insists that his servant travel to his native land to find a wife for Isaac, rather than to allow him to marry a woman from the tribes of Canaan. A similar sentiment is reflected in Deuteronomy: "When *Adonai,* your God, brings you to the land which you will inherit, God will cast out many nations from before you: the Hittite, the Girgashite, the Amorite, the Canaanite, the Perizite, the Hivite, and the Jebusite . . . . You shall not make a covenant with them, nor show mercy to them, nor marry them . . . because one of them will cause your sons to turn away from Me, and they will serve other gods" (Deuteronomy 7:1-4).

The primary concern of this text appears to be that Hebrew men who marry women from one of the local peoples would turn from the God of the Hebrews to worship other gods. However, this attitude is expressed only toward the seven nations of Canaan. Although Moses marries Zipporah, the daughter of a priest of Midian, and Joseph marries Osnat, the daughter of a priest of On, neither are condemned for marrying an outsider. (When Miriam chastises Moses for having married a Kushite woman, which may or may not refer to Zipporah, she is punished.) Furthermore, there is no question that their children are considered to be part of the people of Israel.

In the prophetic literature, we find Isaiah expressing a positive attitude toward those who embrace the God of Israel. "Don't let the foreigner who has joined himself to *Adonai* say, 'Adonai will certainly separate me from God's people . . .' For the foreigners who join themselves to *Adonai* to serve god and to love God's name . . . all who keep from profaning the Sabbath and cling to My covenant, I will bring them to My holy mountain, and make them joyful in My house of prayer . . . For My house shall be called a house of prayer for all people" (Isaiah 56:3-7).

One biblical figure who embraced the God of Israel was Ruth, a Moabite. She married an Israelite who had come to Moab because of a famine in Israel. After her husband dies, her mother-in-law, Naomi, decides to return to Israel. She tells Ruth, and her other widowed daughter-in-law, Orpah, to remain in Moab. Orpah reluctantly agrees, but Ruth insists on staying with Naomi. She says: "Don't urge me to leave you or to return from following you. For where you go, I will go, and where you live, I will live. Your people will be my people and your God will be my God. Where you die, I will die, and there will I be buried. Thus and more may *Adonai* do to me if anything but death separates me from you" (Ruth 1:16-17).

Ruth, therefore, expresses her commitment to Naomi's people and God. After going to Israel with Naomi, Ruth meets and marries Boaz, a relative of Naomi's late husband. Their child, Obed, becomes the grandfather of King David. Thus Ruth, who chose Judaism, is an ancestor of King David.

Another biblical reference to conversion occurs in the book of Esther. After Esther reveals Haman's plot to the king, Ahasuerus appoints Mordecai to become prime minister. Mordecai quickly issues an edict allowing the Jews to fight back when they are attacked. The text reports, "And many of the people of the land became Jewish, for the fear of the Jews had fallen upon them" (Esther 8:17). However, the historicity of this story is questioned by many scholars.

Nevertheless, the acceptance of foreigners is not universal. Ezra, for example, demands that the Jews returning from Babylonia to the land of Israel divorce their foreign wives. They apparently do so, expelling the women and the children born to them (Ezra 9-10). There does not seem to be any consideration that these women or children could become part of the Jewish people.

Rabbinic Period

Moving to the Rabbinic period (100 B.C.E.-500 C.E.), one finds significant material in the Talmud and *midrash* about conversion, most of it quite positive. During this Rabbinic period, the term *ger* came to refer to a person who had converted to Judaism. In a famous Talmudic passage, a pagan offers to convert if someone can teach him all about Judaism while standing on one foot. He first approaches Shammai, who, thinking he is making fun of Judaism, angrily chases him away. He then approaches Hillel with the same challenge. Hillel responds, "What is hateful to you do not do to your fellow human being. This is the entire Torah, the rest is commentary. Now, go and learn it" (*Shabbat* 31a).

Other passages praise those who have become Jewish. "Dearer to God than all of the Israelites who stood at Mt. Sinai is the convert. Had the Israelites not witnessed the lightning, thunder, quaking mountain, and sounding trumpets, they would not have accepted the Torah. But the convert, who did not see or hear any of these things, came and surrendered to God and accepted the yoke of heaven. Can anyone be dearer to God than such a person?" (*Tanchuma Buber, Lech Lecha* 6, 32a).

The Rabbis referred to a person who accepted Judaism out of personal conviction and without any ulterior motives as a *ger tzedek,* a righteous convert.

According to another *midrash*, Abraham and Sarah were the first to convert others. "What is meant by the verse: '. . .the souls which [Abraham and Sarah] had made?' (Genesis 12:5). These are their converts. Why is the word 'made' used? To teach that if you bring an idolator to conversion, it is as if you created the person" (*Genesis Rabbah* 39:14).

While much of the Rabbinic material presents a positive attitude toward converts, concern about their motivation is sometimes expressed. For example, the Talmud says that no converts were accepted during the reigns of King David and King Solomon because it was suspected that they might be converting for financial gain.

Furthermore, in the Jerusalem Talmud we find this debate: "Those who seek to become converts because of their love for a Jew are not received. Neither are those who seek to become Jewish out of fear or because of some advantage. But Rav said: 'They are to be received.' This is the law: They are to be welcomed immediately. They are not to be repelled at the beginning; and they must be treated kindly for perhaps they will become converts with pure intent" (*Kiddushin* iv:i, 65b). The debate about how to respond to one who wishes to become Jewish and what motivations are acceptable continues to this day.

A *midrash* supports the idea that one who seeks to become Jewish should not be turned away. "God said: 'I am the one who brought Jethro [Moses' father-in-law] near and did not repel him. So, too, when a person comes in the name of heaven to convert, you should draw him/her near and not repel him/her.' From this one learns that a person should repel with the left hand and draw near with the right" (*Mechilta, Amalek* 3).

During the Rabbinic period, the process for conversion became formalized. The Talmud offers this instruction about how to respond to perspective converts. "Our Rabbis taught: Currently, a person who comes to convert is addressed as follows: 'What have you seen that you came to be a proselyte? Don't you know that Israel at the present time is persecuted and oppressed, despised, harassed, and overcome by afflictions?' One who replies, 'I know and yet am unworthy,' is accepted immediately, and is given instruction in some of the minor and some of the major *mitzvot* . . . The person is also told of the punishment for the transgression of the commandments . . . and is informed of the reward granted for their fulfillment . . . The person is not, however, persuaded or dissuaded too much. If he accepts [the *mitzvot*], he is circumcised . . . As soon as he is healed, arrangements are made for his immediate immersion in a *mikvah*, where two learned men must stand by his side and acquaint him with some of the minor commandments and with some of the major ones. When he comes up after his immersion, he is deemed to be an Israelite in all respects" (*Yevamot* 47a).

Many of the contemporary practices related to conversion can be traced to this teaching, including instruction about the *mitzvot*, circumcision, and immersion in a *mikvah*.

While converts were clearly welcomed in the Rabbinic period, the extent of Jewish proselytizing is greatly debated. A well-known Christian text states, "Woe to you, scribes and Pharisees, hypocrites! For you compass sea and land to make one convert" (Matthew 23:15). While this statement may be an exaggeration, historians assert that Jews actively sought converts during the Rabbinic period and that they had significant success. However, when Christianity became the official religion of the land, such proselytizing was prohibited.

Sidney Hoenig concludes that while Judaism did not use trained missionaries, "converts were won through the religious propaganda spread by deeply consecrated and well learned Rabbis and Jewish laymen, and by the powerful example of the good lives which these dedicated people lived" ("Conversion During the Talmudic Period," in *Conversion to Judaism,* edited by David Max Eichhorn, p. 49).

Not all the material in Rabbinic literature pertaining to converts, however, looks upon them favorably. "Do not trust a convert, even to the twenty-fourth generation, because the inherent evil is still within him" (*Ruth Zutra* 1:12). Another source claims, "Converts are as hard for Israel as a sore" (*Yevamot* 109b).

Such statements may at least in part be in response to bad experiences certain Rabbis had with proselytes who subsequently turned against Jews and became Roman informers. Despite these experiences, the Rabbinic material displays a primarily positive attitude toward converts.

Middle Ages

During the Middle Ages, most Jews resided in countries dominated by Christian or Islamic rule. Both Christianity and Islam strongly condemned those who abandoned their faith, making it a capital offense. Nevertheless, conversion to Judaism continued in certain places and time periods.

In the fifth century, for example, the kings of Himyar, a province in southern Arabia, became Jewish, as did many of its citizens. And in the eighth century, the upper classes of the Khazars, a national group of Turkish origin, adopted Judaism. Among the converts to Judaism during the Middle Ages were Christian clergy such as Bodo-Eleazar, a ninth century deacon of Louis the Pious, and Vicilinus, an eleventh century priest of Mainz, Germany.

One scholar concludes, "It is difficult to ascertain with certainty the extent of proselytism in the Middle Ages. The historical sources mention isolated cases only. However, the fact that such cases recurred in every generation, despite the preachings and admonitions by the heads of Church against Judaizing and the many regulations and decrees they issued to prevent this danger, testifies to the persistence of the phenomenon, at least to a limited extent" (*Encyclopaedia Judaica,* "Proselytes," Vol. 13, col. 1189).

Modern Period

At the dawn of the modern period of Jewish history (usually dated from the emancipation of the Jews in France in 1791), most Jewish communities were reluctant to accept converts. In Poland, for example, Rabbi Akiba Eger insisted that the Jews abide by the law of the land which prohibited the Jews from accepting converts. Rabbi Solomon Luria also forbid receiving converts, and in Lithuania, the Jewish council established serious penalties for those who accepted converts. Nathan Adler, Chief Rabbi of the British Empire in the late nineteenth century, required that all conversions in Britain be approved by him.

In North America a more tolerant position toward accepting converts began evolving in the twentieth century. Reform Judaism was particularly open to accepting sincere converts, even before its active Outreach Program was established in the early 1980s. In recent years, a far more open attitude toward welcoming converts has developed in all the movements of Judaism in North America and in many other countries. This development is in part a result of the significant increase in intermarriages, but also reflects the tolerance of society in general toward Judaism.

It is now common to refer to individuals who have become Jewish as Jews-by-Choice, rather than converts or proselytes. This term reflects the decision of the person to choose Judaism freely, and avoids the terms convert and proselyte, which can be seen as perjorative or as having Christological overtones. It is estimated that between 5,000 and 10,000 people convert to Judaism each year in North America.

The Conversion Process

The process for becoming Jewish first described in the Talmud (see above, p. 44) has remained fairly consistent over the centuries. When approached by a person who wishes to become Jewish, many Rabbis follow the tradition of discouraging him or her three times, in order to assure that the person is sincere. Other Rabbis prefer to be more encouraging to the prospective Jew, while at the same time asking many questions to determine the person's sincerity.

Many people who express an interest in converting, do so at first because they wish to marry a Jew. Because this motive was considered insufficient by the sages, some Rabbis follow the tradition of refusing to convert such a person. However, most Rabbis will agree to work with that person if convinced of his or her sincerity and strong desire to become Jewish. In some cases, the person is not ready to become Jewish prior to the marriage, and converts months or years later.

The conversion process consists primarily of a period of study which can range from a few months to a few years. The study usually includes group classes (such as Introduction to Judaism), as well as private instruction with a Rabbi or tutor. Among the topics studied are Jewish holidays, life cycle ceremonies, home rituals, theology, beliefs, values, history, and liturgy. Learning Hebrew is sometimes required. Orthodox Rabbis usually spend more time focusing on the requirements of Jewish law.

In addition to study, the prospective convert is expected to begin to lead a Jewish life. This process might include attending worship services, celebrating Shabbat and holidays, engaging in acts of *tzedakah,* and observing the dietary laws.

When the Rabbi is satisfied that the person has attained the requisite knowledge and has demonstrated his/her readiness to live as a Jew, the conversion ceremony is arranged. Traditionally, this begins with the candidate meeting with a *Bet Din,* a court of three Rabbis, or learned Jews at least one of whom is a Rabbi. They ask the candidate a variety of questions, testing his/her knowledge of and commitment to Judaism. Some liberal Rabbis do not require that a candidate for conversion meet with a *Bet Din.*

The next step in the process are the rituals of circumcision for males and *mikvah* for males and females. Since it is a requirement for all male Jews to be circumcised, a male candidate is circumcised by a *mohel.* If, however, he has already been circumcised (or if he can't be circumcised for health reasons), then as a symbol of circumcision, a drop of blood is taken from the penis. This ritual is called *Hatafat Dam Brit,* the dripping of the blood of the covenant. Many Reform and Reconstructionist Rabbis do not require *Hatafat Dam Brit.*

Both male and female converts traditionally undergo immersion in a *mikvah.* This practice is required by all Orthodox and Conservative Rabbis, and by many if not most Reform and Reconstructionist Rabbis. This ritual symbolizes a spiritual rebirthing as a Jew. Before a witness, the candidate submerges himself/herself three times and recites the blessing:

בָּרוּךְ אַתָּה יְיָ אֱלֹהֵינוּ מֶלֶךְ הָעוֹלָם,
אֲשֶׁר קִדְּשָׁנוּ בְּמִצְוֹתָיו וְצִוָּנוּ עַל הַטְּבִילָה.

Baruch Atah Adonai Elohaynu Melech HaOlam,
Asher Kidshanu B'Mitzvotav V'Tzivanu Al HaTevilah.

Blessed are You, Adonai our God, Sovereign of the universe, who made us holy with *mitzvot* and commanded us concerning immersion.

The witness will then report to the Rabbi that the immersion was done properly. The conversion is completed with a short ceremony during which the convert receives the Hebrew name he or she has chosen. The name includes the phrase *ben Avraham*

v'Sarah (son of Abraham and Sarah) for a male or *bat Avraham v'Sarah* (daughter of Abraham and Sarah) for a female. Most often the word *Avinu* (our Patriarch) is inserted after Avraham and *Imaynu* (our Matriarch) is inserted after v'Sarah.

It is now common practice in Reform communities for there to be a public conversion ceremony, often during a Shabbat service. This ceremony allows the entire congregation or community to celebrate the completion of the conversion process and welcome a new member into the Jewish people.

The Attitude toward Converts

While Jewish texts express a variety of opinions about conversion, they are in agreement that a person who has become Jewish is not different from any other Jew. In his "Letter to Obadiah the Proselyte," Rambam (Maimonides) wrote: "You ask me if you are allowed to use the words of blessing: 'Our God and God of our fathers' . . . 'you have brought us out of the land of Egypt' . . . Yes, you may say all of this in the prescribed order and not change it in the least. In the same way that every Jew by birth says prayers and blessings, you, too, may pray and bless . . . Do not consider your origin as inferior. While we are the descendants of Abraham, Isaac, and Jacob, you derive from the One through whose word the world was created" (*A Maimonides Reader,* Abraham Twersky, ed., pp. 475-6).

In response to a convert who was ridiculed by his teacher, Rambam wrote, "He called you a fool? Astounding! A man who has left his mother and father, his birthplace, his country and its power, and attached himself to this lowly despised, and enslaved people who recognized the truth and righteousness of this people's Law, and cast the things of this world from his heart — shall such a one be called a fool? God forbid" (Twersky, p. 477).

A Jew-by-Choice may therefore do virtually everything that Jews-by-birth are able to do. One exception is that a female convert may not marry a *kohen* (priest), unless she became Jewish at age three or younger (*Yevamot* 60b). In the Talmudic period, a convert also could not hold public office or serve as a judge in most cases.

The positive and accepting attitude toward one who has chosen Judaism has endured to this day.

In fact, one is not supposed to even remind such a person that he or she was not born Jewish, but converted. (It is therefore important to be sensitive when asking a Jew-by-Choice to share his/her experience with your students. Your Rabbi or educator can be helpful in identifying individuals who would be willing to do this.)

The Conversion of a Child

There are a number of situations in which a child (one who has not reached the age of Bar or Bat Mitzvah) would require conversion to Judaism: (1) if a couple adopts a child whose birth mother is not Jewish, or if the mother's religion is not known; (2) in an intermarriage, if the father is Jewish, but the mother is not, according to Orthodox and Conservative Judaism. (In Reconstructionism and Reform Judaism, however, if one parent is Jewish — either father or mother — and the child is raised solely as a Jew, the child is considered Jewish and no conversion is necessary.); (3) if an entire family converts to Judaism.

For a child, conversion consists of immersion in a *mikvah,* and boys must undergo circumcision or *Hatafat Dam Brit.* The child receives a Hebrew name. At the age of Bar/Bat Mitzvah, the child may choose to annul the conversion, but must do so immediately.

The Acceptance of Converts and Who Is a Jew

Because Rabbis of different denominations have different standards for conversions, not all conversions are recognized by all Rabbis or denominations. While it is difficult to generalize, the following guidelines usually apply.

Most Reform and Reconstructionist Rabbis will accept a conversion by any other Rabbi. Some of these Rabbis will only accept the conversion if the person has gone to the *mikvah.* Most Conservative Rabbis will accept the conversions by other Conservative and Orthodox Rabbis, and by Reform and Reconstructionist Rabbis if the person has gone to the *mikvah* and if males have been circumcised or performed *Hatafat Dam Brit.* Orthodox Rabbis will usually accept only conversions performed by other Orthodox Rabbis. Some, however, will accept conversions by non-Orthodox Rabbis if the requirements meet Orthodox *halachic* standards.

The issue is further confusing in Israel. The Chief Rabbinate has consistently refused to recognize non-Orthodox conversions and has attempted to refuse to recognize as Jews those who have converted to Judaism under non-Orthodox Rabbis. However, according to the Law of Return, as interpreted by Israel's Supreme Court, all converts must be recognized as Jews for the purpose of citizenship.

SOURCES FROM THE TRADITION

Rabbi Elazar ben Pedat taught: "The Holy One who is blessed, dispersed Israel among the nations only in order to gain converts."

(Pesachim 87b)

God loves converts exceedingly. To what is this matter compared? To a king who had a flock. Once, a stag entered the flock; he went with the goats and grazed with them. When the flock came in to rest, the stag came in with them. The king was told. He liked the stag and ordered: "When the stag is in the field, let him have a nice shepherd. Let no one harm him; be careful with him. When the stag comes in with the flock, give him something to drink." The shepherds said to the king: "Master, you have so many male goats, and so many lambs and you don't warn us about them. Yet, concerning the stag you warn us every day." The king said to them: "The flock has no choice, for it is their nature to graze in the field all day and come in each night to sleep in the stable. Stags, however, sleep in the wilderness. It is not their nature to enter the living places of human beings. Shall we not consider it a merit for this one who has left behind all the vast wilderness, the place of all wild animals, and has come and stood in the yard?" Similarly, shouldn't we be grateful to the convert who has left a family and a father's house and a people and all the other peoples of the earth, and comes to us? Therefore, God provided extra protection, for God warned Israel that they should be careful not to harm them. And thus Scripture says: "You shall love the convert" (Deuteronomy 10:19).

(Numbers Rabbah 8:2)

"The souls which they made in Haran" (Genesis 12:5). R. Elazar b. Simeon said: If all the people of the world came together to create even a single fly, they could not put life into it. Why does it say, "The souls which they made?" These souls are the converts. Why is the word "made" used? To teach that if anyone brings near an idolater and converts him, it is as if he had created him. And why does it say

"They made?" R. Huna said: Abraham converted the men, and Sarah converted the women.

(Genesis Rabbah 39:14)

Those who wish to become a convert because of love of a Jew are not received. Nor are converts from fear or because of advantage received. Rav said: "They are to be received." This is the law: they are to be considered proselytes; they are not to be pushed away as they are at the outset, and they must have friendly treatment, because maybe they want to become a convert from a pure motive.

(Yerushalmi Kiddushin iv:1)

Under the present conditions, when we live in a country that is not ours, like slaves under the rod of a master, a Jew who encourages someone to convert to Judaism becomes a rebel against the government, subject to the death penalty . . . . Therefore, I caution anyone against being a party to such activity when the law of the state forbids it, for he thereby forfeits his life.

(Rabbi Solomon Luria, sixteenth century, commentary to *Yevamot* 49a in *Jewish Wisdom* by Joseph Telushkin)

Once a Hasid, a *Tzadik,* was asked why Jews don't proselytize. He answered, simply, that a candle glows without making an effort to give off light. Religion should do that too, he said.

(Paul Cowan, *An Orphan in History,* p. 195)

We understand conversion to be a process, the goal of which is a wholehearted and informed acceptance of Judaism for its own sake. We consider the formal adoption of Judaism by a person who has been born a non-Jew to be a decision that is to be accorded respect and a process to be invested with a seriousness of purpose and dignity.

The preparation, counseling, and final ceremonies should give expression to the fact that even though conversion to Judaism is primarily a religious act, its dimensions and consequences are more encompassing. A person seeking to become a Jew should be sensitized to the realization and manifest an awareness that there is involved also an act of incorporation into a people whose civilization values are now entrusted to him/her to internalize and express in attitude and practice.

We deem it the responsibility of Jewish congregations and of the Jewish community at large to welcome warmly into their midst, and involve in all their activities, persons who have converted to Judaism.

(Reconstructionist Rabbinical Association Guidelines on Conversion. In *Your People, My people: Finding Acceptance and Fulfillment as a Jew by Choice* by Lena Romanoff, pp. 271-272)

Why not open our arms to those who seek a spiritual way to life? Are we not told in the classic text of *Avoth DeRebbe Nathan* (2ba) that Jews are urged to bring people beneath the wings of the divine presence exactly as Abraham and Sarah had done?

The logic is clear, and so is the theology. Judaism is not an exclusive club of born Jews. It is a universal faith with an ancient tradition that has deep resonance for people today . . . . If Judaism is a world religion, then it has something valuable to offer the world.

Conversion to Judaism is not for the sake of the survival of a group or for ethinic comfort. Becoming Jewish is not a matter of culinary taste, a familiar dialect, or insider jokes. Genuine conversion affects the native born as well as the Jew by choice. Conversion means that Judaism is not genes and chromosomes but a free, reasoned, and personal choice. Conversion is to fulfill the covenanted promise of our father Abraham, the first convert.

("Seek Converts!" by Harold M. Schulweis. In *Moment*, April 1997/Nissan 5757, pp. 43-45)

ACTIVITIES

Primary

1. Read to the class *Mommy Never Went To Hebrew School* by Mindy Portnoy. Discuss: Why didn't the girl's mother go to Hebrew school? How did she become Jewish? How does her daughter feel about her mother having become Jewish? This may be the opportune time to share with the students that Jews-by-Choice are not to be thought of any differently than Jews-by-birth.

2. Read to the students a primary version of the Book of Ruth. Discuss: Why did Ruth decide to go with her mother-in-law? Why did Orpah decide to stay behind? What does "Your people will be my people, and your God will be my God" mean? Explain that Ruth is considered to be a woman who converted to Judaism. Resources: *Lessons from Our Living Past* edited by Jules Harlow, pp. 31-33; *A Child's Bible: Lessons from the Prophets and Writings* by Seymour Rossel, pp. 55-61; *Prophets, Writings and You* by Ruth Samuels, pp. 36-39; *Let's Discover the Bible* by Shirley Rose, Set II, #13, Ruth & Naomi.

3. Invite a Jew-by-Choice (perhaps the parent of one of the students) to speak to the class. He or she should explain, on a simple level, about conversion, why he or she chose Judaism, and how he or she became Jewish. Leave time for questions.

4. Distribute chalk pastels and large sheets of white paper to the students. As the class listens to the song "Ruth and Naomi" from the recording *Sparks of Torah* by Kol B'seder, each student creates a picture describing his/her reaction to the music. The students move the chalk pastel on the paper showing how the music makes them feel, changing colors as they go. After completing the pictures, ask students to explain them. Write the students' explanations on a large sheet of paper. Mount the pictures and the paper with the students' words on a bulletin board.

5. Introduce the theme of choice to the students with the following activity. Make a list of about 20 things and ask the students whether each item is something that they choose or don't choose. Among the items on the list might be: color of eyes, parents, clothes they are wearing, what they ate for breakfast, color of hair, school they attend, their name, their religion. Point out how they will be making more choices as they get older. Conclude by explaining how and why some people choose to be Jewish.

6. Read a simplified version of the story of Ruth to the students (see activity #2 above for resources). Discuss Ruth's decision to leave home. Ask each student to write (or dictate to an older student) a letter that Ruth might have written to her parents telling them about her decision to leave her home and go to the land of Israel with Naomi.

7. Primary age children are just beginning to understand that there are different religions. Begin the class by asking the students what being Jewish means, i.e., what do they do because they are Jewish? Do they wear special symbols, celebrate certain holidays, eat special foods (ask for specific examples). List their responses on the board. Explain that all these answers help identify Judaism. Write the word "Religion" on the board. Ask the children if they can read this word and what it means. Write the word "Judaism" under the word Religion. Ask students if they can name any other religions. You may need to prompt them by asking: What are people who celebrate Easter and go to church called? Explain that some people belong to a religion because they are born into it, while others choose their religion.

8. To help students learn about the Jewish value of welcoming the stranger (which has been interpreted to mean Jews-by-Choice), create welcome gifts with your class. These gifts could be a *challah* with a *challah* cover, hand-made candle holders for Shabbat and holidays along with beeswax rolled candles, or a *mezuzah*

case for the home. Arrange for the class to present their gifts to the Jews-by-Choice at an assembly, service, or other special program.

9. Another activity which teaches students the important value of welcoming Jews-by-Choice to Judaism begins with each child drawing a picture of his or her favorite Jewish activity. Invite to the class adults who are in the process of becoming Jewish or who are Jews-by-Choice. Pair up the adults and the children. Each student explains his or her picture and presents it as a gift. The pairs should then do an activity together, such as baking *challah* or doing a *tzedakah* project.

10. Gather students in a circle for reading time. Read *No Friends* by James Stevenson or choose a similar story about being a new child in class. Discuss: Who are the main characters? What is the story about? Who is the "new kid"? How did the new kid feel? Was it easy to make new friends? Was anyone helpful to the new kid? How? Did the feelings of the characters change from the beginning of the story to the end? Ask the students if any of them were ever new to a group. What did others do to make them feel welcome? Was it easy or hard to make friends and become part of the group? Has anyone ever been part of a group which welcomed someone new? What did they do to welcome that person? Ask the students what they could do to help welcome a newcomer to Judaism. Brainstorm ideas and implement at least one of them.

Intermediate

1. Explain to the class the tradition of the *Bet Din* and its role in conversion. With the students brainstorm questions that a *Bet Din* might ask a prospective Jew-by-Choice. Be sure that there are questions both about knowledge of Judaism and commitment to Judaism. Choose some of the questions and see if the students are able to answer them. Discuss: Is it fair to expect Jews-by-Choice to know more than other Jews? To extend this activity, role play a *Bet Din* question-ing a Jew-by-Choice, using the questions that the students identified.

2. Design a conversion certificate. The certificate should include the English name and Hebrew name of the Jew-by-Choice, the date of the conversion and place, and room for at least three signatures. Students should choose appropriate quotations and illustrate. (A Rabbi from your synagogue or a local congregation may be able to provide you with examples of printed conversion certificates.)

3. As a class, interview a Jew-by-Choice. Each student should be prepared to ask at least one question. After the interview, ask each student to state one thing that he or she learned about conversion to Judaism.

4. Create an informational bulletin board about conversion to Judaism. One section might be about well-known converts, another about the requirements of conversion, and another about Jewish texts relating to conversion. You may also want an interactive section, asking questions about conversion, with paper that can be folded up to reveal the answers.

5. Using the Book of Ruth, construct a family tree for Ruth, tracing her lineage as far back as possible and forward to King David. Discuss the importance of David in Judaism and the tradition that the Messiah will be a descendant of David.

6. Create an advertising campaign for inviting people to consider becoming Jewish. Divide the class into groups. Each group should create a billboard, posters, radio, television, newspaper or magazine ad, or a short video. Select the best material and display for the congregation or school.

7. Put on the play "Stranger in the Land: The Story of Ruth" from *Heroes, Heroines & Holidays: Plays for Jewish Youth* by Elaine Rembrandt. (See pp. 121ff. for complete text of this play.)

After the play, interact with audience members, focusing on the role of Ruth and why she chose to follow her mother-in-law Naomi.

8. Read to your class the story *Are You There God? It's Me, Margaret* by Judy Blume over the course of a number of sessions. Although it is not a book about conversion, it is a story about exploring one's religious identity. After each reading session, students should write a short journal entry, summarizing what was read and their thoughts about it. Ask one or two specific questions to help the students focus their writing.

9. Read to your students the *midrash* on Deuteronomy 10:19 from *Numbers Rabbah* 8:2 (see above, page 49). Also read the biblical text on which this *midrash* is based. (Use this opportunity to describe what *midrash* is, how it was and is currently being written, and its relationship to the biblical text.) Ask the students to explain what relationship the biblical text has to the *midrash*. Individually or in pairs, have students write their own *midrash* on this verse. It may take the form of an illustrated story, a skit, a poem, or another format. Gather all the *midrashim* the students have created, and reproduce for the entire class.

10. As a class, attend a public conversion ceremony. At the next class session, ask students to describe the ceremony, the reactions of members of the congregation, and the students' own reactions. Review the ceremony, making sure the students understood each part of it. Ask the students if they felt any different about being Jewish after witnessing the ceremony.

11. Discuss with students what they would choose to give someone who is becoming Jewish. Besides material objects such as books, ritual objects, etc., students should also be encouraged to think about giving a particular Jewish value or a Jewish skill, such as reading Hebrew or conducting a Passover *Seder*. Students should give a reason for their choice.

List responses on the board. In small groups, go over the list and choose 5-8 of the items that are most important to them. Each group presents its list to the other students. Finally, try to agree on a common list for the entire class. Students should then discuss: How many of these items do they have or hope to acquire?

12. Have the class perform "The Story of Ruth (A Puppet Play)" from *Kings and Things: 20 Jewish Plays for Kids 8 to 18* by Meridith Shaw Patera, pp. 128-135.

Secondary

1. Divide the students into small groups. Each group is to prepare a unit to teach to those who are studying to become Jewish. Each group chooses a topic and then researches it. The students can prepare an oral presentation, a written report, a game, a video, or any other format to teach the material.

2. Most Jews-by-Choice go to the *mikvah* as part of the conversion process. Discuss how immersion in a *mikvah* symbolizes one's spiritual rebirth as a Jew. If possible, invite a Jew-by-Choice to talk about his/her experience. Also discuss other uses of a *mikvah* in Judaism. Resource: *Teaching Mitzvot: Concepts, Values, and Activities* by Barbara Binder Kadden and Bruce Kadden, Unit 14: Immersing in a Ritual Bath.

3. Assign students individually or in small groups to do a brief report on a Jew-by- Choice. Among the people to choose from: Jethro; Rahab; Ruth; Onkelos; Izates II; Keti'a bar Shalom; Aquila; Yusaf Dhu Nuwas of Himyar; Kahina, Queen of the Berbers; Bulan, King of the Khazars; Obadiah the Norman; Lope de Vera y Alarcon; Catherine Weigel; Count Valentine Potocki; Warder Cresson; Sesuzo Kotsuji; Nahida Ruth Lazarus. Among the information to learn: when and where the person lived, religion before becoming Jewish, significance in history, and reason for converting. Students can share their information by giving first person reports, saying: "My name is . . . . I lived in . . . ."

Resources: *Conversion to Judaism: A History and Analysis* edited by David Max Eichhorn; *Encyclopaedia Judaica.*

4. Role play challenges which Jews-by-Choice sometimes encounter. Set up each situation and assign a part to students. After each role play discuss. Suggested scenarios:

   a. Ellen, who was raised Christian, has fallen in love with Jonathan, a Jew. She has decided to convert. Role play Ellen telling her parents.

   b. Jeff, who was raised without a religion, has recently decided to become Jewish. Role play Jeff telling his co-workers, some of whom are Jewish and some of whom are not, about his decision.

   c. Jennifer became Jewish ten years ago, when she married Steven. They have two children and are planning to visit Jennifer's parents (who are Christian) in late December, during Chanukah and Christmas. Role play a discussion between Jennifer, Steven, and Jennifer's parents about how they will observe the holidays.

5. Ask students to write an editorial about whether Jews should actively seek converts. Students can take either a pro or con position, and should support their point with material from Jewish tradition.

6. As a class, create a list of guidelines for the sensitive treatment of Jews-by-Choice. Begin by discussing Judaism's attitude toward those who have become Jewish. Next, consider a variety of circumstances in which someone might be insensitive, for example, a person saying "you don't look Jewish" to someone who was not born Jewish, or assuming a person who converted had done so because he or she was marrying a Jew. Then write up a list of guidelines. Publish in the synagogue bulletin or school newsletter.

7. Tell your students the story of the pagan who said that he would convert to Judaism if Hillel could teach him the entire Torah while standing on one foot (see above, page 44). Ask the students how they would respond to the pagan? How would they best summarize the teachings of Judaism? Stage a photograph of each student playing the role of Hillel responding to the pagan (another student) standing on one foot. Write the student's response to the pagan as a caption for this picture.

8. Brainstorm a list of reasons that someone might want to convert to Judaism. Discuss each reason and whether or not it should be an acceptable reason for becoming Jewish.

9. Survey members of your synagogue or community about attitudes toward Jews-by-Choice. With the class create a list of potential survey items such as: Jews-by-Choice should be full members of the Jewish community. Jews-by-Choice will never know how it feels to be Jewish. Jews-by-Choice are more committed to Judaism than Jews-by-Birth. (Answers to these items should be: strongly agree, agree, uncertain, disagree, strongly disagree.) Choose the most appropriate items and create the survey. Make copies for each student to distribute. Students should bring completed surveys back to class, compile the results and discuss. If students are disturbed by any of the results, the class may wish to create a presentation to sensitize the congregation or community to Jewish attitudes toward Jews-by-Choice.

10. Create a videotape library of interviews with Jews-by-Choice. As a group compile a list of questions to be asked during the interviews. Put an announcement in your synagogue bulletin asking for Jews-by-Choice who would like to participate in this activity. The Rabbi or educator might also be able to help identify others who might want to take part. Choose one of the following formats: one-on-one interviews, panel discussions, an interview at home as the Jew-by-Choice prepares for a holiday celebration, or a format of your choice.

11. Invent a fictional correspondence between a Jew-by-Choice and a friend or family member. Students should work in pairs, with one student taking each role. The Jew-by-Choice should begin the correspondence by writing to his/her friend or family member about the decision to convert. The other student then writes a response, congratulating the person or questioning this decision and asking for a more detailed explanation. A follow-up letter in response should be written by each student. Students may wish to reverse roles and repeat the activity. Conclude the activity by discussing the responses and what the students learned from writing the letters.

12. The Overview and Sources from the Tradition in this chapter contain a variety of reactions to conversion. Write each of these on a separate sheet of paper and post around the room. Read each of the statements to the students and ask students if they agree or disagree with each statement and share the reasons for their responses. After discussing the statements, each student writes a personal reaction to conversion. Offer an opportunity for those who wish to share their reactions with the class.

13. Write on the board this quotation: "A candle glows without making an effort to give off light. Religion should do that too" (*An Orphan in History*, Paul Cowan, p. 195). Read the quotation to the class and explain that it was made by a Hasidic Jew to explain why Jews don't proselytize. Turn off the lights in the room and light a candle in the middle of room to demonstrate this quote. Ask students to think quietly about what it means to give off light without making an effort. How does one do this as a Jew? Distribute white paper and markers, crayons, or chalk to the students. Instruct the students to draw a glowing candle. In the candle's glow, students should write what they do as Jews to give off light (i.e., to show others that they are Jews).

Hebrew

1. Teach the students the terms: *ger, gioret, gerim, gerut, ger tzedek,* and *ger toshav* (see Overview to this chapter, pages 43 and 44). Discuss the difference in meaning of the term *ger* in the Bible, where it refers to a stranger, and in Rabbinic Judaism, where it means a convert (as the term is used today). Older students might use a biblical concordance to see how the word is used in different verses, such as in Exodus 22:2, 23:9; Leviticus 19:34; Deuteronomy 10:19.

2. Teach the students the Hebrew blessing one says when immersing in a *mikvah* for the purpose of conversion. Compare to other blessings with which the students are familiar.

בָּרוּךְ אַתָּה יְיָ אֱלֹהֵינוּ מֶלֶךְ הָעוֹלָם,
אֲשֶׁר קִדְּשָׁנוּ בְּמִצְוֹתָיו וְצִוָּנוּ עַל הַטְּבִילָה.

Baruch Atah Adonai Elohaynu Melech HaOlam, Asher Kidshanu B'Mitzvotav V'Tzivanu Al HaTevilah.

Blessed are You, Adonai our God, Sovereign of the universe, Who has made us holy with *mitzvot* and commanded us concerning immersion.

3. Jews-by-Choice are usually expected to learn Hebrew as part of the conversion process. Team these adults up with students in the Hebrew school for reading practice sessions with a partner or small groups.

4. As part of the conversion process, Jews-by-Choice select a Hebrew name, followed by *ben Avraham (Avinu) v'Sarah (Imaynu)* for a male and *bat Avraham (Avinu) v'Sarah (Imaynu)* for a female. This name usually has special meaning to the person. Have your students investigate the meaning of their Hebrew names. Discuss: In what ways does their personality or character reflect the meaning of their name? If they were to choose a Hebrew name, would they choose the name they were given?

Adult

1. Refusal to recognize conversions of other Jewish denominations is one of the issues that threat-

ens Jewish unity in the modern world. Most Orthodox Rabbis will recognize a conversion only if it follows Orthodox procedures. Most Conservative Rabbis require *mikvah* and circumcision (or *Hatafat Dam Brit*) for a conversion to be recognized. Hold a forum with representatives from different denominations on this issue. Include Jews-by-Choice on the panel.

2. A *Ba'al Teshuvah,* a previously non-observant Jew who embraces Orthodox Judaism, is a type of Jew-by-Choice. Invite one or more *Ba'alay Teshuvah* or *Ba'alot Teshuvah* to share their stories. What was missing from their Jewish upbringing? What led them back to Judaism? Why did they choose Orthodox Judaism?

3. Should Jews proselytize? This question has been seriously debated recently. Hold a panel discussion presenting both sides of the issue. Each side should make clear which methods of reaching out to non-Jews are appropriate and which are not. Also, consider whether the target should be only those who are not affiliated with another religion, particularly non-Jews who are married to Jews.

4. An issue related to the previous activity is whether the Jewish community should focus on Outreach or Inreach. Distribute or summarize the article "How to Save American Jews" by Jack Wertheimer, Charles S. Liebman, and Steven M. Cohen, which argues that we should spend more of our community resources on those who are already active as part of the community. You may want to invite community leaders to comment. Discuss what programs can be offered that meet both goals.

5. View the video *Choosing Judaism: Some Personal Perspectives.* Discuss: What were the reasons that the people in the video became Jewish? What obstacles did they encounter? How can their stories serve as inspirations to all Jews?

6. Form a Literary Cafe to read and discuss books which deal with the themes of conversion or rediscovering one's Jewish roots. Participants should read a book and come prepared to share their reactions to it. One member of the group should facilitate the discussion by preparing questions.
Resources: *An Orphan in History: Retrieving a Jewish Legacy* by Paul Cowan; *Lovesong: Becoming a Jew* by Julius Lester; *So Strange My Path: A Spiritual Pilgrimage* by Abraham Carmel; *Ordained to be a Jew* by John David Scalamonti.

Family

1. Create a host-family program to help welcome Jews-by-Choice to Judaism. Invite families that are interested and prospective Jews-by-Choice to a workshop where they learn about conversion to Judaism. Then match the families to the prospective Jews-by-Choice based on the common interests. Host families should sit with the Jew-by-Choice at services, invite him/her for a Shabbat or holiday meal, and share other Jewish experiences.

2. Design a program which focuses on special challenges faced by families of Jews-by-Choice. Ask a few Jews-by-Choice to prepare brief remarks on some or all of the following topics: "How to Create a Jewish family," "The December Dilemma," "Dealing with Parents and In-laws," "Developing a Jewish Identity," etc. Each session should focus on one of these topics and be led by those who have prepared the topic.

3. Create a brochure for introducing prospective Jews-by-Choice to Judaism and the local Jewish community. Divide participants into groups, with each group examining a different topic, such as: Synagogues, Jewish Institutions, Celebrating the Jewish Holidays, Who's Who in the Jewish Community, etc. Each group should write up its findings, and then a committee should edit a booklet from the material. Parallel sessions should be held for children to discuss challenges they face.

All-School

1. Hold a creative Shabbat or Shavuot service on the theme of conversion to Judaism. Select

Jewish texts relating to conversion. Invite Jews-by-Choice to participate in the service, including sharing about why they chose to be Jewish. Shabbat *Yitro,* when the story of Jethro is read, would be especially appropriate.

2. Stage an all-school production of the Book of Ruth. Divide the Book of Ruth into sections, with one section per class. Each class is to create a presentation about its assigned portion of the story. This presentation can be a song, skit, dance, news report, etc. Each class presents its creation in the order of the story. Alternatively, the older grades may present the story to the younger grades.

3. Sponsor a Shabbat dinner or *Oneg Shabbat* for the current Introduction to Judaism class and other individuals studying for conversion. Prior to the dinner or *Oneg,* match students and their families with guests. Introduce the students to the *mitzvah* of welcoming the stranger and practice how to make introductions and conversation.

4. With your school, do the dance *midrash* "Love the Stranger" from *Torah in Motion: Creating Dance Midrash* by JoAnne Tucker and Susan Freeman, pp. 146-147.

GLOSSARY

Bet Din – A Rabbinic court, usually comprised of three Rabbis, which oversees a conversion process.

Ger (*Gerim,* pl.) – In biblical Hebrew, stranger. In post-biblical Hebrew, a male convert.

Ger Toshav – In biblical Hebrew, a resident alien.

Ger Tzedek – A righteous convert.

Gerut – The process of conversion.

Gioret – A female convert.

Hatafat Dam Brit – Ritual of taking a drop of blood from the penis to symbolize circumcision in a male convert who is already circumcised.

Ivri – A Hebrew

Kohen – A member of the priestly class descended from Aaron.

Midrash – Stories or teachings, usually based upon a biblical text.

Mikvah – Ritual bath.

Mitzvah (*Mitzvot,* pl.) – Commandment.

Mohel – Ritual circumciser.

RESOURCES

For the Teacher

Belin, David. *Why Choose Judaism: New Dimensions of Jewish Outreach.* New York: UAHC Press, 1985.

Berkowitz, Allan L., and Patti Moskovitz, eds. *Embracing the Covenant: Converts to Judaism Talk about Why & How.* Woodstock, VT: Jewish Lights Publishing, 1996.

Carmel, Abraham. *So Strange My Path: A Spiritual Pilgrimage.* Rev. ed. New York: Bloch Publishing Company, 1993.

Cohen, Jack S. *Intermarriage and Conversion: A Halakhic Solution.* Hoboken, NJ: KTAV Publishing House, Inc., n.d.

Cowan, Paul. *An Orphan in History: Retrieving a Jewish Legacy.* Garden City, NY: William Morrow & Co., Inc., 1996.

Diamant, Anita. *Choosing a Jewish Life: A Handbook for the New Jewish Convert.* New York: Schocken Books, 1997.

Divre Gerut: Guidelines Concerning Proselytism. New York: Central Conference of American Rabbis, 1983.

Eichhorn, David Max, ed. *Conversion to Judaism: A History and Analysis.* Hoboken, NJ: KTAV Publishing House, Inc., 1965.

Encyclopaedia Judaica. Jerusalem: Keter Publishing House Jerusalem Ltd., 1972.

Epstein, Lawrence. *Conversion to Judaism: A Guidebook.* Northvale, NJ: Jason Aronson Inc., 1994.

————, ed. *Readings on Conversion to Judaism.* Northdale, NJ: Jason Aronson Inc., 1995.

Huberman, Steven, *New Jews: The Dynamics of Religious Conversion.* New York: UAHC Press, 1979.

Kadden, Barbara Binder, and Bruce Kadden. *Teaching Mitzvot: Concepts, Values, and Activities.* Rev. ed. Denver: A.R.E. Publishing. Inc., 1996.

Kukoff, Lydia. *Choosing Judaism.* New York: UAHC Press, 1981.

Lamm, Maurice. *Becoming a Jew.* Middle Village, NY: Jonathan David Publishers, Inc., 1991.

Lester, Julius. *Lovesong: Becoming a Jew.* New York: Arcade Publishing, Inc., 1995.

Myrowitz, Catherine Hall. *Finding a Home for the Soul: Interviews with Converts to Judaism.* Northvale, NJ: Jason Aronson Inc., 1995.

Patera, Meridith Shaw. *Kings and Things: 20 Jewish Plays for Kids 8 to 18.* Denver: A.R.E. Publishing, Inc., 1996.

Romanoff, Lena, with Lisa Hostein. *Your People, My People: Finding Acceptance and Fulfillment as a Jew by Choice.* Philadelphia: Jewish Publication Society, 1990.

Rosenbloom, Joseph R. *Conversion to Judaism: From the Biblical Period to the Present.* Cincinnati: Hebrew Union College Press, 1978, o.p. (Available from Books on Demand, 300 N. Zeeb Rd., Ann Arbor, MI 48106-1346)

Scalamonti, John David. *Ordained to Be a Jew: A Catholic Priest's Conversion to Judaism.* Hoboken, NJ: KTAV Publishing House, Inc., 1992.

Telushkin, Joseph. *Jewish Wisdom: Ethical, Spiritual, and Historical Lessons from the Great Works and Thinkers.* New York: William Morrow & Company, Inc., 1994.

Tucker, JoAnne, and Susan Freeman. *Torah in Motion: Creating Dance Midrash.* Denver: A.R.E. Publishing, Inc., 1990.

Twersky, Isadore, ed. *A Maimonides Reader.* West Orange, NJ: Behrman House, Inc., 1972.

Wertheimer, Jack; Charles S. Liebman; and Steven M. Cohen. "How to Save American Jews." In *Commentary,* vol. 101, no. 1, January 1996, pp. 47-51.

For the Students

Blume, Judy. *Are You There God? It's Me, Margaret.* New York: Bradbury Press, 1990.

Harlow, Jules, ed. *Lessons from Our Living Past.* West Orange, NJ: Behrman House, Inc., 1972.

"Is Judaism a Missionary Faith? Should Jews Proselytize?" In *Keeping Posted,* November, 1975.

Portnoy, Mindy. *Mommy Never Went To Hebrew School.* Rockville, MD: Kar-Ben Copies, Inc., 1989.

Rose, Shirley. *Let's Discover the Bible.* West Orange, NJ: Behrman House, Inc., 1992.

Rossel, Seymour. *Lessons from the Prophets and Writings.* West Orange, NJ: Behrman House, Inc., 1989.

Samuels, Ruth. *Prophets, Writings and You.* Hoboken, NJ: KTAV Publishing House, Inc., 1989.

Shekel, Michal. *The Jewish Lifecycle Book.* Hoboken, NJ: KTAV Publishing House, Inc., 1989.

Stevenson, James. *No Friends.* New York: Greenwillow Books, 1986.

Audiovisual

Choosing Judaism: Some Personal Perspectives. UAHC Press. Videocassette.

Sparks of Torah. Kol B'seder. A.R.E. Publishing, Inc. Audiocassette/CD.

CHAPTER FOUR
RELATIONSHIPS
MARRIAGE • DIVORCE

OVERVIEW

ACCORDING TO JEWISH TRADITION, TWO primary purposes of marriage are companionship and procreation. Both of these values are reflected at the very beginning of the Torah. God blesses the first man and woman saying: "Be fruitful and multiply and fill the earth and rule over it" (Genesis 1:28). In the second account of creation, God proclaims: "It is not good for man to be alone. I will make a helper opposite him" (Genesis 2:18).

As Maurice Lamm notes, "Loneliness is not felt by animals; only man can experience loneliness, the fragmentary and incomplete nature of this world. It is the genuine companionship of Adam and Eve that humanity requires, and which is the stated purpose for marriage in the scheme of creation" (*The Jewish Way in Love & Marriage,* p. 123). This companionship is reflected in the statement "Therefore a man shall leave his father and mother and shall cleave to his wife, and they shall be as one flesh" (Genesis 2:24).

The laws, traditions, and rituals related to Jewish marriage reflect the dual purposes of companionship and procreation. Some of these laws, traditions, and rituals have their origin in the Torah; others developed over the centuries as Jews faced new conditions, situations, and challenges. As with other life cycle ceremonies, the Jewish wedding often reflects customs which developed in a variety of times and places. The original reason for and meaning of certain symbols and practices is often shrouded in mystery, generating a variety of homiletical explanations.

Selecting a Mate

According to one Talmudic passage, marriages are preordained: "Forty days before the birth of a child, a voice in heaven announces: 'The daughter of so-and-so will marry the son of so-and-so'" (*Sota* 2a). A legend states that a Roman matron once asked Rabbi Yosi: "What has your God been doing since finishing the creation of the world?" The Rabbi replied: "God has been busy making matches" (*Pesikta d'Rav Kahana* 2:4; for the continuation of this *midrash,* see Sources from the Tradition, p. 71). According to the mystics, each soul is created both male and female. The soul is divided before birth, and is reunited when a man and a woman marry (*Zohar* 1.91b).

For much of Jewish history, the responsibility of selecting a mate has been given to the matchmaker. The Hebrew word for a pair is *shidduch,* hence a matchmaker is a *shadchan.* The first *shadchan* was God, Who brought Eve to Adam. Later in Genesis, Eliezer, the servant of Abraham, finds Rebecca at the well in Haran and brings her back to Canaan as a spouse for Isaac.

"Much care and thought was given to selecting the right person to marry. From the days of the Talmud and for centuries thereafter, it was the headmasters of the Higher Torah Academies who were customarily asked to recommend eligible students for marriage" (Lamm, p. 5). During the Middle Ages and in some communities throughout the modern era, matchmakers continued to find appropriate husbands and wives for their clients. A competent *shadchan* was careful to take into account family background and wealth, scholarship and piety, as well as the personal characteristics of each individual.

The process of matchmaking was always fraught with potential pitfalls. First a match was proposed. Then the arrangement and details had to be worked out and agreed upon by both sets of parents, and then, before any public announcements were made, the prospective bride and groom would meet each other, and either could decide to nullify the match. (In practice, however, this rarely happened.)

With the rise and spread of romantic love in the late Middle Ages and early Modern Era, most Jews began to take matters into their own hands — choosing their own mates. Jewish tradition, however, has much to say about whom one may and may not marry. That one will marry is not an option, but an obligation (*Shulchan Aruch, Even HaEzer* 1:1). Even Reform Judaism, which respects the autonomy of an individual, teaches that "It is a *mitzvah* for a Jew to marry" (*Gates of Mitzvah,* Simeon J. Maslin, ed., p. 29).

Forbidden marriages according to Jewish law include the following.

Incestuous relations delineated in the Torah, such as marriages with one's mother, father, sister, brother, son, daughter, aunt (Leviticus 18), and expanded upon by the Rabbis (*Yevamot* 21a) to include grandmother, great-aunt, etc. (Lamm, p. 41).

Adulterous relationships (Exodus 20:13 and Deuteronomy 5:17). It is forbidden for a woman who is already married to have sexual relations with another man or to marry him. (While both biblical and Talmudic law permit a man to have more than one wife, Rabbenu Gershom issued an edict in the eleventh century banning polygamy. This applied only to the Ashkenazi community until 1950, at which time the Chief Rabbinate of Israel extended the ban to include the Sephardi and Oriental Jewish communities.)

Interfaith marriages. Jewish law forbids the marriage of a Jew to a non-Jew (see below).

Homosexual marriages. Jewish law does not permit marriages between members of the same sex. Some liberal Rabbis will, however, officiate at a same-sex commitment ceremony.

Kohanim, men who are descended from Aaron's priestly line, are forbidden to marry a divorcee or a convert to Judaism.

Interfaith marriage has been one of the most controversial topics in contemporary Jewish life. While all branches of Judaism urge Jews to marry other Jews, the response to intermarriage varies greatly. Throughout much of Jewish history, such a marriage usually meant that the Jewish spouse was lost to the community. After all, how could one expect a non-Jew to adopt the religion and enter the community of a people reviled and persecuted by the outside world? And so, the parents and other family members responded to their child's inter-marriage by sitting *shiva* — as if the child had died.

Today, however, many Jews who marry non-Jews maintain ties to Judaism and to the Jewish community. In many if not most cases, the non-Jewish partner will accept an invitation to study Judaism and even convert. Some Reform and Reconstructionist Rabbis will officiate at intermarriages, usually under certain conditions — that the couple will create a Jewish home and that the children will receive a Jewish education. Reform, Reconstructionist, and most Conservative Congregations accept as members Jews who have intermarried. Most of these congregations will welcome the participation of the non-Jewish spouse as well, though usually with certain restrictions as to their ritual and leadership involvement.

A major effort has been undertaken in recent years to involve interfaith couples and their children in Jewish life. Rather than viewing intermarriage as a threat to Jewish survival, many Jews view it as a reality of the times and an opportunity to bring Judaism to more people.

Levirite Marriage

According to biblical tradition, a woman whose husband died before fathering a child was required to marry the husband's eldest brother (*levir*). The purpose of this requirement was to provide a descendant for the deceased husband and to ensure continuing support for the widow. Such an arrangement was called a Levirite marriage.

If the eldest brother refused to marry his brother's widow, he was required to perform a ceremony of release called *chalitzah* (Deuteronomy 25:5-10; see also Ruth 4:1-14). In time, *chalitzah* became the required practice for such a situation, with marriage to one's brother's widow no longer an option. Only in the most traditional of communities is this practice followed today.

Tennaim – Conditions of Marriage

Agreements between the parents of the bride and the parents of the groom are referred to as *tennaim* — conditions. At first these conditions were agreed to orally, but by the eleventh century they were put in writing and a ceremony was created to formalize them. Among the items usually included in the *tennaim* were: the date and place of the wedding, the dowry, the gift for the groom, the parents' financial commitment to the couple, delineation and separation of the bride's estate, and inheritance rights.

The ceremony for signing the *tennaim* was called *Erusin* or *Kiddushin* — espousal or sanctification. In earlier times, *Erusin* was performed as much as a year prior to the wedding. But the announcement of engagement obligated the couple as much as if they were married. In order to break the engagement, they would have to go through the process of divorce. Also, if something befell the groom-to-be (e.g., he was taken captive or he died in battle without witnesses), the engaged woman would become an *agunah* (see below, p. 69) — chained to a relationship that could never be, and forbidden to enter into marriage with anyone else. Because of this, it became common for the ceremony of accepting the *tennaim* to be held very close to the wedding day. In this day and age, when it is done, it is done on the eve of the wedding or on the wedding day itself.

The ceremony includes: writing of the *tennaim;* the act of *kinyan,* in which an object (usually a handkerchief) is taken by the groom from the person delivering the contract to signify acceptance of the terms and conditions; the reading and signing of the document; and the smashing of a plate to finalize the act.

Time and Place of the Wedding

For much of Jewish history, the third day of the week (Tuesday) was considered an especially auspicious day for a wedding. This was so because concerning the account of the third day of creation, the phrase " . . . and God saw that it was good" (Genesis 1:10,12) appears twice. Therefore, Tuesday is a doubly good day for a wedding. In some communities couples would choose Rosh Chodesh, the first day of the month (when it did not conflict with Shabbat or other prohibited days), perhaps because the moon waxing in the sky was considered "a symbol of growth and fertility" (*The New Jewish Wedding,* Anita Diamant, p. 51). In Talmudic times, Sunday and Wednesday were especially good marriage days because the court met on Monday and Thursday and any contention as to virginity of the bride could be lodged immediately after the wedding night.

While some days may have been preferred for one reason or another, certain days were explicitly prohibited. Jewish weddings are not held on Shabbat because work and travel are not permitted then. Also, a new agreement may not be entered into on that day. Further, each opportunity for joy and celebration is to be observed individually, and not combined with another. For this last reason also, two members of the same family could not be married on the same day.

Similarly, weddings are forbidden on the holidays of Rosh HaShanah, Yom Kippur, Pesach, Shavuot, and the first and last days of Sukkot. But weddings may be held on Purim, the intermediate days of Sukkot, and during Chanukah. Traditionally, the entire three week period between the 17th of Tammuz through Tisha B'Av is considered a period of semi-mourning for the destruction of the Temple; therefore, weddings are not held then. Similarly, the seven week period from Pesach through Shavuot is a time of mourning for the death of Rabbi Akiba's students. However, there is a variety of traditions as to which days during this period are permissible for marriages and which are not. Usually the two Rosh Chodesh dates (of Iyar and Sivan) and Lag B'Omer are permitted days for weddings. Some Rabbis permit weddings on Yom HaAtzma'ut also. Still other Rabbis take an even less stringent approach as to which days during these semi-mourning periods are permissible for weddings.

Weddings may take place anywhere, but it has been customary to hold them in certain locations. They were sometimes held in the home of the groom or the bride. In fact, in ancient times, "the groom's father built special quarters in the family home for the married couple" (Lamm, p. 183). They are also often held in the synagogue, or on the synagogue grounds, in a courtyard.

Aufruf

It is traditional for the groom to receive an *aliyah* to the Torah on the Shabbat prior to his wedding. In Reform, Reconstructionist, and Conservative synagogues, both bride and groom are usually called to the Torah. This ceremony is called *aufruf,* which, in Yiddish, means "calling up." After reciting the blessings, the Rabbi usually offers a *Mi Sheberach* blessing for the couple. After that, the groom (or couple), as they leave the *bimah,* is showered with candy and raisins, symbolizing sweetness and fruitfulness, or nuts, because the Hebrew word for nut, *egoz,* has the same numerical value (17) as the Hebrew word for good (*tov*).

Mikvah

It is traditional for the bride to immerse herself in a *mikvah,* a ritual bath, before her wedding. "The bridal *mikvah* was a woman's first trip to a place that would be part of her life's rhythms for as long as she menstruated, and for traditional Jews *mikvah* remains a crucial part of married life" (Diamant, p. 151). Many non-Orthodox brides use the *mikvah* before their weddings and some have developed new rituals for this occasion (Diamant, pp. 155-156).

Symbols and Rituals

Chupah

A Jewish wedding takes place under a *chupah,* a canopy held aloft by four poles. It is thought that the word *chupah* may be a variation of the two Hebrew words *chai po,* meaning "live here." Originally, it referred to the bridal chamber — usually a room in the groom's house — where in ancient times the marital act would be consummated. In medieval times, when the marriage ceremony was commonly held outdoors, a *tallit* was held over the couple by four attendants to represent that chamber. A *tallit* may still be used for a *chupah.* However, today, a decorative cloth is more often used. The couple might honor close friends and/or relatives by asking them to hold one of the *chupah* poles.

Ketubah

The Jewish wedding document, *ketubah,* means "that which is written" or "a writing." It is certainly one of the oldest of documents, the earliest form of which comes down to us on papyrus from Aswan, Egypt, dating to the fifth century B.C.E. In this agreement, the husband pledges at least a minimum settlement (200 *zuzim* if she is a virgin, 100 *zuzim* if a divorcee, often considerably more in the case of a divorce). Additionally, he promises his wife that he will fulfill the interpersonal and financial responsibilities of marriage. As further protection, it stipulated her inheritance rights if he were to die. It is signed by two witnesses and is considered a binding contract. The bride takes possession of the document, and if it becomes lost, a new one is to be written and witnessed immediately.

Written in Aramaic, the traditional *ketubah* includes the date and place of the wedding, the names of the bride and groom, the groom's statement of proposal, the obligations of the groom during marriage and if the marriage should terminate, the bride's acceptance of the proposal, her dowry, his *mohayr* (dowry), any special terms, and the signatures of two male witnesses who are not related to either side of the family.

The *ketubah* is usually signed immediately prior to the ceremony, then read aloud and presented to the bride during the wedding.

In modern times, some couples choose to replace the traditional text of the *ketubah* with a contemporary text, the focus of which is upon the vows which the bride and groom make during the ceremony and their profession of love for one another. A rich medieval tradition of illuminating the *ketubah* with decorative art goes back at least to the fourteenth century, with the tradition being most wide-spread in the sixteenth to eighteenth centuries in Italy, Persia, and other Middle Eastern countries. The *ketubah* as art form has been revived of late by a significant number of Jewish artists and calligraphers.

Ring

A Jewish marriage is, according to tradition, a legal act in which the groom "acquires" the bride. In earliest times, the purchase price was a *prutah* — the smallest of coins. But since the seventh century, it has been customary to use a ring worth at least a *prutah*.

Jewish law stipulates that the ring be a solid band, without holes or gemstones, so that its value could easily be assessed. The ring must belong to the groom and be given without provisions to the bride. It is placed on the strongest finger of the bride (usually the right index) so that she may grasp it firmly upon accepting it and show it clearly to the witnesses. (Another explanation, which is clearly more romantically correct than medically valid, contends that this finger is connected directly to the heart by a vein.) In non-Orthodox modern ceremonies, the bride may also give a ring to the groom.

Breaking of the Glass

The most widely recognized symbol of the Jewish wedding — the breaking of the glass — is actually of no legal importance. This custom is based upon Talmudic legends of wedding feasts which occurred soon after the destruction of the Jerusalem Temple. In both stories, it was the groom's father who smashed an expensive goblet or plate against the mantle to quiet down the celebration.

Over the centuries, many explanations have arisen for the breaking of the glass. For example, it reminds us of the destruction of the Temple and thus teaches that marriage should endure both the joyous and the sad times. It was said to keep away evil spirits which do not like loud noises. The broken glass is also interpreted to symbolize the broken vessels which represent the world according to Jewish mysticism. The couple is reminded that it is their task to participate in the *mitzvah* of *tikkun olam,* of repairing a shattered world symbolized by the glass. The broken glass also reminds the couple that the ceremony makes a life-altering change which cannot be undone, just as the broken glass cannot be returned to its former shape.

Fasting

It is customary for the bride and groom to fast on their wedding day from dawn until the ceremony and to break their fast (except for the wine that is sipped during the ceremony) during *yichud* immediately following the ceremony (see below, p. 69). If the wedding occurs on Rosh Chodesh, Purim, or another day of joy when fasting is not allowed, the couple does not fast.

Because the bride and groom are beginning their lives anew as a married couple, the wedding day (until the ceremony) is considered a mini-Yom Kippur for them. Besides fasting, the *Viddui* and *Al Chayt* prayers of confessional are recited by the couple during the daily service. In addition, the groom traditionally wears a *kittel,* a white linen robe normally worn on Yom Kippur, as a sign of purity and renewal.

The Wedding Ceremony

Bedeken

If it is her first marriage, it is traditional for a bride to wear a veil, and for the groom to place the veil over the bride's face immediately prior to the ceremony. As he does so, he recites Genesis 24:60: "Our sister, may you be the mother of thousands upon ten thousands." This blessing was offered to Rebecca by her mother and brother before she left her house in Haran for Canaan to become Isaac's bride. Indeed, Rebecca covered her face with a veil (Genesis 24:65) before meeting Isaac, which is one source for this custom.

Another reason for the *bedeken* is so the groom clearly identifies his bride before she is veiled — to make certain that this is his betrothed and no other, for did not Jacob receive Leah instead of his beloved Rachel? (Genesis 29:23-28)

After the veiling, the Rabbi and the couple's parents offer personal blessings for the couple; the bride's father sometimes recites the priestly blessing (Numbers 6:24-26).

Kabbalat Panim

Before a traditional wedding ceremony, the men and women gather in separate spaces. The bride is occupied at a *Kabbalat Panim* — a gathering of women who fuss over her and entertain her with songs and poems and speak to her of love and marriage. The men, meanwhile, gather around the *chossen's tish* (groom's table). At this *tish,* the men sing, offer toasts, and study appropriate texts. The groom may offer a *D'var Torah.* In some communities it is the custom to interrupt the *D'var Torah* time and again with Hebrew songs and clapping. The *ketubah* is usually signed during this time.

The Processional

In a traditional Jewish wedding, the men — including both fathers — escort the groom from the *tish* to the bride for *bedeken* and then to the *chupah.* The women — including both mothers — escort the bride to the *chupah.* In some communities it is customary to hold candles while walking to the *chupah.*

Another custom is for the groom and the bride to walk with both their respective parents, who then remain under the *chupah* with the couple. However, these traditions are a matter of custom rather than law, and so are open to great variation.

When under the *chupah,* the bride stands to the groom's right (which is opposite the common practice in non-Jewish weddings). This custom is based on the verse "The queen stands on your right hand in fine gold of Ophir" (Psalms 45:10).

Circling

It is traditional for the bride, upon arriving at the *chupah,* to walk around the groom three (or in some communities seven) times. Sometimes one or both mothers lead the bride around the groom or follow holding her train.

This custom is based upon the phrase "A woman encompasses a man" (Jeremiah 31:22). In medieval times, it was thought that the circle was a protective shield for the groom to ward off evil spirits. It might also have its origin in the custom of walking around property in order to define and proclaim ownership. It also symbolizes the fact that the bride is set aside for him and no other man, and that he is at the center of her life.

Many feminists consider this ritual to be sexist and either do not include it in the ceremony (it is a custom, not a legal requirement) or follow it with the groom walking around the bride.

The Ceremony

The contemporary Jewish wedding ceremony is a combination of two separate ceremonies brought together sometime in the eleventh century. The first ceremony is called *Erusin* (betrothal) or *Kiddushin* (sanctification). Replacing the old engagement period (see *Tennaim* above, p. 63), it consists of the betrothal blessings and the giving and receiving of the ring.

The second ceremony is called *Nissuin* (literally, lifting up). This part of the ceremony consists of the *Sheva Brachot* (seven blessings) and *yichud,* during which the bride and groom spend time in privacy, to symbolize the consummation of the relationship.

Anita Diamant notes, "The two ceremonies differ in function and feeling. *Kiddushin* is a legal contract involving the precise formulas and transactions of *ketubah* and *kinyan; Nissuin* is a far less tangible process, sealed not with documents but with actions. Betrothal designates the bride and groom for each other only, but nuptials gives them to each other. *Kiddushin* forges the connection between bride and groom; *Nissuin,* which can also mean 'elevation,' connects a husband and wife with God." (p. 168-9)

Today, *Kiddushin* begins with words of welcome to the bride and groom and guests, from Psalm 118:26:

בָּרוּךְ הַבָּא (בְּרוּכִים הַבָּאִים) בְּשֵׁם יְיָ.

Baruch HaBa (B'ruchim Haba'im) B'Shem Adonai.

Welcome in the name of *Adonai.*

בֵּרַכְנוּכֶם מִבֵּית יְיָ.

Bayrachnuchem MiBayt Adonai.

We welcome you from God's house.

Next is a short prayer asking God to bless the bride and groom:

מִי אַדִּיר עַל הַכֹּל, מִי בָּרוּךְ עַל הַכֹּל, מִי גָּדוֹל
עַל הַכֹּל, הוּא יְבָרֵךְ הֶחָתָן וְהַכַּלָּה.

Mi Adir Al HaKol
Mi Baruch Al HaKol
Mi Gadol Al HaKol
Hu Y'varech HeChatan v'HaKallah.

May the One who is more adored than all,
May the One who is more blessed than all,
May the One who is greater than all,
Bless this groom and bride.

After this introduction, the betrothal blessings follow. First is the blessing over the wine. Second is *Birkat Erusin,* which affirms God's commandments prohibiting certain relationships while permitting others.

בָּרוּךְ אַתָּה יְיָ אֱלֹהֵינוּ מֶלֶךְ הָעוֹלָם,
בּוֹרֵא פְּרִי הַגָּפֶן.
בָּרוּךְ אַתָּה יְיָ אֱלֹהֵינוּ מֶלֶךְ הָעוֹלָם, אֲשֶׁר קִדְּשָׁנוּ
בְּמִצְוֹתָיו וְצִוָּנוּ עַל הָעֲרָיוֹת, וְאָסַר לָנוּ
אֶת־הָאֲרוּסוֹת, וְהִתִּיר לָנוּ אֶת־הַנְּשׂוּאוֹת לָנוּ עַל יְדֵי
חֻפָּה וְקִדּוּשִׁין. בָּרוּךְ אַתָּה יְיָ, מְקַדֵּשׁ עַמּוֹ יִשְׂרָאֵל
עַל יְדֵי חֻפָּה וְקִדּוּשִׁין.

Baruch Atah Adonai Elohaynu Melech HaOlam Borei P'ri HaGafen.
Baruch Atah Adonai Elohaynu Melech HaOlam Asher Kidshanu b'Mitzvotav v'Tzivanu Al Ha'arayot V'asar Lanu Et Ha'arusot V'hitir Lanu Et Han'suot Lanu Al Y'day Chupah v'Kidushin. Baruch Atah Adonai M'kadaysh Amo Yisrael Al Y'day Chupah v'Kiddushin.

Blessed are You, *Adonai,* our God, Sovereign of the universe, Creator of the fruit of the vine.
Blessed are You, *Adonai* our God, Sovereign of the universe, Who has made us holy with *mitzvot* and commanded us concerning illicit relations. Who has forbidden to us women who are betrothed, but permitted to us women who have been taken according to *chupah* and *Kiddushin.* Blessed are You, *Adonai,* who sanctifies the people Israel through *chupah* and *Kiddushin.*

The couple then drinks from the first cup of wine. Sometimes this cup of wine is also shared by the immediate family members of the bride and groom.

The second part of the *Kiddushin* is the ring ceremony. This ritual is considered the core of the Jewish ceremony. In fact, according to the Talmud, the giving of a ring (or other object of value) from the groom to the bride accompanied by the formula for the ring in front of witnesses is enough to constitute a valid marriage.

The groom places the ring on the bride's right index finger (see Ring, p. 65) and recites these words to her:

הֲרֵי אַתְּ מְקֻדֶּשֶׁת לִי בְּטַבַּעַת זוֹ כְּדַת מֹשֶׁה וְיִשְׂרָאֵל.

Haray At M'kudeshet Li b'Taba'at Zu k'Dat Mosheh v'Yisrael.

Behold, you are consecrated to me with this ring, according to the tradition of Moses and Israel.

In liberal communities, the bride then places a ring on the finger of the groom and says to him one of the following:

אֲנִי לְדוֹדִי וְדוֹדִי לִי.

Ani l'Dodi v'Dodi Li.

I am my beloved's and my beloved is mine.

הֲרֵי אַתָּה מְקֻדָּשׁ לִי בְּטַבַּעַת זוֹ כְּדַת מֹשֶׁה וְיִשְׂרָאֵל.

Haray Atah M'kudash Li b'Taba'at Zu k'Dat Mosheh v'Yisrael.

Behold, you are consecrated to me with this ring, according to the tradition of Moses and Israel.

Most traditional Jews do not permit the bride to give the groom a ring as part of the ceremony because it calls into question the legal validity of the groom's giving a ring to the bride.

The ring ceremony ends *Kiddushin.* To make the distinction between the two parts of the ceremony, the *ketubah* is sometimes read at this point. Also, the Rabbi often address the couple at this time.

Nissuin begins with the *Sheva Brachot.* The first of these seven blessings is recited over a second cup of wine. The three blessings that follow praise God for creation, particularly for creating human beings. The fifth blessing invites Jerusalem (referred to as Zion) to rejoice as her children marry.

The sixth blessing links the rejoicing of the bride and groom to God's rejoicing at creation. The final and longest blessing acknowledges God's creation and links it to the joy and happiness of the groom and bride.

בָּרוּךְ אַתָּה יְיָ אֱלֹהֵינוּ מֶלֶךְ הָעוֹלָם, בּוֹרֵא פְּרִי הַגָּפֶן.

בָּרוּךְ אַתָּה יְיָ אֱלֹהֵינוּ מֶלֶךְ הָעוֹלָם, שֶׁהַכֹּל בָּרָא לִכְבוֹדוֹ.

בָּרוּךְ אַתָּה יְיָ אֱלֹהֵינוּ מֶלֶךְ הָעוֹלָם, יוֹצֵר הָאָדָם.

בָּרוּךְ אַתָּה יְיָ אֱלֹהֵינוּ מֶלֶךְ הָעוֹלָם, אֲשֶׁר יָצַר אֶת־הָאָדָם בְּצַלְמוֹ, בְּצֶלֶם דְּמוּת תַּבְנִיתוֹ, וְהִתְקִין לוֹ מִמֶּנּוּ בִּנְיַן עֲדֵי עַד. בָּרוּךְ אַתָּה יְיָ, יוֹצֵר הָאָדָם. שׂוֹשׂ תָּשִׂישׂ וְתָגֵל הָעֲקָרָה בְּקִבּוּץ בָּנֶיהָ לְתוֹכָהּ בְּשִׂמְחָה. בָּרוּךְ אַתָּה יְיָ, מְשַׂמֵּחַ צִיּוֹן בְּבָנֶיהָ.

שַׂמֵּחַ תְּשַׂמַּח רֵעִים הָאֲהוּבִים. כְּשַׂמֵּחֲךָ יְצִירְךָ בְּגַן עֵדֶן מִקֶּדֶם. בָּרוּךְ אַתָּה יְיָ, מְשַׂמֵּחַ חָתָן וְכַלָּה.

בָּרוּךְ אַתָּה יְיָ אֱלֹהֵינוּ מֶלֶךְ הָעוֹלָם, אֲשֶׁר בָּרָא שָׂשׂוֹן וְשִׂמְחָה, חָתָן וְכַלָּה, גִּילָה רִנָּה דִּיצָה וְחֶדְוָה, אַהֲבָה וְאַחֲוָה וְשָׁלוֹם וְרֵעוּת. מְהֵרָה יְיָ אֱלֹהֵינוּ יִשָּׁמַע בְּעָרֵי יְהוּדָה וּבְחוּצוֹת יְרוּשָׁלָיִם קוֹל שָׂשׂוֹן וְקוֹל שִׂמְחָה, קוֹל חָתָן וְקוֹל כַּלָּה, קוֹל מִצְהֲלוֹת חֲתָנִים מֵחֻפָּתָם וּנְעָרִים מִמִּשְׁתֵּה נְגִינָתָם. בָּרוּךְ אַתָּה יְיָ, מְשַׂמֵּחַ חָתָן עִם הַכַּלָּה.

Baruch Atah Adonai, Elohayu Melech HaOlam, Boray P'ri HaGafen.

Baruch Atah Adonai, Elohaynu Melech HaOlam, Shehakol Bara Lichvodo.

Baruch Atah Adonai, Elohaynu Melech HaOlam, Yotzayr HaAdam.

Baruch Atah Adonai, Elohaynu Melech HaOlam, Asher Yatzar Et HaAdam B'tzalmo, B'tzelem D'mut Tavnito V'hitkin Lo Mimenu Binyan Aday Ahd. Baruch Atah Adonai, Yotzayr HaAdam.

Sos Tasis V'tagel HaAkarah B'kibbutz Baneha L'tochah B'simchah. Baruch Atah Adonai, M'samay'ach Tzion B'vaneha.

Samay'ach T'samach Rayim HaAhuvim, K'samay-chacha Y'tzircha b'Gan Ayden Mikedem. Baruch Atah Adonai, M'samayach Chatan v'Kallah. Baruch Atah Adonai, Elohaynu Melech HaOlam, Asher Bara Sason V'simcha, Chatan v'Kallah, Gilah, Rinah, Ditzah, v'Chedvah, Ahavah, v'Achavah, Shalom v'Ray'ut. M'hayra Adonai Elohaynu Yishama B'aray Yehudah Uv'Chutzot Yerushalayim, Kol Sasson v'Kol Simchah, Kol Chatan v'Kol Kallah, Kol Mitzhalot Chatanim Maychupatam u'Na'arim Mimishtay N'ginatam. Baruch Atah Adonai, M'samayach Chatan Im HaKallah.

Blessed are You, *Adonai* our God, Sovereign of the universe, Creator of the fruit of the vine.

Blessed are You, *Adonai* our God, Sovereign of the universe, Who created everything for Your glory.

Blessed are You, *Adonai* our God, Sovereign of the universe, Creator of human beings.

Blessed are You, *Adonai* our God, Sovereign of the universe, Who created human beings in Your image, according to Your likeness, and has fashioned from it a lasting mold. Blessed are You, Adonai, Creator of human beings.

May the barren one [Jerusalem] be joyful and glad when her children gather in her midst in happiness. Blessed are You, *Adonai,* Who causes Zion to rejoice with her children.

Cause these beloved companions to rejoice as You caused your creation to rejoice in the Garden of Eden. Blessed are You, *Adonai,* Who causes the groom and bride to rejoice.

Blessed are You, *Adonai* our God, Sovereign of the universe, Who created joy and happiness, groom and bride, rejoicing, celebration, pleasure and delight, love and friendship, peace and fellowship. Soon, *Adonai* our God, may there be heard in the cities of Judah and within the walls of Jerusalem the voice of joy and voice of happiness, the voice of the groom and the voice of the bride, the voice of grooms from their canopies and young men from their festivals of songs. Blessed are You, *Adonai,* Who causes the groom and bride to rejoice.

After these blessings are recited, the groom and bride sip the wine. Some couples use a cup different from the one that was used for the betrothal blessings.

The ceremony concludes with the Rabbi pronouncing the couple husband and wife and offering a closing blessing (such as the priestly benediction, Numbers 6:24-26). The groom then steps on the glass which is wrapped in a cloth. Sometimes one of the glasses of wine is used, but often a different glass is broken.

The couple then leads the recessional from the *chupah* and goes directly to *yichud* (alone time, together). *Yichud* is the assumption that the marriage has been consummated. If the couple has fasted, they break their fast during this time.

Some Jewish wedding ceremonies include other readings, such as verses from Song of Songs, or contemporary poetry, or prose pertaining to the themes of love and marriage. Some ceremonies include English vows similar to those at non-Jewish weddings (e.g., Do you _____ take _____ to be your wife/husband, promising to cherish and protect her/him, whether in good fortune or adversity and to create together a home hallowed by the faith of Israel?).

It is customary for the wedding ceremony to be followed by a *Seudah Mitzvah,* a meal (to celebrate) the *mitzvah* of getting married. A *Seudah Mitzvah* is also held after other life cycle events, such as circumcision and Bar/Bat Mitzvah. While there are few explicit laws pertaining to this celebratory meal, it is a *mitzvah* to rejoice with the bride and groom.

In Eastern Europe, the center of attention at such a meal was the *badchan* — an entertainer or joker. He was paid to entertain the couple and guests through song, humor, words of wisdom, and other antics. Music and dancing are also part of traditional wedding celebrations.

In traditional communities, the wedding celebration continues for a week, with the *Sheva Brachot* being recited as part of the *Birkat HaMazon* at each meal where there is a *minyan* present and a new guest present, as a way of extending the celebration of the wedding. At certain times in Jewish history, lavish parties were discouraged by sumptuary laws instituted by the Rabbis.

Divorce and the Agunah

Not all marriages will be successful and, therefore, Jewish custom allows for divorce if it is necessary. Since marriage is traditionally viewed as a contractual relationship of mutual consent between a husband and wife, a formal writ of Jewish divorce, a *get,* is required in addition to the civil divorce. Such a document goes back to biblical times, as in Deuteronomy 23:1-4. The procedure for Jewish divorce is made explicit in the Talmud, tractate *Gittin.*

While either husband or wife is permitted to initiate divorce proceedings, the husband must of his own free will give the *get* to his wife.

Some husbands, either out of spite or out of greed, refuse to give a *get.* Without a *get,* a divorcee becomes an *agunah* — literally, a bound woman. (A woman can also become an *agunah* if her husband's death cannot be adequately verified or if he becomes mentally ill and therefore is not considered competent to grant a divorce.) Since an *agunah* is considered "chained" to a former spouse, she may not take another husband, since to do so would be considered adultery. Furthermore, any offspring to another union would be a *mamzer* (see Chapter 1, p. 7).

Currently, no remedy exists to permit an *agunah* to be able to remarry. Some communities pressure the husband to give his wife a *get,* but he must do so of his own will for it to be valid. Some Orthodox Rabbis permit the use of a prenuptial agreement which compels them to go to a *Bet Din* if they decide to divorce.

Conservative Judaism has attempted to remedy this situation by including an extra paragraph as part of the *ketubah* which authorizes the *Bet Din* "to impose such terms of compensation as it may see fit for failure to respond to its summons or to carry out its decision" (*A Guide to Jewish Religious Practice,* Isaac Klein, p. 393). This statement would allow a woman to bring a civil lawsuit against her husband if he refused to agree to giving a *get* or to its terms.

The Reform Movement does not require couples to obtain a *get,* accepting as fully sufficient a civil divorce agreement. However, some Reform Rabbis support a *get* being obtained for purposes of peace in the community.

The procedure for obtaining a get is straightforward. A Rabbi or *Bet Din* oversees a *sofer* (scribe) who writes the *get* in Torah script. A brief ceremony is then held during which witnesses attest to the writing of the *get*. The Rabbi asks the husband whether he gives the *get* of his own free will, and the wife whether she receives it of her own free will. The Rabbi gives the *get* to the husband who drops it into the hands of the wife and recites the phrase: "This is your *get*, and by receiving it you are divorced from me from now on, and you are now permitted to any man." The wife tucks the *get* under her arm and walks to the door, symbolizing her release or freedom. The *get* is then returned to the Rabbi, who reads it again, and then cuts each of its corners or makes slashes through the document to indicate it has been delivered and may never be used by anyone else.

If the husband and wife cannot be present together, the *get* may be delivered by the husband to an agent, who then delivers it to the wife.

Isaac mourned for his mother Sarah for three years. After three years, he married Rebecca and stopped mourning for his mother. Therefore we learn that until a man takes a wife, he directs his love toward his parents. Once he marries, he directs his love toward his wife.

(*Pirke d'Rabbi Eliezer* 32:2)

A man who reaches 20 years of age and is not married, spends his days in sin. In sin! Is it really so? Rather, say that he spends all his days in sinful thoughts.

(*Kiddushin* 29b)

Our Rabbis taught: "How does one dance before the bride?" The school of Shammai said: "Describe the bride as she is." The school of Hillel said: "Praise her as a beautiful and graceful bride." The school of Shammai said to the school of Hillel: "If she were lame or blind would you still say, 'beautiful and graceful bride?' For it is written in the Torah, 'Keep far from a false matter'" (Exodus 23:7).

The school of Hillel said to the school of Shammai: "According to your view, if a person made a bad purchase in the market, should you praise it in front of him or should you criticize it? You should certainly praise it. Therefore the sages said: 'A person should always have a pleasant disposition toward others.'"

(*Ketubot* 16b-17a)

A Roman woman asked Rabbi Yosi ben Chalafta: "How many days did God take to create the world?"

He answered: "In six days, as it is written, 'In six days *Adonai* made heaven and earth'" (Exodus 31:17).

"And what has God been doing since?" she asked.

"God has been arranging marriages — the daughter of so and so to the son of so and so . . . . "

"That is something I can do. I have many servants, and I can match them."

Rabbi Yosi responded, "Arranging marriages may be easy in your eyes, but for God it is as hard as dividing the Sea of Reeds."

After Rabbi Yosi left the woman, she arranged for a row of 1000 male servants to be placed across from a row of 1000 female servants. Then she ordered: "So and so is going to marry so and so, and so and so is going to marry so and so." They were married that very night.

In the morning, the couples came before the woman, one with a cracked skull, another with a missing eye, a third with a broken leg. One said: "I don't want that woman." Another said, "I don't want that man."

The woman sent for Rabbi Yosi and said, "Your Torah is right; what you told me is true."

(*Pesikta d'Rav Kahana* 2:4)

Once a woman and man in Sidon were married, but after many years they had no children. On account of that, the couple went to Rabbi Shimon bar Yochai and asked him for a divorce.

The Rabbi said: "By your lives, just as you were married with a great feast, so you shall start your separation with a great feast."

The couple followed the Rabbi's orders and made a great feast. During the meal, the woman gave the man too much to drink. After the meal, he said, "My dear, take a close look at all of the valuable things in this house. Take the one thing that is most valuable to you and return to your father's house."

What did she do? When he fell asleep, she told her servants to carry her husband on his bed to her father's house. In the middle of the night, he awoke and said: "What am I doing in your father's house?"

She replied: "Didn't you tell me this evening to take whatever is most precious and bring it with me to my father's house? There is nothing more precious to me in the whole world than you."

They returned to Rabbi Shimon bar Yochai. He prayed for them and they had children.

(*Song of Songs Rabbah* 1:1)

ACTIVITIES

Primary

1. Create a dress-up box for your students which includes wedding attire for the bride, groom, attendants, Rabbi, and other participants. Play the game: Who are the people in the wedding? Call on one student at a time to come forward and dress up as one of the people in the wedding (whisper the role the child is to play). The other students guess who the child is portraying.

2. Read to the class the description of a wedding from *More All-of-a-Kind Family* by Sydney Taylor, (pp. 139-149). Begin with the words, "At last it was . . ." In small groups build miniature Jewish wedding scenes which include the major symbols of the ceremony, such as the *chupah*, the ring ceremony, the drinking of wine, the *ketubah,* and the breaking of the glass. Invite parents or other classes to view the scenes.

3. Teach students the words *chatan* (groom) and *kallah* (bride). Hold up pictures of weddings and ask students to identify the *kallah* and *chatan*. Teach the song *"Od Yishama,"* which includes the words *chatan* and *kallah*.
   Resource: *Mazel Tov! Music for a Jewish Wedding and Other Joyous Occasions.*

4. To introduce your students to the Jewish tradition of using a *chupah* at a wedding, read to the class the story *The Keeping Quilt* by Patricia Polacco. Have children make their own version of a "keeping quilt" for the classroom. They can use these to sit on for story or circle time, to decorate the classroom wall, or as a tent.

5. Arrange for the parents of students to bring in their wedding albums. Give students the opportunity to look through the albums. Ask them if they saw similar pictures in the different albums. What were some of the special items or traditions that they can identify? Try to include the following: *chupah,* drinking the wine, *ketubah,* rings, and breaking the glass.

6. Create a family photo album for the couples in the book of Genesis: Adam and Eve; Abraham and Sarah; Isaac and Rebecca; and Jacob, Rachel, and Leah. Use your imagination to stage photographs of the meeting, wedding, and honeymoon of these couples. Wherever possible, use biblical material, such as Jacob and Rachel meeting at the well (Genesis 29:9-20), Isaac and Rebecca meeting each other (Genesis 24:62-67), and Jacob discovering that he had been deceived with Leah (Genesis 29:21-30). Write appropriate captions for each of the pictures.

7. Read to the class *Who Will Lead Kiddush?* by Barbara Pomerantz, which introduces the theme of divorce. Discuss: What is different about Debby's life now that her parents are divorced? How did she feel about the divorce at first? How does she feel now? How does she resolve the problem of who will lead *Kiddush* when her father is not present?

8. Define for the class the Jewish value of *sh'lom bayit* (creating and maintaining a peaceful and loving home). Take dictation or have each student write his or her advice about *sh'lom bayit*. Students may illustrate their advice. Assemble the students' work into a booklet; duplicate it, and give it to the Rabbi for distribution to engaged couples.

Intermediate

1. Read to the class *The Return of Morris Schumsky* by Steven Schnur, about the disappearance of a bride's grandfather on her wedding day. Discuss: What is the family doing to prepare for the wedding? Are they enjoying these preparations or are they under stress? Has your family ever prepared for a large event, such as a wedding, Bar/Bat Mitzvah, or graduation? Was the family enjoying it or was there a lot of pressure? Before Morris Schumsky returns (page 20), ask the students to predict what he is doing. How does the family react to his surprise? What did the family learn from this experience?

2. Interview parents, grandparents, and other relatives about how they met each other. Each student should choose one of the accounts and write a short story incorporating that account. Students should display their stories on a bulletin board, read each others' stories, and discuss similarities and differences. Did anyone have an arranged marriage? Did anyone meet in an unusual way, such as via the Internet?

3. Provide each student with a copy of the *Sheva Brachot* in English (see Overview, page 68). As a class, read and discuss each blessing. Divide the class into seven groups and assign each group one blessing. Have the group design and paint a section of a mural based on the blessing. Assemble the mural in order of the blessings and display.

4. Interview the Rabbi or Cantor about how he or she prepares for a wedding. Among the topics to consider: What are the first things that are usually discussed with the bride and groom? How is the date selected? What type of premarital counseling takes place? Why is it important? What rituals are a required part of the wedding? What are optional?

5. With the class, create a *chupah*. Distribute to each child a 10½" square of white or off-white, pre-washed, 100 percent cotton fabric. Using fabric markers, have the students illustrate aspects of the Jewish wedding ceremony (you may wish to have them sketch their drawings in pencil first.) Sew the squares together with ¼" seams. Add a backing fabric and use as a wall-hanging or a chupah.

6. Listen to the song "Matchmaker, Matchmaker" from *Fiddler on the Roof*. Distribute the lyrics of the song to the students. Ask students: What is a matchmaker? From the words of the song, what does a matchmaker do? How do the young people singing the song feel about a matchmaker? Divide students into four groups. Assign one to take the perspective of the young man, another the young woman, a third the

matchmaker, and the fourth the parents. Each group should write another stanza for the song and then sing it for the other groups.

7. Present to your students the story of the Rabbanit Bracha Kapach, who — among her many *mitzvah* activities — collects used wedding gowns for use by poor brides in Israel. Begin a campaign to collect wedding gowns. Advertise in the synagogue bulletin, local Jewish and general newspapers, church bulletins, and other places. The collected gowns may be sent to the Rabbanit or kept in the community to be used by poor brides. Wedding gowns or donations may be sent to the Rabbanit Bracha Kapach, 12 Lod Street, Jerusalem, Israel. Resource: *Munbaz II and Other Mitzvah Heroes* by Danny Siegel, pp. 83-90.

8. Introduce the lesson by saying that many families have experienced divorce. Then present Judaism's attitude toward divorce (see Overview, p. 69). Distribute a piece of paper to each student and ask the class members to write one way that a divorce affects a family. Each student places the completed piece of paper in a bag. Draw one slip of paper at a time from the bag and share with the class. Discuss the issues that are addressed by the students.

9. With the class, read the skit "Stan and Judi Got Married" from *Class Acts: Plays & Skits for Jewish Settings* by Stan J. Beiner. Identify each of the words written in italics and review with the students their meanings, which are explained in the context of the skit. As a class or in small groups, write a new skit using these words. Alternatively, have groups of students write the scene that would come before this one or the scene that would follow.

10. Help students to compile a list of questions about marriage that each of them will ask parents, grandparents, and other relatives. Include questions such as: How did you meet? What was the funniest thing that happened at your wedding? What do you remember most about your

wedding? Did you have a honeymoon? Where did you go? From the students' questions, create a survey for the students to use with their relatives. Students return to class with the completed surveys and share the responses.

11. Write a story about a Jewish wedding from the perspective of one of the ritual objects used at the wedding ceremony: the *Kiddush* cup, the *chupah*, the glass which is to be broken, the *ketubah*, or a wedding ring. Students may choose to write a story in which all of these objects have speaking parts. Share stories with the class. To expand this activity, stage skits based on the stories.

Secondary

1. In some ways, *tennaim* are very much like contemporary prenuptial agreements. Read and discuss what *tennaim* contain and the protections given the bride. Are protections given for the groom also? Subsequently, invite an attorney to your class to discuss what a prenuptial agreement contains and what kinds of protections it gives to the marriage partners. Create a Venn diagram to illustrate the similarities and differences. A Venn diagram consists of two large circles which partially overlap each other. One circle is labeled *tennaim* and the other labeled prenuptial agreement. Similar characteristics are written in the overlapped area and differences are listed in the separated areas of the two circles.

2. Obtain copies of one or more forms used by Jewish dating or matchmaking services. Distribute to each student. Divide in small groups and examine the form. Discuss: What questions/information is most important? Are there any other questions/information that should be included? Each group should design its own form and report to the class. What are the most important qualities and characteristics in a prospective partner.

3. Provide for students a variety of English texts from *ketuvot*. Begin with a traditional version and create a list of what is included. Explain the purpose of the tractional *ketubah*, i.e., what rights are guaranteed to the bride. Then read contemporary English versions and compare to the traditional version. How are they the same? How are they different? What would the students want to include in their *ketubah*? Resources: *The New Jewish Wedding* by Anita Diamant, pp. 83-91; *The Jewish Way in Love & Marriage* by Maurice Lamm, pp. 199-205; or ask a Rabbi for examples.

4. Share with students copies of selected letters pertaining to marriage from *Bintel Brief*, which was an advice column published in *The Jewish Daily Forward*, a Yiddish newspaper. Identify the types of issues which confronted couples in the early twentieth century. Which problems are similar to those faced by couples today? Which are unique to that period? Each student should select one letter and write his or her own response.
Resource: *A Bintel Brief* by Isaac Metzger.

5. It is traditional for a woman to visit the *mikvah* (ritual bath) for the first time prior to her wedding. If there is a *mikvah* in your community, arrange a tour. If there is no *mikvah*, arrange for a woman who went to the *mikvah* before her wedding to speak to the class about her experience. You may also want to show the video *Mikva, Marriage, and Mazel Tov* to the students.

6. Invite a Rabbi to discuss the significance of Jewish divorce. Prepare the students by presenting key information about divorce from the Overview. Students should then write questions. After the Rabbi's talk, ask each student to summarize what Judaism teaches about divorce.

7. Although we have come a long way from the time of arranged marriages, parents are still involved to varying extents in the process. Discuss the following questions with your class: What have your parents told you about who you could date or not date? How much influence should parents have about who you will date and marry? If you are committed to marrying a Jew,

should you date non-Jews? Encourage the students to ask their friends what limits their parents have set with regard to dating someone of a different religious or ethnic background and to share their findings with the class.

8. Read with the class the skit "Intermarriage" from *Class Acts: Plays & Skits for Jewish Settings* by Stan J. Beiner. Invite two or three intermarried couples to the class and one couple in which the non-Jewish partner converted to Judaism. Each couple should give a short presentation about their experiences dealing with intermarriage and/or conversion. Students then ask questions of the couples. After the couples have left, discuss how each couple dealt with the challenges of their marriage. What were the best strategies for dealing with the holidays, non-Jewish families, religious education, etc.

9. Use dance *midrash* to enable the students to understand better the marriages of the Matriarchs Sarah, Rebecca, Leah, and Rachel. Divide the class into three groups and assign each group a different dance *midrash* from *Torah in Motion: Creating Dance Midrash* by JoAnne Tucker and Susan Freeman, pp. 18-19, 30-31, 40-41.

10. Complete the mini-course *Marriage in Jewish Life and Tradition* by Raymond A. Zwerin and Audrey Friedman Marcus.

11. Complete the mini-course *Relationships: A Jewish View* by Barbara Mirel and Jeff Mirel.

12. Complete the instant lesson *Mikvah and the Jewish Laws of Sex and Marriage* by Fran Hirshman.

13. Complete the instant lesson *What Should the Fish Tell the Bird?* by Havi Wolfson, which focuses on the issue of interdating.

Hebrew

1. Using the Cantor or music specialist as a resource, learn some or all of the following

songs associated with Jewish weddings: "*Siman Tov Umazal Tov,*" "*Od Yishama,*" and "*Dodi Li.*" Perform them at an assembly or service and explain their relationship to the wedding. Resources: *Mazel Tov! Music for a Jewish Wedding and Other Joyful Occasions; Ani Ma-amin* by Debbie Friedman.

2. Design a Jewish wedding invitation using a Hebrew phrase such as אֲנִי לְדוֹדִי וְדוֹדִי לִי (I am my beloved's and my beloved is mine) or קוֹל שָׂשׂוֹן וְקוֹל שִׂמְחָה, קוֹל חָתָן וְקוֹל כַּלָּה (The voice of joy and the voice of happiness, the voice of the groom and the voice of the bride.) Also include the Hebrew date and the Hebrew names of the bride and groom.

3. Use the following Hebrew words relating to the Jewish wedding to create one or more of the suggested games. Hebrew words:

חָתָן	– *chatan*/groom
כַּלָּה	– *kallah*/bride
חֻפָּה	– *chupah*/wedding canopy
כְּתוּבָה	– *ketubah*/marriage contract
שֶׁבַע בְּרָכוֹת	– *Sheva Brachot*/seven wedding blessings
מַזָּל טוֹב	– *mazal tov*/congratulations
שִׁיר הַשִּׁירִים	– *Shir HaShirim*/Song of Songs
קִדּוּשִׁין	– *Kiddushin*/Consecration
טַבַּעַת	– *taba'at*/ring
יִחוּד	– *yichud*/private time
שַׁדְכָן	– *shadchan*/matchmaker

Suggested games: *Concentration; Around the World* (say the Hebrew word and the first student to give the English definition wins); *What Am I?* (one person chooses an object; other students ask three questions that are answered yes or no and then must guess what the object is). You could also put these words into a word search or crossword puzzle.

4. The *ketubah* and *get* are both traditionally handwritten documents. Show some examples of *ketubot* or *gittin* to your class. Introduce students to Hebrew calligraphy using chisel point

markers. After practicing, each student should choose one phrase from the wedding as a calligraphy project. Display the finished works of art. Resource: *A Guide to Hebrew Lettering* by Peretz Prusan.

Adult

1. Ask participants to read the story of Ruth from the Bible prior to attending the class. Focus the discussion on the tradition of marriage to the closest relative in cases where a woman's husband dies without leaving an heir. Include in the discussion information about the tradition of Levirite marriage (see Overview, p. 62), which is similar to, but not the same as, the remarriage of Ruth. Explore reasons why it was important to require such marriages in ancient days and why the custom eventually fell into disuse. For an extended program, view the film *I Love You Rosa,* on the theme of Levirite marriage.

2. View the movie *The Imported Bridegroom.* Create a list of advantages and disadvantages of arranged marriages. Ask the participants if they could imagine themselves being party to an arranged marriage as spouse, parent, or matchmaker. Why or why not? Distribute copies of "Personals" from a Jewish newspaper as well as advertisements from Jewish dating services. Compare these methods of matchmaking with the traditions of arranged marriages and matchmakers.

3. Traditionally, *tennaim* were conditions which were agreed to by the parents of the bride and groom as to the date and financial arrangements pertaining to their children's marriage. Some contemporary couples have expanded on this concept to create a list of promises and mutual commitments which will guide them in their marriage. For example, among the *tennaim* agreed to by Einat Ramon and her husband Arik Ascherman are: clean the house thoroughly every week before Shabbat, study Jewish texts together at least two hours per week, compliment each other daily, share a day off each week. As part of a marriage preparation class (or for couples who are already married, but who wish to renew their commitment to each other), hold a workshop on creating modern *tennaim.* Share with the couples information about traditional *tennaim* as well as the contemporary examples above. Each couple should then create their own *tennaim.* Allow opportunities to share ideas with each other before each couple finalizes its list. Hold a ceremony with the couples during which they read their *tennaim.* Include prayers such as the "*Shehecheyanu*" and songs such as "*Dodi Li*" and "*Erev Shel Shoshanim.*"

4. Invite a minister, priest, and Rabbi to be on a panel about the meaning and symbols of marriage in Judaism and Christianity. Each may also want to share views about intermarriage.

5. View the video *Chicks in White Satin* which deals with the issue of same sex marriage. Invite a panel of individuals to share their reactions to the movie and their views on this sensitive issue. If possible, include a Rabbi, a gay or lesbian couple, and a marriage and family counselor on the panel. Allow time for questions.

6. One of the tragedies of modern Jewish life that many adults are not aware of is the plight of the *agunah* (literally, a chained woman). An *agunah* is a woman who may not remarry, usually because her husband has refused to give her a *get.* Discuss this issue and examine the practice of using prenuptial agreements to avoid this problem. Create a pamphlet for your synagogue about this topic to be given to prospective brides and grooms.
   Resources: *Women in Chains: A Sourcebook on the Agunah* edited by Jack Nusan Porter; "The Plight of the Agunah" by Debra Nussbaum Cohen in *The Jewish Monthly;* the organization G.E.T. (Getting Equitable Treatment), P. O. Box 131, Brooklyn, NY 11230.

7. Hold a film series on the theme of Jewish marriage.

Suggested videos: *Enemies: A Love Story; Crossing Delancey; Chicks in White Satin; I Love You, Rosa; Uncle Moses; Polonaise; The Shidduch; The Mountain; Interlove Story; Intermarriage: When Love Meets Tradition; The Imported Bridegroom; Seal upon Thy Heart.*

8. In a marriage education workshop, do the "Pre-Marital Interview" exercise from *Jewish Guided Imagery: A How-To Book for Rabbis, Educators and Groups Leaders* by Dov Peretz Elkins, pp. 122-123.

Family

1. Create a Jewish Wedding Museum. Send home instructions for each family to gather memorabilia from weddings which might include: the *chupah, ketubah,* invitation, pictures, wedding gowns, remnants of the broken glass, videocassette, bridal Bible. Each item should be labeled with the family's name. Before families arrive, set up tables and place signs designating where each type of item should be displayed. As families arrive, they put each object in its appropriate spot and fill out an index card describing the object, its approximate age, at whose wedding it was used. Distribute to each family a sheet of paper with questions they can answer as they tour the museum such as: What was the oldest object they saw? What was the most interesting object? What was the most unusual? What was your favorite? Conclude the program with a reception celebrating the opening (and closing!) of the Jewish Wedding Museum.

2. Create a "Celebration of Marriage" for your synagogue or school. Divide into groups of three or four families. Each married couple should share about its experiences, including the date and place of the marriage, political issues and historical events of that time, what it cost to get married, what life situation or financial circumstances affected the wedding celebration, what Jewish traditions were included in the ceremony. Those who have been married may also share if they wish. Also ask

the couples where they honeymooned and what kind of home and lifestyle they came back to. Create a ceremony to celebrate the marriages, honoring the couple married the longest and the couple most recently married.

3. Hold a program for families which have experienced divorce. Invite social workers and marriage and family counselors to present appropriate workshops for children and adults. (Jewish Family Service is an excellent resource.) Workshops might include: Celebrating Holidays in Separate or Single-Parent Households, Keeping the Battle off the Bimah: Dealing with Life Cycle Events, Raising Children in a Blended Family, Co-Parenting in Two Households. Conclude with an activity or ritual which affirms the sense of family. For example, each family could write a statement and create a banner which expresses their view of being a family. Display the banners and have a member from each family read their statement. Consider including appropriate music.

All-School

1. Create a mock Jewish wedding. Divide families into groups, with each group being responsible for one aspect of the wedding. These should include: creating the ceremony, preparing a *ketubah,* preparing invitations, preparing the reception, organizing entertainment for the reception, assembling the ritual objects, and setting up the *chupah.* Each group should first study material pertaining to their assigned aspect. For example, the group preparing the invitations should study about the dates weddings can and cannot take place, favored days for weddings in Jewish tradition, and how to compose the invitation in both Hebrew and English. The group should choose an appropriate verse to include on the invitation and deliver a copy of the invitation to the other groups. The group preparing the entertainment should study the tradition of the *badchan* and prepare songs and dances to entertain the bride and groom. The group preparing the ceremony should assign all of the traditional roles.

Hold the ceremony, having each group deliver a brief report at the appropriate time during the wedding. (This program can be organized to be done in about 2 to 2½ hours on one day.)

2. Each class reenacts a scene of a wedding from a different time in Jewish history. For example: biblical (Adam and Eve, Abraham and Sarah, David and Bathsheba, Ruth and Boaz); Rabbinic (Rabbi Meir and Beruriah, Rabbi Akiba and Rachel); medieval (Gluckel of Hameln, Converso); modern (*shtetl, kibbutz,* Yemenite,

Moroccan, American, Ethiopian); futuristic. If possible, assign classes a historical period for their wedding that relates to their curriculum. The classes present their scenes for each other.

3. Organize an all-school choir to learn and perform a medley of Jewish wedding songs. Hold a performance for the entire synagogue. Resources: *Mazel Tov! Music For a Jewish Wedding and Other Joyous Occasions; From the Song of Songs; The Best of Debbie Friedman* (songbook).

GLOSSARY

Agunah – Literally, a chained woman. This is a woman whose husband refuses to give her a Jewish divorce (or who disappears during war or at sea without witnesses), preventing her from marrying another man.

Aufruf – Yiddish word for "calling up" the groom (and bride) to the Torah on the Shabbat before their wedding

Badchan – Entertainer at a wedding ceremony, who often served as the master of ceremonies.

Bedeken – Ritual of placing the veil over the bride's face prior to the wedding.

Bet Din – Court, composed of three Rabbis, or at least one Rabbi and two learned Jews, which rules on matters of Jewish law, such as divorce.

Birkat Erusin – Betrothal blessing.

Chalitzah – Ceremony of release performed when a Levirate marriage was traditionally required.

Chatan – Groom (Yiddish, *chossen*).

Chossen's Tish – Groom's table: the gathering of men for song, study, and celebration prior to the wedding.

Chupah – Originally the room in which the wedding was held and consummated; now the wedding canopy which represents that room.

Erusin – First part of the Jewish wedding ceremony which marks the betrothal.

Get – Jewish divorce document.

Hachnasat Kallah – *Mitzvah* of providing a dowry for the bride.

Kabbalat Panim – Gathering of women prior to the wedding. Also used as a general term for a pre-nuptial reception.

Kallah – Bride.

Ketubah (Ketuvot, pl.) – Jewish marriage contract.

Kiddushin – Literally, sanctification. The first part of the Jewish wedding.

Kinyan – Ritual which formalizes the acceptance of the *tennaim*.

Kittel – White linen robe traditionally worn by the groom.

Levirate Marriage – Marriage between a woman (whose husband died before fathering a child) and her husband's eldest brother. While practiced in ancient times, such a marriage is now replaced with the ceremony of *chalitzah*.

Mikvah – Ritual bath.

Nissuin – Second part of the Jewish wedding ceremony, consisting primarily of the *Sheva Brachot*.

Shadchan – Matchmaker or marriage broker.

Sheva Brachot – Seven wedding blessings recited during the ceremony, and after the meal at the reception, and, in Orthodox communities, for the entire week when there is a *minyan*.

Shidduch – A pairing or match for marriage.

Tennaim – Literally, conditions. Stipulations agreed to by the families of the bride and groom as part of the engagement.

Yichud – Private time together observed by the bride and groom immediately following the wedding ceremony.

RESOURCES

For the Teacher

Aiken, Lisa. *Beyond Bashert: A Guide to Dating and Marriage Enrichment.* Northvale, NJ: Jason Aronson Inc., 1996.

Bulka, Reuven. *Jewish Divorce Ethics: The Right Way to Say Goodbye.* Ogdensburg, NY: Ivy League Press, 1992.

———. *Jewish Marriage: A Halakhic Ethic.* Hoboken, NJ: KTAV Publishing House, Inc., 1986.

———. *Judaism on Pleasure.* Northvale, NJ: Jason Aronson Inc., 1995.

Cohen, Debra Nussbaum. "The Plight of the Agunah." In *The Jewish Monthly,* January–February 1996.

Cohen, Jack S. *Intermarriage and Conversion: A Halakhic Solution.* Hoboken NJ: KTAV Publishing House, Inc., n.d.

Cowan, Paul, with Rachel Cowan. *Mixed Blessings: Overcoming the Stumbling Blocks in an Interfaith Marriage.* New York: Penguin Books, 1987.

Diamant, Anita. *The New Jewish Wedding.* New York: Summit Books, 1985.

Elkins, Dov Peretz. *Jewish Guided Imagery: A How-To Book for Rabbis, Educators and Groups Leaders.* Princeton, NJ: Growth Associates, 1996.

Friedman, Debbie. *The Best of Debbie Friedman.* Cedarhurst, NY: Tara Publications, 1987. (songbook)

Isaacs, Ronald H. *The Bride and Groom Handbook.* West Orange, NJ: Behrman House, Inc., 1989.

Kaufman, Michael. *Love, Marriage, and Family in Jewish Law and Tradition.* Northvale, NJ: Jason Aronson Inc., 1992

Klein, Isaac. A *Guide to Jewish Religious Practice.* New York: The Jewish Theological Seminary of America, 1979.

Lamm, Maurice. *The Jewish Way in Love & Marriage.* San Francisco: Harper & Row, 1980.

Lewittees, Mendell. *Jewish Marriage: Rabbinic Law, Legend, & Custom.* Northvale, NJ: Jason Aronson Inc., 1994.

Maslin, Simeon J., ed. *Gates of Mitzvah.* New York: Central Conference of American Rabbis, 1979.

Mayer, Egon. *Love & Tradition: Marriage Between Jews & Christians.* New York: Plenum Press, 1985.

Metzker, Isaac. *A Bintel Brief.* New York: Schocken Books, 1990.

Pasternak, Velvel, ed. *From the Song of Songs.* Cedarhurst, NY: Tara Publications, 1988. (songbook)

———. *Mazel Tov! Music For a Jewish Wedding and Other Joyous Occasions.* Cedarhurst, NY: Tara Publications, 1992. (songbook)

Porter, Jack Nusan, ed., *Women in Chains: A Sourcebook on the Agunah.* Northvale, NJ: Jason Aronson, Inc., 1996.

Prusan, Peretz. *A Guide to Hebrew Lettering.* New York: UAHC Press, 1982.

Stopler, Pinchas. *Jewish Alternatives in Love, Dating and Marriage.* New York: National Conference of Synagogue Youth and University Press of America, Inc., 1984.

Tucker, JoAnne, and Susan Freeman. *Torah in Motion: Creating Dance Midrash.* Denver: A.R.E. Publishing, Inc., 1990.

For the Students

Beiner, Stan J. *Class Acts: Plays & Skits for Jewish Settings.* Denver: A.R.E. Publishing, Inc., 1992.

Hirshman, Fran. *Mikvah and the Jewish Laws of Sex and Marriage.* Los Angeles: Torah Aura Productions, 1996.

Mirel, Barbara, and Jeff Mirel. *Relationships: A Jewish View.* Denver: A.R.E. Publishing, Inc., 1981.

Polacco, Patricia. *The Keeping Quilt.* New York: Simon & Schuster, Inc., 1988.

Pomerantz, Barbara. *Who Will Lead Kiddush?* New York: UAHC Press, 1985.

Schnur, Steven. *The Return of Morris Schumsky.* New York: UAHC Press, 1987.

Siegal, Danny. *Munbaz II and Other Mitzvah Heroes.* Spring Valley, NY: The Town House Press, 1991.

Taylor, Sydney. *More All-of-a-Kind Family.* New York: Dell Publishing Co., Inc., 1954.

Wolfson, Havi. *What Should the Bird Tell the Fish?* Los Angeles: Torah Aura Productions, 1995.

Zwerin, Raymond A., and Audrey Friedman Marcus. *Marriage in Jewish Life and Tradition.* Denver: A.R.E. Publishing, Inc., 1978.

Audiovisual

Chicks in White Satin. Elaine Holliman. Videocassette.

Crossing Delancey. Swank Motion Pictures. Videocassette.

Enemies: A Love Story. Facets Multimedia, Inc. Videocassette.

Fiddler on the Roof. RCA Cassette #OK-1005; CD #RCDI-7060. Audiocassette.

Friedman, Debbie. *Ani Ma-amin.* A.R.E. Publishing, Inc. Audiocassette.

I Love You, Rosa. Facets Multimedia, Inc. Videocassette.

The Imported Bridegroom. Ergo Media Inc. Videocassette.

Interlove Story. Anne Flatte. Videocassette.

Intermarriage: When Love Meets Tradition. Direct Cinema Ltd. Videocassette.

Mazel Tov! Music for a Jewish Wedding and Other Joyous Occasions. Tara Publications. Arranged by Velvel Pasternak. Audiocassette/CD.

Mikva, Marriage and Mazel Tov. Alden Films. Videocassette.

The Mountain. Jarmaq Productions. Videocassette.

Polonaise. Polygram Beneluk. Videocassette.

Seal Upon Thy Heart. Ergo Media Inc. Videocassette.

The Shidduch. U.S.C. Film School. Videocassette.

Uncle Moses. Facets Multimedia, Inc. Videocassette.

CHAPTER FIVE

GROWING OLDER

ADULTHOOD · AGING · ILLNESS

OVERVIEW

IT IS IRONIC THAT THE LONGEST STRETCH of life, adulthood, has the least number of life cycle events associated with it — only marriage . . . and divorce. Could this be because in previous generations life was so short and uncertain that traditions were seen as tenuous and therefore failed to develop? But now, with a longer life span and more settled conditions, there is an ever increasing number of important concerns and transitions that mark the adult years, and beg our attention.

Parenting and grandparenting, roles once learned as if by osmosis, are today the subject of numerous books, studies, and school courses. Subsets of the same theme include single parenthood, parenting of blended families, as well as living as a single person.

While the growing diversity of life-style affects and changes society in general, the Jewish community is especially challenged by its impact. For example: What does it mean to be a single Jewish adult in a culture that through the ages has emphasized the importance of marriage and family? What roles can grandparents who are not steeped in the tradition play in the transmission of Jewish customs and values?

One phase of adulthood that has been given significant attention is aging. On the whole, we have recognized the unique contributions that the elderly can make to the community, as well as the responsibilities we have in caring for the elderly.

While illnesses might occur at any phase of life, when they afflict the elderly they are usually acute and serious. Therefore, that subject will be included in this chapter.

In recent years, celebrations and rituals have been developed for adults. These include: Adult Bar/Bat Mitzvah; Mid-life; Ceremony of the Wise Woman; *Eshet Hazon*: A Woman of Vision; Menopause; and Retirement. Some of these rituals build on earlier Jewish traditions; some are new creations. All endeavor to bring the wealth of insight and wisdom of our heritage to important moments of life, turning what is often an ordinary transition into a sacred occasion.

Parenting

For many Jewish adults, parenthood presents both the greatest challenge and provides the most significant rewards. Jewish tradition imposes specific expectations on parents. A father, for example, is responsible for circumcising his son, or more commonly for arranging for him to be circumcised. A father is also responsible for, among other things, the Jewish education of his son, teaching him a trade, and teaching him to swim.

A mother's major responsibilities are traditionally to assure the proper celebration of Shabbat and holidays, to keep a kosher kitchen, and to teach her daughters these skills. As Judith Abrams and Steven Abrams say in their book, "In essence, then, what is it that parents are obligated to provide for their children? They must see that their children observe the *mitzvot* in their youth, and that they are prepared to live a productive, righteous life (*Jewish Parenting: Rabbinic Insights*, pp. 209-210).

Until recent times, most Jewish parents were well prepared for these responsibilities. They had been raised in observant Jewish homes in which such knowledge and values were passed down from parents and grandparents. They received a comprehensive Jewish education within the context of a community whose families lived a religiously homogeneous life-style with shared values. While they may have faced severe challenges ranging from poverty to anti-Semitism, these often served to reinforce the importance of the family and the Jewish heritage. Indeed, the ability of the Jewish family to remain cohesive and nurturing may be attributed, at least in part, to such outside influences.

In contrast to previous generations, Jewish parents today face an array of challenges which threaten to hinder, if not undermine, Jewish parenting. In many households, one parent might not have been raised Jewish. Or, parents who were raised Jewish might not have received the education necessary to pass basic Jewish practices along to their children.

In a majority of two-parent families, both parents work, often at 40 plus hours a week jobs. This cuts significantly into time they have to spend with children. Unless parents make a concerted effort, Shabbat and holiday observances often fall by the wayside or take a back seat to other family or outside activities.

Single parents, interfaith couples, and blended families, which make up an increasing percentage of all Jewish families, each face unique challenges to Jewish parenting. Sheila Peltz Weinberg notes that: "Single-parent families are often cut off from the source of strength and nurture they seek in Judaism . . . they are sometimes hindered by Jewish communal structures and activities geared to the traditional family. Furthermore, they are at a disadvantage because they have less time to give and greater need for counseling, legal assistance, job training, and child care ("The Single Parent and the Community," in *The Hadassah Magazine Jewish Parenting Book*, Roselyn Bell, ed., p. 295).

With respect to interfaith households, the degree of commitment to Judaism also varies widely. Some are totally committed to having a Jewish family, with no other religious tradition in the household. Others find the non-Jewish partner practicing his or her religion, while being supportive of raising the children in the Jewish religion. In yet other families, the commitment to Judaism is minimal or non-existent.

Regardless of the degree of their commitment to creating a Jewish home, intermarried families face unique challenges to accomplishing that goal. These include: Christian or other religious holidays brought into the home; dealing with non-Jewish in-laws and grandparents and extended family; and the pervasive influences of a non-Jewish, secularized society. Any or all of these can diffuse and confuse the religious identity of the children. As for blended families, whether both parents and all siblings are Jewish or not, the issues can be even more complex.

Confronted by all of these hurdles, some consider it incredible that any parents are successful in creating a Jewish home. Remarkably, many parents are. Many parents do create an intensely Jewish environment in which the holidays are observed with festive meals and traditional rituals, in which the values of *tzedakah*, *ahavah* (love), and *sh'lom bayit* (peace in the home) are practiced on a daily basis, and in which the spirit and beauty of Judaism are continuously experienced.

Fortunately, for those who want to enrich and deepen their commitment to Judaism, the contemporary Jewish community offers a wide variety of resources, including: books on Jewish practice, including many which focus on parenting (see Resources, p. 99), newsletters for Jewish parents and families, information on the Internet and the World Wide Web, parenting centers at synagogues and Jewish Community Centers featuring classes and resources on every aspect of being a parent, family education programs and classes in which parents learn together with (or parallel to) their children, family education programs for interfaith families, family camp experiences, adult education programs specifically designed to improve Jewish parenting skills, and more.

The stimulus for renewed efforts in this area by local synagogues, Federations, Jewish foundations, as well as by the national Reform, Conservative, and Reconstructionist Movements, was the 1990 Jewish Population Study. This study revealed among other things that a significant percentage of those born Jewish were not actively involved in Jewish life as adults, that the intermarriage rate had skyrocketed, and that only a small percentage of the children from such intermarriages were being raised as

Jews. With excellent resources and programs as potential Jewish entry and reentry portals, and with an emphasis being placed on Jewish continuity, the Jewish community seems to have refocused its attention on attracting and welcoming assimilated Jews and intermarried Jewish couples into its midst.

The Reform, Conservative, and Reconstructionist Movements have each created programs and directed resources toward interfaith couples, encouraging them to participate in Judaism, to raise their children as Jews, and inviting the non-Jewish partner to consider becoming Jewish. For example, Stepping Stones to a Jewish Me, created by Congregation Emanuel of Denver with funding in part from the Allied Jewish Federation of that city and dissemination by the Outreach Commission of the Reform Movement, is a two year program which teaches families about Jewish holidays and practices. For several hours each week, adults learn the basics of Judaism while their children attend the equivalent of Religious School classes. Many of these families subsequently affiliate with synagogues, send their children to Religious School, and become active participants in Jewish life.

Concern about intermarriage has even spurred cross-denominational cooperation as leaders recognize that this is a problem which needs to be addressed on a communal level. For example, organizations such as the National Jewish Outreach Program have spearheaded a national effort to confront the challenges of intermarriage and assimilation by sponsoring a variety of programs such as the Hebrew Reading Crash Course (a class to teach Hebrew) and Shabbat Across America (an effort to get Jews to attend the synagogue of their choice for a Shabbat dinner and service). What all of these have in common is an effort to stimulate and educate Jewish adults, particularly parents, to become active participants in the Jewish community and to make Judaism a more central part of their lives.

Single Adults

With the Jewish community putting so much energy and resources into the education of children and parenting, single adults — particularly those without children — often feel marginalized or alienated from synagogues and Jewish life. In recent years,

more and more Jewish adults are facing the challenge of "Being Single in a Noah's Ark World," as a workshop addressing the issue was titled.

Until the last half of the twentieth century, the percentage of single Jewish adults was relatively small, and consisted mostly of elderly widows and widowers. Most Jews were married in their twenties and stayed married. Jews who never married or who divorced were the exception. In recent decades, however, a variety of factors have lead to an increase in the number of Jewish singles.

First of all, a high percentage of Jews pursue a college education as well as advanced degrees, and only a small fraction of these marry before the end of their education.

Secondly, marriage and children, which were once clear cultural and communal expectations in Judaism, are now often viewed (outside of Orthodox Judaism) as options that one may choose or not choose based on personal preference. With significantly reduced social pressure to marry and have children, many Jews are choosing to remain single.

Thirdly, as the age for getting married increases from early twenties to mid-thirties, many Jews simply remain single longer. Either they marry later, thus skewing the statistic of the percentage of non-married Jews, or they never do marry. It is not rare, however, that the latter go on to adopt or bear children, thus creating yet another sub-category — single, never married, with children.

Finally, an increasing divorce rate among Jews has led to an increasing number of single parents. While some of these single parents remarry, many remain single for significant periods of time or for the rest of their lives.

The Jewish community has responded to the issue of singles in several ways. Many synagogues, Jewish Community Centers, and other organizations have created singles groups to facilitate Jews meeting and dating one another. Programs have been developed and implemented which address some of the particular challenges that single adults and single parents face in the modern world. In some communities there are private dating services run by Jewish individuals or communal dating books housed in a synagogue into which men and women place their pictures and some personal information for the purpose of connecting with one another.

Still, many single adults do not feel welcomed by the Jewish community. When a couple divorces, one or both partners often drop out of active Jewish life, regardless of the efforts of friends, the synagogue, or the community to keep them involved. Singles often perceive that synagogue programs are geared toward children or toward two-parent families, whether this is true or not.

As the Jewish community comes to terms with the ever increasing diversity of its members, singles should begin to feel more at home. And as more singles become involved in the Jewish community, the more likely it is that other singles will follow their example and choose to participate.

Grandparenting

If parents today face new challenges, so much the more so do grandparents. Due to the mobility of the Jewish community, fewer and fewer grandparents live in the same community as their grandchildren. Yet, as people live longer and healthier lives, grandparents are often able to interact with their grandchildren over a greater number of years, often celebrating B'nai Mitzvah, weddings, and the birth of great-grandchildren.

Commenting on the new reality, Gladys Rosen writes: "Grandmothers today bear little resemblance to the stereotypical grandma always there making curative chicken soup or baking restorative cookies. Nor do we see many *Zaydes* going over the *parasha* (Torah portion) of the week or checking on the Hebrew progress of their grandchildren. Given the dramatic social changes we have witnessed during the past two decades, it is not surprising that the image and roles of grandparents have been affected by shifting family relationships, geographic mobility, and technological advances" ("Grandparenting," in *The Hadassah Magazine Jewish Parenting Book*, Roselyn Bell, ed., p. 70).

Some grandparents are playing a more important role in the raising and nurturing of their grandchildren. It is not unusual for a single parent to move home or closer to home so that grandparents can provide part-time or full-time child care while the parent works. And, in cases in which a parent is not able to raise a child (due to physical or social problems), grandparents are often called upon to

take over this responsibility completely.

Even when grandparents do not play such a key role in the daily life of their grandchildren, they often have the opportunity to be a significant Jewish influence in their lives. This is especially so if the parents are intermarried. Grandparents often host holiday celebrations, Shabbat dinners, and other Jewish family gatherings. With the approval and support of parents, grandparents can play a vital role in the informal Jewish education of their grandchildren by teaching them how to make traditional Jewish foods, taking them to Jewish events, and by sharing their love for Judaism with them.

Even when distance separates family members, transportation and technology (telephone, videotapes, E-mail) can facilitate visits and communication. Most parents encourage the development of a relationship between the generations. And most grandparents look forward to the time they spend with their grandchildren.

A reality of our day is that Jewish grandparents sometimes have non-Jewish grandchildren, and Jewish grandchildren sometimes have non-Jewish grandparents. Each such family needs to deal sensitively with these realities, respecting the religion of each person, while at the same time endeavoring to develop the unique relationships that grandparents can have with their grandchildren.

Aging and the Elderly

"Throughout most of history, elders occupied honored roles in society as sages and seers, leaders and judges, guardians of the traditions, and instructors of the young. They were revered as gurus, shamans, wise old men and women who helped guide the social order and who initiated spiritual seekers into the mysteries of inner space. Beginning with the Industrial Revolution, with its emphasis on technological knowledge that often was beyond their ken, elders lost their esteemed place in society and fell into the disempowered state that we now ascribe to a 'normal' old age" (*From Age-ing to Sage-ing: A Profound New Vision of Growing Older*, Zalman Schachter-Shalomi and Ronald S. Miller, p. 6).

Beginning in biblical times, Judaism emphasized the importance of honoring the elderly. "You shall rise before the aged and show deference to the old . . ." (Leviticus 19:32). The Bible accounts living to an old age as being a reward for having observed such *mitzvot* as honoring one's parents (Exodus 20:12), not taking a mother bird and her young on the same day (Deuteronomy 22:6-7), and having accurate weights and measures (Deuteronomy 25:13-15). The ages of the Patriarchs — Abraham (175), Isaac (180), and Jacob (147) — in part reflect the belief that one was rewarded for living a righteous life with many years.

A corrupt generation, according to Isaiah, is one in which "the young bully the old" (Isaiah 3:5). One of the sins which contributed to the destruction of the Temple was that "no respect has been shown to elders" (Lamentations 5:12). And the Psalmist offered the following plea: "Do not reject us in old age. Do not abandon us when our strength leaves us" (Psalms 71:9). These texts indicate that proper treatment of the elderly was a well established value during the biblical period.

This concern for the elderly continued during the Rabbinic period. "Every profession in the world is of help to a person only in one's youth, but in one's old age, one is exposed to hunger" (*Kiddushin* 82b). The Rabbis also acknowledge that with advanced age came physical deterioration. A *midrash* says, "A young man should pray that when he is old his eyes see, his mouth eats, and his legs walk, for in old age, all powers fail" (*Tanchuma Miketz* 10).

The Rabbis recognized that with age came wisdom. For example, Rabbi Simeon ben Eliezer taught: "If the old say 'tear down' but the children say 'build,' tear down, because the 'tearing down' of the old is building and the 'building' of the young is tearing down" (*Megillah* 31b).

However, other sources indicate that age of itself was not sufficient for having one's advice heeded. Rabbi Abbahu and Rabbi Jeremiah were once arguing. When the former claimed that his opinion should be accepted because of his age, Rabbi Jeremiah disputed his claim, saying, "Is the matter decided by age? It is decided by reason" (*Baba Batra* 102b). Furthermore, there was recognition that with age sometimes came loss of intellectual ability. Elisha ben Abuyah said, "What does learning when old resemble? It resembles writing

on blotted-out paper" (*Pirke Avot* 4:20).

It is therefore impossible to conclude that one view of the elderly is found in the Talmud or in other literature of the Rabbinic period. Rabbi Dayle Friedman, a chaplain for many years in a Home for the Aged, sums it up by saying: "On the one hand, old age is envisioned as a blessing, a reward for meritorious living, a time when one is deserving of special honor; on the other hand, it is also depicted as a time of loss and incapacity ("The Crown of Glory: Aging in the Jewish Tradition," in *Celebration & Renewal: Rites of Passage in Judaism*, Rela M. Geffen, ed., p. 203).

Later Jewish tradition built onto the teachings of Bible and Talmud. In the ethical and legal literature of the medieval period we are instructed that the elderly be treated with respect and care and that charity be set aside to support them. While the immediate family assumed primary responsibility for the care of elderly relatives, the community was expected to step in when a family failed in its duty or when a person had no family. After the Chmielnicki pogroms in seventeenth century Poland, the Council of Lithuania offered financial assistance to the elderly. A first Jewish home for the aged was founded in eighteenth century Amsterdam; similar institutions were established in Jewish communities in Western Europe and in the United States.

With the elderly comprising an ever increasing percentage of the North American Jewish community, more programs and resources are now being channeled toward providing services and facilities for this segment of the population. One of the greatest challenges facing the Jewish community in the twenty-first century is in developing creative, often new ways to fulfill the age-old *mitzvah* of honoring the elderly.

Rituals of Adulthood

In recent years, it has become common in liberal synagogues for adults to celebrate a Bar or Bat Mitzvah. By and large, these adults had not had a Bar or Bat Mitzvah ceremony as youths because: they are converts to Judaism and did not grow up in a Jewish home, their childhood congregations did not provide Bat Mitzvah ceremonies for girls (or Bar Mitzvah ceremonies for boys), their families for one reason or another did not offer their children a

Jewish education or the opportunity for Bar or Bat Mitzvah preparation.

As explained above (see Chapter 2, p. 27), according to Jewish tradition, one automatically becomes a Bat Mitzvah at age 12½ and a Bar Mitzvah at age 13, regardless of whether or not this rite of passage is marked by a ceremony or ritual. Adults, in preparing for the ceremony, view it as an affirmation of their personal choice to learn to read Hebrew and to participate more fully in Jewish worship. Although there is no standardized course of study, most adult study offerings focus on the basic prayers of the liturgy, Torah and *Haftarah* blessings, and a selection from the Torah and *Haftarah* of the week.

Sometimes an adult will celebrate becoming a Bar or Bat Mitzvah individually. Sometimes, a parent or even a grandparent will use the occasion of child or grandchild becoming Bar/Bat Mitzvah as the stimulus for personal study — tagging onto the child's ceremony by reading several lines of the Torah. More often, a class which studied together will become B'nai Mitzvah all together in a service at which class members lead different parts of the service, read from the Torah and *Haftarah*, and deliver *Divray Torah*.

Some synagogues also offer adult Confirmation classes which conclude with a ritual or worship experience that affirms the students' continuing study of Judaism.

A variety of ceremonies has also been developed to mark the transition to mid-life. Rabbi Barry D. Cytron observes: "Many circumstances, such as an individual's profession, marital status, and socio-economic background, shape the timing and texture of the midlife years. Moreover, because no specific age inaugurates midlife, and because individuals approach it in so many different ways, this transition is significantly different from the other [life cycle] passages ("Midlife: From Understanding to Wisdom," in Geffen, pp. 132-133).

Psychologists and other commentators on the human condition have identified a variety of issues that one confronts as part of passing through mid-life. These include coming to terms with: the fading of physical or athletic prowess, changing physical features, one's accomplishments as opposed to long held goals and dreams, the moving on and moving out of children, recognizing one's own mortality as peers die or face serious illness.

The challenge of dealing with such profound issues sometimes leads to a so-called mid-life crisis — a confrontation with one's own sense of self and place in the universe. For the first time, one must confront the prospect of growing older in a society whose popular culture venerates youth and deprecates old age.

For some, mid-life is easily navigated because they have a clear perspective about issues of identity and goals. For others, issues can be worked through with the help of books and articles, support groups, personal counselors, members of the clergy, health professionals, or through meditation and introspection techniques.

Some Jews have created rituals to help identify and clarify the most significant issues of this stage of life and that celebrate reaching a state of personal satisfaction and peace. For example, Irene Fine in her book *Midlife: A Rite of Passage*, has created a ritual that affirms the transition "from a young adult to a midlife adult, decision-maker, responsible Jew" (p. 19). It includes keeping a journal, changing one's name, and renegotiating one's personal covenant with God. Another mid-life ceremony, created by Bonnie Feinman, is called *Ma-aseh B're-shit*, The Work of Creation. It includes ritual hand washing, affirmation of the covenant, taking of a new name, and an opportunity for friends and family to share their blessings (Fine, pp. 29-39). These and other mid-life ceremonies draw heavily on Jewish tradition for their texts and rituals, but use them in a creative manner.

Rituals have been created to mark the major physiological changes that women undergo at mid-life with menopause. The purpose of such ceremonies is "to understand and recognize the meaning of menopause for women who have experienced it or will soon enter its phases" (*Miriam's Well*, Penina V. Adelman, p. 75).

Other rituals focus on the recognition, rooted in Jewish texts, that with old age comes wisdom. "One who learns from the young, to whom is that person similar? To a person who eats unripe grapes and drinks wine from its vat. But one who learns from the elderly, to whom is that person similar? To a person who eats ripe grapes and drinks aged wine" (*Pirke Avot* 4:26).

Marcia Spiegel created "Becoming a Crone: Ceremony at 60" to pay recognition to a woman's coming to wisdom (*Lilith,* no. 21, Fall, 1988, pp. 18-19). A particularly striking part of this ceremony is the wearing of a burial shroud to symbolize coming to terms with one's mortality.

Irene Fine concludes in her book that: ". . . midlife is now a recognizable, separate stage in our life cycle. This period between young adulthood and old age requires developmental work including critical self-examination and reevaluation of both internal goals and external objectives . . . Just as change of status at other times in our lives . . . necessitates a celebration with witnesses, so, too, does midlife require a communal rite of passage ceremony to validate, acknowledge, and reaffirm the new status of the individual Jew" (p. 27).

Illness

Everyone faces illness. The possibility of contracting diseases or sustaining injuries at any stage of life is ever present. The elderly being less agile and less resilient are more prone to injury and to certain illnesses. In addition, frailty makes illness in the elderly much more serious than it would be for the young.

Earliest Jewish writings called certain diseases afflictions from God. From a traditional theological perspective, God was ultimately responsible for all illness and disease. As J. David Bleich has explained: "A personal God does not allow His creatures, over whom He exercises providential guardianship, to become ill unless the affliction is divinely ordained as a means of punishment, for purposes of expiation of sin, or for some other beneficial purpose entirely comprehensible to the Deity, if not to man" (*Judaism and Healing: Halakhic Perspectives,* pp. 1-2).

Nevertheless, according to Jewish thought, not only is it appropriate for one who was ill to seek medical attention, it is mandatory. One must recognize that God is the source of healing by directing prayer toward the Divine, but one must also seek the help of a physician.

Furthermore, it is a *mitzvah* as well as an important part of the healing process for Jews to visit the sick (*bikur cholim*). The Talmud teaches, "Whoever visits a sick person helps the person to recover" (*Nedarim* 40a). Visiting the sick was said to take away one sixtieth of a person's illness. Rabbi Akiba even claimed that failing to fulfill this *mitzvah* could be considered as if one sheds blood (*Nedarim* 40a).

With renewed interest in spirituality of late, more attention has been paid to the spiritual aspects of illness and healing. Many synagogues now hold healing services on a regular basis, and a *"Mi Shebayrach"* for the sick has become a regular part of the liturgy.

One who learns from the young, to what may he be compared? To a person who eats unripe grades and drinks wine from the vat. But the one who learns from the old, to what may he be compared? To a person who eats ripe grapes and drinks wine that is aged.

(*Pirke Avot* 4:26)

Rabbi Joshua ben Levi said: "Honor and respect the aged and saintly scholar whose physical powers are broken, equally with the young and strong one. For the broken tablets [of the Ten Commandments], as well as the whole ones, had a place in the Ark of the Covenant."

(*Berachot* 8b)

Until Abraham's time, the young and the old were not distinguished from each other. A person lived a hundred or two hundred years and would not look old. Abraham said: "My son and I enter a town, and nobody knows who is the father and who is the son."

So Abraham said to God, "Sovereign of the Universe, there must be some outward sign of distinction between a father and a son, between an old man and a young one."

And God said, "I will begin with you."

Abraham went to sleep and when he woke up in the morning, he saw that his hair and beard were white. He said, "Sovereign of the Universe, You have made me an example."

(*Tanchuma Chayay Sarah* 1)

Rabbi Ishmael and Rabbi Akiba were once walking in the streets of Jerusalem when they encountered a sick person who said to them: "My teachers, tell me how I may be cured."

They answered, "Do such and such until you are cured."

He asked them, "And who afflicted me?"

They replied, "The Holy One Who is blessed."

He said, "You have entered into a matter which does not pertain to you. God has afflicted and you want to cure! Do you not transgress God's will?"

They asked him, "What is your occupation?"

He replied, "I am a tiller of the soil, and here is the sickle in my hand."

They asked him, "Who created the vineyard?"

He answered, "The Holy One Who is blessed."

They said to him, "And you enter into a matter which does not pertain to you! God created the vineyard and you cut God's fruits from it!"

He said to them, "Do you not see the sickle in my hand? If I did not plow, sow, fertilize, and weed, nothing would sprout."

They said to him, "Foolish man! Have you never in your life heard what is written: 'A person's days are as grass, as a flower of the field, so does one flourish' (Psalms 103:15). Just as if one does not weed, fertilize, and plow, the trees will not provide fruit, and if fruit is provided but is not watered or fertilized, it will not live but will die, so with regard to the body. Drugs and medication are the fertilizer and the physician is the tiller of the soil."

(*Midrash Temurah, Otzar Midrashim*, II, 580-581)

ACTIVITIES

Primary

1. Arrange for students to invite their grandparents or other senior adults to class to share special times and memories from their childhood. Divide into small groups with one or two students and one or two adults per group. Students should also talk about their daily activities and the groups should discuss similarities and differences. Give each participant a sheet of drawing paper and crayons. The elders make a picture about something the children describe, and the children make a picture about something the elders describe. Display the pictures for the congregation or school.

2. Read to students (or have the students read) a variety of books which depict a relationship between a young person and an elderly person. Each student chooses one of the books and creates a poster based on the story. The poster should contain the title of the book and author, a brief summary, what the student learned about the elderly from the book, and a drawing of a scene from the book which reflects the relationship.
   Resources: *Mrs. Katz and Tush* by Patricia Polacco; *Grandma's Soup* by Nancy Karkowsky; *Inside-Out Grandma* by Joan Rothenberg; *Watch the Stars Come Out* by Riki Levinson; *Grandfather's Pencil and the Room of Stories* by Michael Foreman; and *The Crack of Dawn Walkers* by Amy Hest.

3. Devote a class session to the Jewish value of honoring parents. Invite parents to the class to participate in a program entitled "Appreciating and Honoring Our Parents." The program should include a service, songs, treats, and a shared activity led by the children. Students should compose a poem, prayer, or story to be included in the service. Students prepare the treat prior to the parent's arrival. The shared activity can be an arts and crafts project related to Shabbat or an upcoming holiday.

Resource: *100+ Jewish Art Projects for Children* by Nina Streisand Sher and Margaret A. Feldman.

4. With the students, brainstorm a list of ideas about how to be a parent and another list of ideas about how to be a grandparent. Follow up by asking the students about the similarities and differences between the lists. Discuss: Which is harder, being a parent or a grandparent?

5. Teach your students the song *"Ema-Abba"* from *Especially Wonderful Days* by Steve Reuben. To extend this activity to include movement, see "Being Mom and Dad" in *Creative Movement for a Song: Activities for Young Children* by JoAnne Tucker.

6. Read to your class *The Keeping Quilt* by Patricia Polacco. Ask your students if they know about a special item that has been passed down in their family. Help students create a list of questions about such an item to ask parents and grandparents. Invite parents and/or grandparents to bring the item to class and share its story.

7. Arrange for students to bring to class a photograph of the oldest living member of the family and a photograph of the youngest member of the family (who might be the student). Mount the pictures on a poster board, leaving room for students' writing. Each student writes what the oldest can teach or do for the youngest and what the youngest can teach or do for the oldest.

8. Each child draws a portrait of his or her family. Each child in turn describes their family portrait to the class.

9. Discuss with your class the *mitzvah* of *bikur cholim*, visiting the sick. Brainstorm ideas about how the students might participate in this *mitzvah* (such as making get well cards or decorations for a sick person's room for an upcoming Jewish holiday). Choose one of the ideas and do it with your students.

10. Provide a dress up box with adult clothing. Ask each child to bring a doll or small stuffed animal to class. Provide each student with a piece of fabric (approximately 20" x 20") to use as a new blanket for his or her "baby." Students dress up as parents and sit in a circle with their "babies." Ask one question at a time and allow each student in turn to respond. Suggested questions: What does a parent need to do for a baby? How does a parent take care of a baby? Is being a parent a hard or easy job?

Intermediate

1. Have your students write a short essay on "My Ideal Parent." Encourage students to include a Jewish perspective in their descriptions of their ideal parents. Students who wish to do so should read their essays aloud.

2. The first Jewish home for the aged in North America was established in 1855 in St. Louis. Identify the nearest Jewish home for the aged and do one or more of the following activities. Learn about its history. Tour the facility. Do a special project with the residents on a one-time basis or establish an ongoing program. Students can interview the residents. Suggested questions: What was Religious School like when you were young? What is your favorite Jewish holiday and why? Did you have a Bar or Bat Mitzvah? What great inventions have happened during your lifetime?

3. View the movie *Close Harmony*, which depicts the creation of a choir of young children and senior adults. Work with the Cantor or music specialist to create an intergenerational choir with seniors in your congregation or with residents of a home for the aged.

4. Create a Grandparent's Hall of Fame. Students should interview their grandparents or other senior citizens and identify one specific accomplishment or talent to feature. This accomplishment or talent can be a serious achievement or something humorous (such as, makes the largest *matzah* balls). Each student makes a large display which includes photographs or pictures, newspaper clippings (real or made up), a written description or the achievement or talent, and other pertinent information. Set up the posters and have the students act as docents for other classes and adults to tour the exhibit.

5. Write a job description for a parent or grandparent. Begin by discussing what are the major responsibilities of being a parent or a grandparent. Individually or in pairs, students then write a job description.

6. Ask students to bring a photo of their grandparents or great-grandparents as youngsters and as elders. Write a creative story which connects the two pictures. The story may be sent to the grandparents or great-grandparents or shared aloud at a family occasion.

7. Invite seniors to your class for students to interview. Among the questions to ask: When you were growing up, who was your best friend? What was he or she like? What did you do together? Where did you go for fun? Was your best friend Jewish? Did you share holidays and other Jewish events? Where did you go to synagogue? Did you have a Bar/Bat Mitzvah ceremony?

8. Using a large appliance carton, build a "Time Traveling Machine" with the class. Ask students to imagine that they can travel in time by entering the machine. At what point in their family's history would they like to emerge? What family member would they like to meet and at what age? Students should write a short story about traveling in time and meeting their relative. Post the stories on the time machine.

9. Direct the students to interview briefly a grandparent or other elderly relative or friend and ask him or her what Jewish hero or heroine would they like to have met. In class, students research the life of the hero or heroine and create a short presentation. Students dress up as this hero or heroine and invite the person they interviewed to meet this historical figure.

10. Students write and illustrate a story describing how their family came to be. Students should interview grandparents and other relatives, as well as their immediately family unit. Distribute to each student a long sheet of light-colored construction paper on which they write the narrative and include photographs or pictures. Students use this illustrated story to introduce their classmates to their family.

11. Do the skit called "Hall of Jewish Adulthood" by Stan J. Beiner (see Appendix 1, p. 127.)

Secondary

1. With the class, prepare an Elders' Guide to your community. List all agencies and organizations with addresses and phone numbers which provide services to the elderly. Collect pamphlets and other material related to these services. This information can be made available at a kiosk in your synagogue or school or individual packets can be distributed to seniors.

2. Ask students if they can identify any significant achievements that an elderly person has accomplished. Challenge students to research important achievements that senior citizens have made. Among the famous people to suggest: George Burns, Golda Meir, Albert Schweitzer, Artur Rubinstein, Henrietta Szold.

3. As a class, start a *mitzvah* service for senior members of your congregation or community. Advertise in the synagogue or school newsletter and ask the Rabbi or Director of Education to help identify potential clients. Offer such services as: raking leaves, mowing lawns, trimming bushes, cleaning out garages or closets, painting, etc. Take pictures of the students at work and display.

4. Invite a theater make-up artist to show students how to make themselves up as elderly people. After applying the make-up, the students should try one or more of the following activities: place a single layer of facial tissue over the eyes and walk 20 feet (simulating loss of vision); using a walker or cane, students walk 20 feet without lifting their feet more than one inch off the floor and without placing the heel of one foot ahead of the toes of the other foot; students put on gloves or mittens and attempt to thread a needle. Conclude the activity by discussing how it felt to "be" an older person and to try to do these activities.

5. Create a scenario which could have happened in any generation between a teenager and a parent. For example, in the seventeenth century, Gluckel of Hameln complained that no matter how much a parent does or spends, the child does not appreciate it. The scenario may be serious or funny. Students should ask grandparents and parents how their parents handled this situation. With this information, students create a four-paneled comic strip for each intergenerational conflict.

6. In many B'nai Mitzvah ceremonies today, the Torah is passed from generation to generation to symbolize the passing down of Jewish tradition. Have students reflect on this ceremony, if they participated in it. Ask students to write a paragraph about the meaning of this ritual, first as if they are the grandparent, then as if they are the parent, and finally as the student receiving the Torah. (If students did not participate in the ceremony, have them write about whether or not they would have liked to do so and why.) Create a bulletin board entitled "From Generation to Generation" with a depiction of a Torah scroll and students' writings around it.

7. Provide a thumbnail sketch of a person who would have been born in the first quarter of the twentieth century. The person may be historical or fictional. As a class, expand on the description, adding details such as name, place, and date of birth, parent's background, education, profession, family life, synagogue, and Jewish community involvement, etc. Students should describe how world events, such as World Wars I and II, the Depression, the creation of Israel, impacted this person's life. Divide the class into groups and assign each group to write a scene

based on one time period of the person's life. Groups come together and present their scenes as a readers theater or dramatic presentation.

8. Do a webbing activity to help students discuss their attitudes about the elderly. On a large sheet of paper or blackboard, write the word Elderly. Students draw lines from that word and write other words that they think of as related to the word Elderly. Students may also draw lines from other words to make another level of words. When the students have finished adding to the web, take a few minutes to examine the words that they have added. Discuss: What positive attributes did the students write? What negative attributes did the students write? Are any of the attributes contradictory? Do these attributes apply to all elderly or just to some?

9. Ask the students what they have learned from a family member and what they want to pass on to the next generation. Create a document with calligraphy and gold seals. On this document each student describes what he or she has received (recipe, story, teaching, memory) and what he or she intends to pass on.

10. Show the film *Avalon*, which recounts the immigration and settling in America of the patriarch of a multi-generational family. Discuss: Is the family Jewish? How can you tell? How would they make the family's Jewishness clearer? Do students know their own family's immigration experience? Students who are aware of their family's experience should share with the class. Encourage other students to ask their parents how their families came to North America.

11. To give students an opportunity to experience the challenges and responsibilities of parenthood, do the following activity. Students, individually or in pairs, take on the role(s) of parenthood. The parents must find a job, housing, a car, health and car insurance, information on synagogue membership, and create a budget for their family, including saving for their child's college education and their retirement. Students create a portfolio with the information collected. After completing this activity discuss: Is parenting harder than it looks? Were the students aware of all the things that one needs to do as a parent? Do they have a different perspective about their own parents after doing this activity? Resources: Newspapers, guest speakers, synagogue administrator or Membership Chairperson.

12. View the film *Lies My Father Told Me* (rated R), the story of a special relationship between a boy and his grandfather in early twentieth century Canada. Ask the students to become film critics and write a review of the film. Students share their reviews. Follow this up with a discussion, beginning with basic recall questions. Discuss each main character (the boy, his father, his mother, and the grandfather). What was their relationship to each other? What was their relationship to Judaism? What were the lies the boy's father told? How could the father have handled better telling the boy about the grandfather's death? Conclude by asking the students, as film critics, who they would recommend should see the film.

13. Do a Readers Theater of the play *Number Our Days* from *Jewish Story Theater* by Eleanor Albert. Follow up this activity by inviting seniors to the class for students to interview as a living history class. Brainstorm questions to be asked. Consider videotaping the interviews to form a library of tapes.

14. Complete the minicourse *Aging and Judaism* by Kerry M. Olitzky and Lee H. Olitzky.

15. Complete the minicourse *The Jewish Family: Past, Present and Future* by Paulette Benson and Joanne Altschuler.

Hebrew

1. Learn the Hebrew words for the different phases of life:

   תִּינוֹק/תִּינוֹקֶת   *tinok/tinoket*/baby;

   יֶלֶד/יַלְדָּה   *yeled/yaldah*/child;

צָעִיר/צְעִירָה   za'ir/tz'irah/teenager;
מְבוּגָּר/מְבוּגֶּרֶת   m'vugar/m'vugeret/adult;
זָקֵן/זְקֵנָה   zakayn/z'kayna/elder.

Cut out appropriate pictures from magazines to create a picture dictionary of these words.

2. Learn the following Hebrew or Yiddish words for parents and grandparents.

אַבָּא   abba/father,
אִמָּא   ima/mother;
סַבָּא   saba/grandfather;
סַבְתָּא   savta/grandmother;
זיידע   zayde/grandfather (Yiddish);
בָּאבּע   bubbe/grandmother (Yiddish);

To reinforce these words, sing "*David Melech Yisrael.*" During the second part of the song, students respond with the opposite word that the leader sings. To extend this activity, perform "The Family: A Musical Puppet Play" in *Creative Puppetry for Jewish Kids* by Gale Solotar Warshawsky, pp. 72-77.

3. Teach the students the "*Mi Shebayrach,*" which is said for one who is ill or who has surgery. Listen to the song version of this prayer by Debbie Friedman.
Resource: *Renewal of Spirit.*

4. Introduce your class to the saying "עַד מֵאָה וְעֶשְׂרִים/*Ad May'ah v'Esrim*" — (Until a hundred and twenty.) This is the traditional Jewish birthday wish. Explain that because Moses lived to 120 years of age according to the Torah, it is considered the ideal life span. Make a cake and write this expression in Hebrew and English on the cake. Invite senior adults to share the cake.

Adult

1. Begin a parent support group focusing on surviving and thriving as Jewish parents. At the first session, each parent should share a funny incident about his or her child or children. Discuss how humor is a necessary ingredient in child rearing. A trained professional should facilitate the discussion. Brainstorm ideas for future sessions.

2. Teach parents how to be Jewishly aware sex educators for their children. Invite a representative from Planned Parenthood or another organization which focuses on sex education to lead a workshop to help parents become comfortable talking about sex with their children. Also invite a Rabbi to present Jewish values pertaining to sex and how to include them in a discussion with children.

3. Invite parents to a program entitled "Hopes and Dreams for My Child." Each parent receives paper and pencil and records the hopes and dreams they have for their child. The group shares these hopes and dreams and then each parent writes a formal letter to his or her child sharing their hopes and dreams. Parents should share the letter with their child at an appropriate time, and each year, at Rosh HaShanah, update the letter and share it again with the child. Alternatively, parents may write and save these letters and present them to the child at an appropriate time, such as graduation from high school or college.

4. Share the Overview and Sources from the Tradition from this chapter with the class and discuss Judaism's attitude toward aging and the elderly. Ask the adults to share experiences from their own lives which pertain to this theme. Consider creating a committee in your synagogue to focus on the needs of the elderly.

5. Hold a panel discussion with a gerontologist, a physician who specializes in gerontology, a nutritionist, and a health educator to speak about how our body naturally ages and how we can take care of ourselves to improve lifelong health.

6. Parents often become caught in the sandwich generation as they raise their children and care for their elderly parents. Create a group for

adults faced with this challenge. Find an appropriate facilitator who will lead discussions, as well as present information about some of the issues that adults face as their parents age. Resource: *Learning to Sit in Silence: A Journal of Caretaking* by Elaine M. Starkman.

7. Set up a book cart with resources on parenting. Suggested titles: *To Raise a Jewish Child: A Guide for Parents* by Hayim Donin; *When Your Jewish Child Asks Why: Answers for Tough Questions* by Kerry M. Olitzky, Steven M. Rosman, and David P. Kasakove; *Jewish Family Celebrations: The Sabbath, Festivals, and Ceremonies* by Arlene Rossen Cardozo; *Jewish Literacy: The Most Important Things to Know about the Jewish Religion, Its People and Its History* by Joseph Telushkin; *Living a Jewish Life: A Guide for Starting, Learning, Celebrating, and Parenting* by Anita Diamant and Howard Cooper; *The Hadassah Magazine Jewish Parenting Book* edited by Roselyn Bell; *Golden Rules: The Ten Ethical Values Parents Need to Teach Their Children* by Wayne Dosick.

8. Hold a film festival on the theme of Aging and the Elderly in the Jewish Community. Suggested films: *Bloomers; Brighton Beach; Complaints of a Dutiful Daughter; The Last and Only Survivor of Flora; The Miracle of Intervale Avenue; Number Our Days; A Private Life; Tell Me a Riddle;* and *Young at Hearts.* For other appropriate films, see *Independent Jewish Film: A Resource Guide* edited by Janis Plotkin, Caroline Libresco, and Josh Feiger.

9. View the documentary *Simchat Chochmah* (Joy of Wisdom), a modern ceremony which celebrates the sixtieth birthday of a Jewish woman. Share reactions to the film. How do the participants feel about new ceremonies evolving? Does it take away from the tradition or strengthen it? Would any of them want to be part of a similar ceremony? Why or why not? Consider beginning an ongoing group for seniors to discuss issues pertaining to aging.

10. Hold a healing service for members of your congregation or community. Create your own ceremony or contact The National Center for Jewish Healing, 9 East 69th Street, New York, NY 10021.

11. For an observance of Rosh Chodesh, hold a study session about contemporary ceremonies relating to menopause and the celebration of aging. Resources: *A Ceremonies Sampler: New Rites, Celebrations, and Observances of Jewish Women* edited by Elizabeth Resnick Levine; *Midlife: A Rite of Passage and The Wise Woman, A Celebration* by Irene Fine; *Celebrating the New Moon: A Rosh Chodesh Anthology* by Susan Berrin.

12. To help adults deal with their aging parents, do the guided fantasy "Fiftieth Wedding Anniversary" from *Jewish Guided Imagery: A How-To Book for Rabbis, Educators and Group Leaders* by Dov Peretz Elkins, pp. 132-133. Ask participants to share from their own experiences the joys and challenges of dealing with their elderly parents. Invite a representative from Jewish Family Service or another agency to offer suggestions and identify resources in the community which serve the elderly.

Family

1. For students in grades four and above and their families, view the film *Gefilte Fish*, which shows three generations of Jewish women and how they prepare gefilte fish. Following the movie, hold a brief discussion about how traditions change from one generation to the next. Prior to the program ask each family to bring traditional Jewish recipes from each generation. The families create a multi-generational Jewish cookbook which includes stories and descriptions of the recipes, where the recipes originated (if known), when the food is served, and why the recipes are special to the family.

2. Have each family create a time line of important family events. Families then make a memory book which contains the time line, photographs, letters, invitations, announcements of births,

deaths, engagements, and marriages, narrative descriptions of celebrations, special occasions, travel, homes, and pets. The family may want to highlight the funniest or most unusual family member or event.

3. Invite a party planner or organizer to share information on how to plan a family reunion. Provide families with paper and pencils for them to begin the process of planning their own family reunion. Encourage families to follow through and hold a reunion. Keep track as reunions are held. Share this information through a newsletter to all participants and/or hold a follow-up gathering during which families report about their reunions. Conclude by having each family member record what the reunion meant to him or her.

4. Invite families to bring family photo albums which include pictures from several generations of the family. Each family gathers as a group to quietly sit and look at the pictures, while the parents (and grandparents, if any) talk about the history of the family. Families then gather, and one person from each family shares what he/ she learned about his or her family.

5. Help families start new Jewish family traditions. Present a variety of ideas for families to choose from, such as baking *challah* for Shabbat, making a *tzedakah* box and creating a plan for giving *tzedakah*, building a *sukkah*, growing vegetables for Passover, planning a trip to Israel. Each group should have a facilitator who will help the families create and implement the new Jewish family tradition they have chosen. Facilitators should have all the basic information necessary for families to learn about the particular tradition. Facilitators should follow up with each family and offer additional support and guidance as necessary.

All-School

1. With the students, publish a newspaper on the theme of parenting and grandparenting, honoring the elderly, or illness and healing. Present an overview of the theme to the students at an assembly, then assign each class to produce one or more articles, pictures, cartoons, editorials, advice columns (e.g., Kids' Tips for Raising Kids), or advertisements for the newspaper.

2. Hold a Grandparents Shabbat service and dinner. Each student should invite his or her grandparents; those without grandparents living nearby can adopt grandparents to invite. Each class in the school leads a prayer or song from the service. Invite a child, a parent, and a grandparent, not necessarily from the same family, to speak about what they have learned from the other generations.

3. Make *Mishloach Manot* packages for Purim or plates of apples and honey for Rosh HaShanah and deliver them to elderly members of the congregation or community. For Purim each plate should have *hamentaschen* (baked by the students), nuts, dried fruit, and a Purim card made by the students. For Rosh HaShanah each plate should have apples, honey, other fruit, and a new year's card made by the students. Recruit parents to drive groups of students to deliver the treats.

4. Divide students into groups, with mixed grade levels in each group. Assign each group one of the quotations from the Overview and Sources from the Tradition sections, or another source pertaining to the elderly. Each group should read and briefly discuss the quotation and then prepare a short skit which reflects its message. Each group in turn presents its skit and the quotation to the other students.

GLOSSARY

Abba – Father

Ayshet Chazon – Woman of Vision, a contemporary ceremony for older women.

Bikur Cholim – *Mitzvah* of visiting the sick.

Bubbe – Grandmother (Yiddish)

Ima – Mother

Mi Shebayrach – A prayer often recited on behalf of those who are ill.

Saba – Grandfather

Savta – Grandmother

Zayde – Grandfather (Yiddish)

RESOURCES

Periodicals for Jewish Parents and Families

Being Jewish: The Hands-on Supplement for Jewish Family Education. (Published three times a year by Isaac Nathan Publishing Co., 22711 Cass Avenue, Woodland Hills, CA 91364.)

Jewish Family & Life. (Bi-monthly newsletter and on-line service published by Rejuvenation, Inc., 3111 Rittenhouse St., N.W., Washington, DC 20015; www.jewishfamily.com.)

The Jewish Parent Connection. (Published September and monthly November to May by Torah Umesorah,160 Broadway, New York, NY 10038.)

For the Teacher

Abrams, Judith Z., and Steven A. Abrams. *Jewish Parenting: Rabbinic Insights.* Northvale, NJ: Jason Aronson Inc., 1994.

Adelman, Penina V. *Miriam's Well: Rituals for Jewish Women around the Year.* 2d ed. New York: Biblio Press, 1990.

Bell, Roselyn, ed. *The Hadassah Magazine Jewish Parenting Book.* New York: The Free Press, 1989.

Berrin, Susan. *Celebrating the New Moon: A Rosh Chodesh Anthology.* Northvale, NJ: Jason Aronson Inc., 1996.

Cardozo, Arlene Rossen. *Jewish Family Celebrations: The Sabbath, Festivals, and Ceremonies.* New York: St. Martin's Press, 1985.

Danan, Julie Hilton. *The Jewish Parents' Almanac.* Northvale, NJ: Jason Aronson Inc., 1996.

Diamant, Anita, and Howard Cooper. *Living a Jewish Life: A Guide for Starting, Learning, Celebrating, and Parenting.* New York: HarperCollins Publishers, 1991.

Donin, Hayim. *To Raise a Jewish Child: A Guide for Parents.* New York: Basic Books, Inc., 1977.

Dosick, Wayne. *Golden Rules: The Ten Ethical Values Parents Need to Teach Their Children.* San Francisco: HarperCollins Publishers, 1995.

Elkins, Dov Peretz. *Jewish Guided Imagery. A How-To Book for Rabbis, Educators and Group Leaders.* Princeton, NJ: Growth Associates, 1996.

Fine, Irene. *Midlife: A Rite of Passage and The Wise Woman, A Celebration.* San Diego, CA: Woman's Institute for Continuing Jewish Education, 1988.

Geffen, Rela, ed. *Celebration and Renewal: Rites of Passage in Judaism.* Philadelphia: Jewish Publication Society, 1993.

Levine, Elizabeth Resnick, ed. *A Ceremonies Sampler: New Rites, Celebrations, and Observances of Jewish Women.* San Diego, CA: Woman's Institute for Continuing Jewish Education, 1991.

Lilith. No. 21, Fall, 1988.

Lilith. Vol. 16, No. 4, Fall, 1991.

Lilith. Vol. 20, No. 3, Fall, 1995.

Mason, Ruth. "Adult Bat Mitzvah: A Revolution for Women and Synagogues." in *Lilith*, Vol. 14, No. 4, Fall 1989.

Olitzky, Kerry M.; Steven M. Rosman; and David P. Kasakove. *When Your Jewish Child Asks Why: Answers for Tough Questions.* Hoboken, NJ: KTAV Publishing House, Inc., 1993.

Plotkin, Janis; Caroline Libresco; and Josh Feiger, eds. *Independent Jewish Film: A Resource Guide.* 3d ed. San Francisco: The San Francisco Jewish Film Festival, 1996.

Schachter-Shalomi, Zalman and Ronald S. Miller. *From Age-ing to Sag-ing: A Profound New Vision of Growing Older.* New York: Warner Books, 1995.

Sher, Nina Streisand, and Margaret A. Feldman. *100+ Jewish Art Projects for Children*. Denver: A.R.E. Publishing, Inc., 1996.

Starkman, Elaine M. *Learning to Sit in Silence: A Journal of Caretaking*. Watsonville, CA: Papier-Mache Press, 1993.

Telushkin, Joseph. *Jewish Literacy: The Most Important Things to Know About the Jewish Religion, Its People, and Its History*. New York: William Morrow & Company, Inc., 1991.

Tucker, JoAnne. *Creative Movement for a Song: Activities for Young Children*. Denver: A.R.E. Publishing, Inc., 1993.

Warshawsky, Gale Solotar. *Creative Puppetry for Jewish Kids*. Denver: A.R.E. Publishing, Inc., 1985.

For the Students

Albert, Eleanor. *Jewish Story Theater*. Los Angeles: Torah Aura Productions, 1989.

Benson, Paulette, and Joanne Altschuler. *The Jewish Family: Past, Present and Future.* Denver: A.R.E. Publishing, Inc., 1979.

Foreman, Michael. *Grandfather's Pencil and the Room of Stories*. New York: Harcourt, Brace & Company, 1994.

Hest, Amy. *The Crack-of-Dawn Walkers*. New York: Macmillan Publishing Company, 1984.

Karkowsky, Nancy. *Grandma's Soup*. Rockville, MD: Kar-Ben Copies, Inc., 1989.

Levinson, Riki. *Watch the Stars Come Out*. New York: E. P. Dutton, 1985.

Olitzky, Kerry M., and Lee H. Olitzky. *Aging and Judaism*. Denver: A.R.E. Publishing, Inc., 1980.

Polacco, Patricia. *Mrs. Katz and Tush*. New York: Bantam Books, 1992.

———. *The Keeping Quilt*. New York: Simon & Schuster, Inc., 1988.

Rothenberg, Joan. *Inside-Out Grandma: A Hanukkah Story*. New York: Hyperion Books for Children, 1995.

Audiovisual

Bloomers. Brooks-Antonio. 16mm film.

Brighton Beach. Arthur Cantor, Inc. Videocassette.

Close Harmony. Cornell University Audio-Visual Resource Center. Videocassette.

Complaints of a Dutiful Daughter. Women Make Movies. 16mm film.

Friedman, Debbie. *Renewal of Spirit*. A.R.E. Publishing, Inc. Audiocassette.

The Last & Only Survivor of Flora. Lee Hirsch. 16mm film.

Lies My Father Told Me. Modern Sound Pictures Inc. Videocassette.

The Miracle of Intervale Avenue. Ergo Media Inc. Videocassette.

Number Our Days. Direct Cinema Ltd. Videocassette.

A Private Life. Museum of Modern Art Circulating Film Library. Videocassette.

Reuben, Steve. *Especially Wonderful Days*. A.R.E. Publishing, Inc. Audiocassette.

Simchat Chochmah. Sounds Write Productions, Inc. Videocassette.

Tell Me a Riddle. The Saul Zaentz Center. Videocassette.

Young at Hearts. Outsider Enterprises. Videocassette.

CHAPTER SIX
END OF LIFE
DEATH · BURIAL · MOURNING

OVERVIEW

FROM A JEWISH PERSPECTIVE, DEATH AND DYING are seen as being a part of life and living. Dr. Ron Wolfson has written, "The Jewish approach is reality-based. There is a time to be born — and a time to die. From dust we are fashioned — to dust we return. No denial. No avoidance. The art of Jewish dying is a fundamental factor in the art of Jewish living" (*A Time to Mourn, A Time to Comfort*, p. 29).

In the Jewish tradition, a person who is dying is to be treated with love, respect, and caring. Following death, the body is to be treated with respect and allowed to decompose naturally in the earth. Another important principle which underlies many of the traditional burial customs is that all human beings are equal in death.

Mourning is recognized as a vital process intended to give appropriate respect to the deceased and to allow close family members and friends to express their grief and sympathy. The various periods of mourning in the Jewish tradition are designed to help a person work through grief by appropriately remembering the deceased and, as time goes on, to return to one's regular routine.

While celebrating the blessing of life, Jews are called upon to recognize the finality of death and to affirm God. It is considered inappropriate to treat death casually or to dwell on it too long.

A variety of practices and traditions accompany the process of death and mourning. Even Jews who are minimally observant in the main, find comfort and hope in many of these mourning customs.

Treatment of the Dying

Bikur cholim, visiting the sick, is a *mitzvah*. Just as we are enjoined to visit a person who is recovering from an illness or surgery, so, too, are we commanded to visit one who is dying. The principle that life is of infinite and inestimable value extends to the very last moments of life as well.

Therefore, it is prohibited to do anything that will shorten life. As Rabbi J. David Bleich has written, "The practice of euthanasia — whether active or passive — is contrary to the teachings of Judaism. Any positive act designed to hasten the death of the patient is equated with murder in Jewish law, even if death is hastened by only a matter of moments. No matter how laudable the intentions of the person performing an act of mercy-killing may be, his deed constitutes an act of homicide" (*Judaism and Healing*, p. 136).

In his code of Jewish law written in the twelfth century, Maimonides wrote, "One who is in a dying condition is regarded as a living person in every respect. One may not bind his jaws, stop up the organs of the lower extremities, or place metallic or cooling vessels upon his navel in order to prevent swelling . . . . One who touches him is guilty of shedding blood" (*Mishneh Torah, Hilchot Avel* 4:5).

Furthermore, any act that is normally done after the person has died, such as closing his eyes or removing the pillow from under his head, may not be done while he is still alive.

On the other hand, concerning a *gosays* (dying person), some sources distinguish between acts which hasten death and those which merely hinder the soul's departure. For example, if someone is chopping wood nearby, one may ask the person to stop, or if there is salt on the patient's tongue, one may remove it, because these are considered impediments to the departure of the soul.

And yet, pain medication may be given to someone who is dying even if it might hasten death, so long as the primary purpose of the medication is to relieve pain. Though carefully circumscribed, certain actions may be taken which could hasten an individual's death. Reform, Conservative, and Reconstructionist teachings tend to be more liberal in interpreting the parameters of such actions.

In recent years, much attention has been given to advance medical directives, by which an individual formally indicates his or her preference concerning end of life issues. There are two basic types of advance directives. The first type — a living will — contains instructions regarding whether or not artificial methods should be used if one has a terminal condition and/or is in an irreversible coma. The second type — usually called a Durable Power of Attorney for Health Care — appoints a friend or family member to make medical decisions for a person who is unable to make decisions. Laws vary from state to state (and country to country) as to the legality of these documents.

Such documents are generally opposed by Orthodox Rabbis, who maintain that competent Rabbinic authorities must be consulted to decide any specific case. The other movements generally support the use of such documents.

When a person is near death, it is traditional to recite *Vidui*, a confessional asking God's forgiveness for all sins of omission or commission. Following this, the last words to be spoken are the *Sh'ma*. A person who is dying should not be left alone. Those present remain until the person has died, and then someone must remain with the body until burial. Usually, a member of the *Chevra Kaddisha* (see immediately below) or others of the community serve as *shomer* (guardian), reciting Psalms while sitting with the body.

Chevra Kaddisha

A *Chevra Kaddisha* or burial society is charged with responsibility for preparing the body for burial in accordance with Jewish customs. It is considered a great honor to be a member of a *Chevra Kaddisha* and to participate in the preparation of the body. Most communities with a significant Jewish population have a *Chevra Kaddisha*. Many Jews today, however, use a Jewish funeral home or a funeral home which is aware of Jewish burial customs.

From Death To Burial

Since ancient times, it has been the custom that burial take place as soon after the death as possible. With regard to a man put to death due to a capital offense, the Torah teaches, "You must not allow his body to remain on the stake overnight, but must bury him the same day. For an impaled body is an affront to God. You shall not defile the land that *Adonai,* your God, is giving you for a possession" (Deuteronomy 21:23).

Traditionally, therefore, burial takes place within 24 hours of death. However, if relatives must travel from a distance to attend the funeral it is permissible to delay it. Furthermore, funerals are not held on Shabbat or on the first or last days of major holidays. Nevertheless, in most communities, burial takes place as soon after death as practical.

Concern for proper treatment of the body includes opposition to the practices of autopsy, cremation, and embalming. While autopsy is discouraged, there are situations when it is mandated or acceptable. These include: when the civil authority requires it (as in the case of homicide or suicide), when death is due to a heredity disease and an autopsy may directly benefit the survivors, when an autopsy may yield medical information that would directly benefit another person.

Embalming is an ancient procedure used to preserve the body after death. The Torah records that Joseph was embalmed after he died (Genesis 50:26). Because embalming inhibits the natural decaying of the body, it is not normally permitted. However, if there is a delay in the funeral service or if the body has to be shipped to another city, embalming may become necessary.

Cremation is also prohibited because it interferes with the natural decay of the body. Cremated ashes may not be buried in a Jewish cemetery according to Orthodox practice. While Reform, Reconstructionist, and Conservative Judaism discourage cremation in favor of the traditional practice of burial of the body, most Rabbis will officiate at a memorial service for someone who has been cremated and the ashes are usually permitted to be buried in the cemetery.

Taharah

One of the most important steps in preparing the body for burial is *taharah*, ritual cleansing. This practice is based on the teaching "As one came [into the world], so shall one leave" (Ecclesiastes 5:5). In other words, just as a baby is washed immediately following birth, so, too, must the body be washed prior to burial. However, this washing is not a cleansing, but a ritual purification in which warm water is poured over the entire body and then dried off.

Tachrichim

After *taharah*, the body is traditionally dressed in *tachrichim*, shrouds. Usually made of either muslin or linen, the shrouds are a simple, white garment without pockets, symbolizing the fact that one takes nothing from this world to the next. *Tachrichim* also reinforce the idea that all are equal in death. Regardless of what we have achieved during our lifetime, death makes no distinctions between rich and poor, educated and illiterate, pious or cynic. It is also traditional for a man to be buried in his *tallit* with the *tzitzit* cut off to indicate that this man will no longer be performing *mitzvot* and that the *tallit* is no longer to be used for worship.

Aron/Casket

The traditional Jewish casket is often referred to as a "plain pine box," though it need not be pine or plain. The teaching that all are equal in death is reflected in the tradition that the *aron* (casket) be simple, not ostentatious. It must be made completely of wood, so that it will decompose. No metal may be used, not even nails. Therefore, the casket is usually held together with dowels and glue. In Israel caskets are not used altogether. Rather, the body is wrapped totally in linen (mummy style) and buried directly in the ground.

In some instances, a small bag of earth from the land of Israel is placed in the coffin. This custom comes from Jewish folklore of the Middle Ages. It was thought that in the end of days when the messiah comes, he will resurrect the dead on the Mount of Olives in Jerusalem. Those who are buried outside of Israel will roll (*gilgul*) underground to that spot when the time comes. So as to enable the body to know when it has arrived at the proper place, the bag of earth will serve as a guide. Others maintain that the bag of Jerusalem earth teaches that even in death we are still connected to *Eretz Yisrael* (the Land of Israel). Another tradition is to have *Shaymot* (sacred books containing the divine Name) that can no longer be used placed in the casket.

Aninut

The period from the moment one learns about the death of a loved one until burial is called *aninut*. One is not yet a mourner, but most of the traditions related to mourning are observed during this period of time. In addition, one is exempt from most *mitzvot* so as to be free to arrange for the funeral and burial. As Rabbi Maurice Lamm has observed: "The *onen* is a person in deep distress, a person yanked out of normal life and abruptly catapulted into the midst of inexpressible grief. He is disoriented, his attitudes are disarrayed, his emotions [are] out of gear. The shock of death paralyzes his consciousness and blocks out all regular patterns of orderly thinking" (*The Jewish Way in Death and Mourning*, p. 21).

Indeed, we are discouraged from trying to comfort the mourner prior to the burial. *Pirke Avot* teaches, "Do not console a person whose deceased relative lies before him" (4:23). Therefore, the common Western customs of viewing the body and visitation are contrary to traditional Jewish practice.

Who Is a Mourner?

According to Jewish tradition, one is obligated to observe mourning rituals for the following relatives: father, mother, sister, brother, son, daughter, and spouse. One may choose to observe some or all of the rituals for other relatives, such as grandparents, aunts, uncles, cousins, etc.

Traditionally, one does not observe mourning customs for an infant under 30 days old. "An infant who does not live for thirty days is called a *nefel*, and is not considered viable in terms of Jewish tradition. The laws of *aninut* and mourning do not apply to the family at all" (Lamm, p. 247). However, *taharah*, ritual purification, is performed and the body is buried, but without the usual service and prayers. These practices were developed at a time when infant mortality was very high in order not to place a burden upon the parents.

In modern times, many Jews feeling a need to mourn for a stillbirth or for a child who dies before reaching one month, as they might for any other death, choose to observe the traditional mourning customs.

Jewish law forbids one to observe the mourning customs for an apostate who renounces Judaism and adopts another religion and for one who commits suicide. In traditional cemeteries the bodies of such individuals are usually buried in a special section, often near the border. However, most Rabbis are lenient in the interpretation of Jewish law relating to suicide, considering one who commits such an act as mentally disturbed or insane. The act is therefore not technically a suicide, the body need not be buried in a special area, and family members may observe mourning rituals.

Funeral, Burial, and Mourning
K'riah

In biblical times, upon learning of the death of a loved, one would tear one's clothing. Jacob rent his garments when he saw his son Joseph's coat torn and covered with blood. King David tore his clothes upon learning of the death of King Saul. This emotional expression of grief served to channel natural feelings of anger, and may also have served to sublimate, or even replace, the pagan practice of tearing at one's flesh upon learning of a relative's death.

This act of tearing a garment is called *k'riah*. The garment torn is usually outer wear — a vest, suit jacket, or tie for a man; a dress, blouse, or scarf for a woman. The garment is torn immediately upon hearing of the death or just prior to the funeral service or the burial. It is common practice among non-Orthodox Jews to cut and tear a black ribbon, which is pinned to a garment of the mourner as a substitute for destroying the garment itself.

Traditionally, the *k'riah* is made on the left side, over the heart, if one is mourning a blood relative, and on the right side for relatives by marriage. If one is mourning a parent, the torn garment or ribbon should be worn during the entire *shivah* period, whereas for other relatives it is not necessary to do so.

When performing *k'riah*, mourners recite the following blessing:

בָּרוּךְ אַתָּה יְיָ אֱלֹהֵינוּ מֶלֶךְ הָעוֹלָם, דַּיָּן הָאֱמֶת.

Baruch Atah Adonai Elohaynu Melech HaOlam, Dayan HaEmet.

Blessed are You, *Adonai* our God, Sovereign of the Universe, who is the Judge of truth.

Funeral Service

The purpose of the funeral service is to honor the memory of the deceased and to comfort the mourners. For much of Jewish history, the funeral was held either at the home of the deceased or at the cemetery. It is now common to hold the service in a funeral chapel and then to proceed to graveside for burial. It is permissible, but less common, for a funeral to be held in a synagogue.

While Jewish tradition discourages the presence of flowers at funerals, the Talmud notes that they were used at one time to cover up the smell of the decaying body. Normally, those who wish to honor the memory of the deceased make a contribution to a synagogue or a charity chosen by the mourning family instead of sending flowers.

The use of music at a funeral, other than the chanting of the funeral liturgy, is also discouraged.

The funeral normally begins with one or more Psalms, often including Psalm 23 ("*Adonai* is my shepherd . . .") and Psalm 121 ("I will lift my eyes to the mountains . . ."). "A Woman of Valor" from Proverbs 31 is sometimes recited for a female.

A significant part of the funeral service is the *hesped* or eulogy. Dr. Ron Wolfson has stated, "One of the most wonderful ways to honor a departed friend or family member, and one of the greatest gifts you can give to a bereaved relative, is to write and offer a personal eulogy at the funeral or at a *shivah minyan*" (Wolfson, p. 139).

While the primary purpose of the eulogy is to praise the deceased, it should be truthful and not exaggerate his or her qualities or accomplishments. The eulogy is normally offered by the Rabbi, but family members or close friends may also elect to speak.

"Ayl Malay Rachamim," the traditional memorial prayer, is read or chanted. It asks God to "Grant perfect rest under the wings of Your presence" to the deceased. This prayer usually ends the service at the funeral home.

The body is then transported to the cemetery. Relatives and close friends are honored by being pallbearers. They carry the coffin to the grave site, traditionally pausing several times (three or seven are the most common numbers) to indicate a reluctance at taking leave of the deceased.

It is traditional for bodies to be buried in the ground, and not in mausoleums where the body remains above ground, although in ancient times, burial was sometimes in caves.

Verses from Psalm 91 are read as the coffin progresses toward the grave or after it arrives. The casket is then lowered to the bottom of the grave as the Rabbi says:

עַל מְקוֹמוֹ יָבֹא בְשָׁלוֹם./עַל מְקוֹמָהּ תָּבֹא בְשָׁלוֹם.

Al M'komo Yavo v'Shalom/Al M'komah Tavo v'Shalom.

May he/she go to his/her resting place in peace.

Mourners and others then participate in filling the grave with dirt so as actually to participate in the *mitzvah* of burying the dead. Usually this practice is symbolic, with each person adding just a shovelful or handful of dirt to the grave, but in some communities the grave is filled to cover the casket or to the top. If a shovel is used, it is customary for each person to place the shovel in the pile of dirt, rather than hand it to the next person in order that death not be contagious.

In some communities, the *Tzidduk HaDin* prayer which proclaims acceptance of death is also recited. Then the mourners rise and recite either the Mourner's *Kaddish* or the Burial *Kaddish*, which includes in the first paragraph a reference to God "reviving the dead and raising them to eternal life."

After the last words of *Kaddish* are recited, two rows are formed by those in attendance and the mourners walk between the rows as the people say to them:

הַמָּקוֹם יְנַחֵם אֶתְכֶם בְּתוֹךְ שְׁאָר אֲבֵלֵי צִיּוֹן וִירוּשָׁלָיִם.

HaMakom Yinachaym Etchem B'toch Sh'ar Avaylay Tzion Virushalayim.

May God comfort you among all the mourners of Zion and Jerusalem.

Shivah

The next stage of the mourning process is called *shivah*, from the Hebrew word for seven. The seven day mourning period was already established in biblical times (see Genesis 50:10, Job 2:13). *Shivah* begins immediately following burial (the day of the funeral being the first day) and lasts seven days, concluding after the morning service on the seventh day. *Shivah* is suspended for Shabbat, and then resumes again after Shabbat. If *shivah* begins before a major holiday (Rosh HaShanah, Yom Kippur, Passover, Shavuot, Sukkot), the remainder of the *shivah* period is cancelled by the holiday. Family members of the deceased "sit *shivah*," usually in the home of the deceased. But, if necessary, *shivah* may be observed in the house of a close relative.

A pitcher of water, a collecting bowl, and paper toweling are usually placed outside the door of the *shivah* house on the first day only, so that those returning from the funeral can ritually wash their hands. This practice reflects an ancient belief that contact with the dead makes a person ritually impure. Being in the proximity of the deceased or at a cemetery jeopardizes that ritual purity.

During *shivah*, worship services are conducted in the home so that mourners may recite *Kaddish* in the presence of a *minyan*. In traditional communities, all three daily services are done in the home; in other communities, only the evening service is done.

Mourners should refrain from working (unless dire economic results would occur). Friends are expected to visit the mourners, to comfort them, and to provide for their needs, especially assuring that they have food and other provisions. Mourners do not rise to greet the comforters. Conversation should focus on the grief of the mourner and on the life of the deceased. Mourners refrain from enjoyable activities such as: attending parties, including wedding and Bar/Bat Mitzvah receptions; listening to music or watching television; studying Torah (except for reading Job, Lamentations, or Jeremiah); wearing leather shoes; wearing new clothes; sexual intercourse; personal grooming, such as shaving, cutting their hair, and wearing cosmetics. In addition, it is traditional for the mourners to sit on low stools or benches (Sephardic Jews sometimes sit on the floor) rather than on regular chairs, reflective of the humbling effect that losing a loved one can have.

Another common practice is to cover the mirrors in the house of mourning. This tradition may reflect an ancient belief that the soul of the deceased or the visage of the angel of death might be captured in the mirror, or that the image of one who looks at the mirror may be trapped therein. Another interpretation of this custom is that it reminds us of the insignificance of our physical image and that we should not be concerned with our physical appearance when we are mourning.

These mourning rituals are observed to a varying extent in the contemporary Jewish world. The *shivah* period is sometimes shortened to three days or less and many of the traditional rituals are ignored. Each community and congregation usually sets its own guidelines.

Seudat Havra'ah/Meal of Condolence

Upon returning home from the funeral to begin *shivah*, it is the obligation of the community to provide a *Seudat Havra'ah*, a meal of condolence, for the mourners. It is traditional to serve foods that are round to symbolize the cyclical nature of life. Among the most common foods are hard-boiled eggs (a poignant symbol of the close nexus between life and death), lentils and garbanzo beans, and even bagels. (Lentils are especially significant because they are round and they have no eye, as most beans have. This is symbolic of the deceased no longer being seen. The lentil was also thought to be the source of the red soup that Jacob served to Esau, who was famished when he arrived at the tent. Jacob was said to have been making the soup because his grandfather Abraham had just died.) Most important, the meal is served to the mourners

by their friends and other family members. Although it is now common for all guests to share in this meal, at one time it was only for the mourners.

Sh'loshim

The next stage of mourning is called sh'loshim, Hebrew for thirty. It is the 30-day period beginning with burial (the first seven days of which are *shivah*). For all relatives except for one's parents, *sh'loshim* constitutes the entire period of mourning.

During *sh'loshim*, mourners begin to return to normal life. One may work and attend to one's daily affairs. The prohibitions against wearing leather shoes, studying Torah, and engaging in sexual intercourse are ended. Mirrors are uncovered, and one may sit on regular chairs. Services are no longer held in the home; the mourners say *Kaddish* at a synagogue *minyan*. However, mourners are expected to refrain from attending parties, shaving, cutting their hair, and wearing new clothes.

Shanah/Kaddish

For parents, the full mourning period is twelve months, beginning from the day of death (rather than at burial as is the case with *shivah* and *sh'loshim*). During this period of time, following *sh'loshim*, mourners return to most activities. However, observant Jews continue to refrain from haircutting and shaving and attending parties.

The most important observance during this period of time is the daily recitation of *Kaddish*. Although the *Kaddish* did not originate as a mourner's prayer and does not mention death, it has become one of the most important mourning rituals in Judaism.

The history of the *Kaddish* is obscure, but by the eighth century the version of the *Kaddish* now called *Kaddish Yatom*, Orphan's or Mourner's *Kaddish*, was recited to conclude a study session, including the study session held to mark the end of *shivah* for a scholar. It then became the practice to recite *Kaddish* at the end of every *shivah* period. By the thirteenth century, it was recited at the end of every worship service.

Eventually, it became the custom to recite the Mourner's *Kaddish* as part of the preliminary prayers during the daily morning service and after

Psalm 93 during *Kabbalat Shabbat*. In addition, it is the custom for mourners to recite *Kaddish d'Rabbanan*, the Rabbi's *Kaddish*, which is included in the liturgy during *Birchot HaShachar* (after studying chapter 5 of *Mishnah Zevachim*, *Ayzohu M'koman*, and Rabbi Ishmael's 13 principles for interpreting scripture) and during *Kabbalat Shabbat* (after studying *Mishnah Shabbat* chapter 2, *Bameh Madlikeen*).

Although it was originally the custom to recite the *Kaddish* for the full 12 months of mourning, it is now traditional to recite the *Kaddish* for only 11 months. The recitation of the *Kaddish*, particularly by a son, was believed to have a positive effect on God's ultimate judgment of the deceased. This judging period was a full year following death. However, only the wicked are presumed to need the entire 12-month period in order to be judged righteous. Since no one would presume their parents to be wicked, it became the custom to recite the *Kaddish* for only 11 months.

Memorial or Headstone

Since ancient times, it has been the custom to mark the grave with a stone or monument. After Rachel died, "Jacob erected a monument on Rachel's grave" (Genesis 35:20). The marker or monument serves to identify the grave so that relatives will find it when they visit, honor the memory of the deceased, and identify a place of burial so that *Kohanim* (priests) will avoid it as required by Jewish law.

Jewish tradition makes no stipulation as to the size or type of marker or monument, but most cemeteries have specific guidelines. The Jewish teaching that all are equal in death often serves as a guide to choosing an appropriate headstone.

The marker usually includes: the English and Hebrew name of the deceased, the dates of birth and death in English and Hebrew, and the relationship to other family members (i.e., father/mother, husband/wife, grandfather/grandmother, sister/brother, etc.). Also, one often finds the Hebrew letters: פ״נ *pay nun*, standing for "*Po Nikbar(ah)* — here is buried," and the letters: ת.נ.צ.ב.ה. *tav, nun, tzadee, bet, hay,* standing for the phrase תְּהְיֶה נִשְׁמָתוֹ/נִשְׁמָתָהּ צְרוּרָה בִּצְרוֹר הַחַיִּים "*Tihyeh Nishmato/ta Tzerurah BiTzror HaChayim*"

(May his/her soul be bound up in the bond of eternal life.)

It is customary for the grave marker to be put in place and for an unveiling ceremony to be held after the *Kaddish* period is over, but no later than one year after the death. While many families wait until almost the full year has passed to do the unveiling, it may be done sooner; in Israel the stone is usually placed soon after *sh'loshim*.

Unveiling

The unveiling ceremony consists of the recitation of Psalms, a very brief eulogy encapsulating the most salient characteristics of the deceased, removing the cloth covering the headstone, the *Ayl Malay Rachamim*, and the Mourner's *Kaddish*. Traditionally, *Kaddish* is not recited aloud if no *minyan* is present.

It is customary, before leaving the gravesite, to place a small stone on the marker to indicate that someone has visited the grave. This tradition may also reflect the biblical practice of marking the grave with a pile of stones. Or, it may be the end result of the custom of writing notes to the deceased and pushing them into crevices in the headstone (just as notes are pushed into the Western Wall in Jerusalem). When no crevice could be found, the note was weighted down with a stone. In time, the paper disintegrated or blew away leaving only the stone. Thus, some began to think that the leaving of a stone was the custom . . . and so it became the custom.

Visiting the Grave

While visitation of the grave is permitted at almost any time, excessive visits are discouraged. "The Rabbis were apprehensive that frequent visiting to the cemetery might become a pattern of living thus preventing the bereaved from placing their dead in proper perspective (Lamm, p. 192).

It is considered especially appropriate to visit the graves of loved ones on the last day of *shiva* and the last day of *sh'loshim*, on *Yahrzeit*, on Jewish fast days, and before or between the High Holy Days. Traditional Jews will often recite Psalms while visiting, study a short passage from the *Mishnah,* or recite "*Ayl Malay Rachamim*."

Yahrzeit

The anniversary of the death is called *Yahrzeit* — Yiddish for year-time. *Yahrzeit* is traditionally observed according to the Jewish calendar, but some people use the Gregorian calendar. One lights a 24-hour *Yahrzeit* candle in the home at sundown on the anniversary of the death. There is no blessing said when lighting this candle.

One is also obligated to recite *Kaddish* at synagogue on the *Yahrzeit*. In congregations without a daily *minyan*, it is often customary to read the name during the Shabbat service nearest to the *Yahrzeit* and for family members to attend so as to recite *Kaddish*. In traditional congregations mourners will sometimes lead the service.

Yizkor

Besides *Yahrzeit*, loved ones are also remembered four times during the year at special memorial services called *Yizkor*. These services are held on Yom Kippur, Shemini Atzeret (the day after Sukkot), the last day of Pesach, and on Shavuot (the second day if two days are observed). This memorial service is usually part of the morning service on these holidays, following the Torah reading, with the exception that many Reform congregations observe *Yizkor* on Yom Kippur in the late afternoon just before *Neilah*. The *Yizkor* service includes readings from Psalms, the *Yizkor* prayer asking God to remember the soul of the deceased, and "*Ayl Malay Rachamim.*" In some traditions the *Kaddish* is also recited.

Life after Death

So far, the focus in this chapter has been on mourning customs and on what happens to the body after death. But Jewish literature also addresses the question: What happens to the soul after a person dies? The Bible has very little to say about life after death, focusing instead on how one should act in this world. Indeed, throughout Jewish history much more attention has been paid to how a Jew should act in this world without regard to what will happen in a next one. Nevertheless, a variety of beliefs about what happens to the soul after one dies has developed.

The Bible mentions the word *Sheol* — a place located under the ground, where one goes after death. Every living being goes to *Sheol* after death, but there is no indication that anything happens after one goes there. However, the biblical text offers hints of other beliefs. For example, two characters, Enoch and Elijah, did not die. "Enoch walked with God and he was no more" (Genesis 5:24), and Elijah is said to have ascended to heaven in a fiery chariot by a whirlwind (II Kings 2:11).

Several laws which oppose inquiring of the dead (Deuteronomy 18:10-11) indicate that the people were aware of that practice, and most likely engaged in it. And in a famous passage, Saul demands that the witch of Endor contact the prophet Samuel (who had died) for guidance. She does, but Samuel is not pleased to have been so conjured (I Samuel 28).

Another well-known passage from Ezekiel uses the metaphor of resurrection to symbolize the restoration of Israel. "And [God] said to me: 'Mortal one, these bones are the whole house of Israel.' They say, 'Our bones are dried up, our hope is gone. We are doomed.' So prophesy and say to them: 'Thus said *Adonai,* God: I am going to open your graves and lift you out of the graves, My people, and bring you to the land of Israel'" (Ezekiel 37:11-12).

During the Rabbinic period, speculations concerning the immortality of the soul and the resurrection of the dead were introduced and became a part of Jewish theology. The Rabbis asserted that following death, the body remains in the grave, while the soul ascends to heaven, where it awaits reunification with the body. The soul is considered to be an independent entity, which has awareness of the world.

The most significant Rabbinic statement about the soul is expressed in the liturgy during *Birchot HaShachar.* "My God, the soul which you have given me is pure. You created it, you formed it, and you breathed it into me. You have preserved it within me and will take it from me, but will restore it to me in the world to come." While many other passages refer to the soul, no definitive teaching developed about it.

The Jewish concept of resurrection of the dead was introduced by the Pharisees, to the staunch opposition of the other major Jewish faction of their day, the Sadducees. The Rabbis insisted that resurrection of the dead was a belief derived from the Torah (see Sources from the Tradition, p. 110). They denied a place in the world to come to one who rejected this belief (*Sanhedrin* 10:1). This resurrection of the bodies and reuniting with the souls would only occur at the end of time when the Messiah came, a time referred to as *Olam HaBa* — "the world to come" — as opposed to "this world."

In addition, the Rabbis speculated about reward and punishment, and heaven and hell. They believed that the righteous would be rewarded and the wicked punished in the world to come. The beliefs in reward, punishment, and resurrection of the dead were among Thirteen Principles of Faith of Maimonides.

Reform Judaism rejected the concept of resurrection of the dead, although it maintained a belief in the immortality of the soul. However, for some Jews, the meaning of immortality of the soul is that we live on through the friends and family we have left behind and through whatever contributions we made to this world during our lives.

Reincarnation is also a concept that is present in Judaism, most significantly in the mystical concept of *gilgul neshamot*, the transmigration of souls. The souls were viewed as having independent existence, and of inhabiting one body after another. This concept continues to be embraced by many Hasidic and other Jews in the modern world.

Judaism, therefore, has offered a wide variety of beliefs pertaining to life after death, with a great deal of speculation and imagination, but no definitive teaching. Whatever a Jew's belief about life after death, virtually all Jews agree that one should focus on life in this world, and let the next world take care of itself.

Rabbi Chama son of Rabbi Chanina also said: "What is the meaning of the text: 'You shall walk after *Adonai* your God' (Deuteronomy 13:5)? The meaning is to walk after the attributes of the Holy One . . . . The Holy One comforted mourners, as it is written, 'And it came to pass after the death of Abraham that God blessed Isaac his son' (Genesis 25:11), so you should comfort mourners. The Holy One buried the dead, as it is written, 'And [God] buried [Moses] in the valley' (Deuteronomy 34:6), so you should bury the dead."

(*Sota* 14a)

At one time, funerals in Israel were more difficult [i.e., more costly] for the relatives [of the deceased] than the death itself, so much so that they would leave [the body] and flee. Then Rabban Gamliel came and behaved simply with regard to himself, [insisting] that they would bring his body out in linen garments. Then everyone followed his example and brought out bodies in linen garments. Rav Papa said: "Now it is the practice to bring out bodies in rough cloth worth only a *zuz*."

(*Ketubot* 8b)

When Rabbi [Judah] was dying, the Rabbis declared a public fast and offered prayers that God have mercy on him [i.e., spare his life] . . . . Rabbi's maid went up to the roof and prayed: "The angels want Rabbi [to join them in heaven] and the people want him to remain with them. May it be the will of God that the people overpower the angels." However, when she saw how often he had to use the bathroom, each time painfully taking off his *tefillin* and putting them on again, she prayed: "May it be the will of God that the angels overpower the people." As the Rabbis continued to pray, she took a jar and threw it off the roof. They stopped praying [because they were startled by the noise], and the soul of Rabbi departed.

(*Ketubot* 104a)

Rabbi Eliezer said: "Repent one day before your death." His students asked him: "Does one know the day of one's death?" That is all the more reason to repent today lest one dies tomorrow. Therefore, all one's days shall be filled with repentance.

(*Shabbat* 153a)

Just as one enters the world, so does one leave the world.

One enters it with a cry and leaves with a cry.

One enters the world with weeping and leaves it with weeping.

One enters the world with love and leaves it with love.

One enters the world with a sigh and leaves it with a sigh.

One enters the world without knowledge and leaves it without knowledge.

It has been taught in the name of R. Meir: "One enters the world with hands clenched as if to say, 'The whole world is mine; I shall inherit it.' But when one leaves the world, one's hands are spread open as if to say, 'I have not taken anything from the world.'"

(*Ecclesiastes Rabbah* 5:14)

A favorite saying of Rav: "The world to come is not like this world. In the world to come there is no eating or drinking or procreation or business or jealousy or hatred or competition. Rather, the righteous sit with their crowns on their heads and enjoy the brightness of the *Shechinah*."

(*Brachot* 17a)

"A human being is equated with a Torah scroll that was impaired and can no longer be used at religious services. While the ancient scroll no longer serves any useful ritual purpose, it is revered for the exalted function it once filled. Man was created in the image of God and, although the pulse of life is no more, the human form must be respected for having once embodied the spirit of God, and for the character and the personality it housed."

(Maurice Lamm, *The Jewish Way in Death and Mourning*, p. 3)

ACTIVITIES

Primary

1. Read to the class *Daddy's Chair* by Sandy Lanton, the story of two young children whose father has died. Discuss these questions: Why doesn't Michael want anyone else to sit in his father's chair? How does his mother answer Michael? How does Michael behave differently after talking with his mother? Why does Michael sit in the chair at the end of the story? Do any of the students have a special place or object that helps them to remember or think about a special person (or animal) who has died?

2. With the students, read *Mrs. Katz and Tush* by Patricia Polacco. Discuss: How did Mrs. Katz and Larnel become friends? What are some of the things that Larnel learned about Judaism from Mrs. Katz? How did Larnel honor Mrs. Katz's memory after she died?

3. Ask the students if they have had a pet which died, and to share with the class what they did after the death. How did the students feel, and how did the actions help them feel better? Do they wish that their family would have done something different? Briefly describe to your students similarities between what they did for their pets and what is done for people. As a class create a story about a pet that died and a family's response to the death, including ritual, discussion, and perhaps replacing the pet.

4. Children have a natural curiosity about death and do not often have an opportunity to express their thoughts and feelings and to ask questions. Take your class to the sanctuary or to the place where memorial plaques are located. Ask the children if they know what these are and why they are there. Discuss the importance of remembering those who have passed away. Invite the Rabbi or other Jewish professional to answer the students' questions about death and dying.

5. Teach the students about preparing a *Seudat Havra'ah*, a meal of consolation for mourners. Bring to class pictures of food. Ask students to divide them by category, such as: vegetarian/non-vegetarian; meat/milk/grains/fruits and vegetables; what we normally eat for breakfast/lunch/dinner; junk food/healthy food; by shape: round/square/long. Explain that Jews eat round food as a reminder of the cycle of the year and the cycle of life. Ask when a round *challah* is eaten (Rosh HaShanah). Explain that it is traditional to prepare round food for mourners to eat after the funeral at a special meal called a *Seudat Havra'ah*. With your students brainstorm a list of round foods that could be prepared for such a meal. Coordinate with the Rabbi so that your class can help prepare or purchase round food for a family in mourning. For example: bagels, hard-cooked eggs, round cookies, lentils, muffins, fruit, etc. With students write a note which explains that your class is studying the *mitzvah* of consoling the bereaved and has prepared round food for the meal of consolation.

6. Teach students one of the melodies to "*Oseh Shalom*," which is the last line of the Mourner's *Kaddish*.
    Resources: *And the Youth Shall See Visions* by Debbie Friedman; *The Bridge* by Kol B'seder; Cantor or music specialist.

Intermediate

1. Bring a *Yahrzeit* candle and a *k'riah* ribbon to class. Pass them around and ask students to identify how they are used. Read to the class *A Candle for Grandpa* by David Techner and Judith Hirt-Manheimer. Ask each student to write down at least one question about the Jewish rituals pertaining to death or mourning. Invite the Rabbi to answer these questions and to discuss Jewish practices related to death.

2. Ask students to bring to class old clothes, particularly shirts, vests, or scarfs that can be torn. Distribute one garment to each student and have them put them on over their regular

clothes. Explain the custom of tearing one's garments upon learning of the death of a relative. Do a brief guided fantasy, in which the Jewish community in ancient times learns of the death of one of its leaders. Tell the students to tear their garments in response to learning of this news. Afterward, ask the students to describe the feelings they had when tearing the clothes. Do the students think that doing this would help express one's distress or anger?

Explain to the students the contemporary custom in many communities of using a black ribbon instead of tearing one's garments, and cutting the ribbon prior to the funeral. Ask the students if this ritual would have the same effect as actually tearing one's garments.
Resource: *Jewish Guided Imagery: A How-To Book for Rabbis, Educators and Group Leaders* by Dov Peretz Elkins.

3. Ask the students to imagine that they are sitting *shiva* for someone who has died. Have them write a diary about their imagined experiences. Students should use words from the Glossary, and can make whatever assumptions they want about the time period, family structure, and their place in it. Ask each student to share one or more diary entries with the class.

4. Bring to the classroom two or three large mirrors and cover them with cloths before the students enter the room. Tell the students that they will be doing a lesson on death and mourning customs in Judaism. Ask the students to guess what is under the cloths and the relationship to death and mourning. If no one is familiar with the ritual, explain the practice of covering the mirrors in the house of mourning during *shivah* and the variety of reasons for doing so (see Overview, p. 106).

Uncover the mirrors and ask students as a group to generate words which describe the experience of looking into a mirror. Write all student responses on the board. Then cover the mirrors and repeat the activity, with the students describing the covered mirrors. Compare the two lists and relate to the reasons for covering

mirrors during *shivah*. To extend this activity, write a poem as a class, in small groups, or individually using the words generated by the group.

5. Have each of the students create a grave marker for a famous Jewish figure from the past. Explain to the students the information traditionally included (see Overview, p. 107). Students should research the individual they chose to get this information (date of birth and death, Hebrew name, etc.). Students may also include a short epitaph which summarizes the person's life.

6. Set up two stations in the classroom. One station should be a sink with soap and towels. The other should be a large bowl of water with a pitcher or water and a towel. Each student in turn washes his or her hands at each station. Discuss the similarities and differences. Explain the Jewish tradition of ritual hand washing upon returning from the cemetery (see Overview, p. 105). Also point out the tradition of ritual hand washing before eating.

7. Create with your students "remembering booklets." Begin by asking students what they remember about someone who has died. List responses on the board. From these responses create general categories such as "What we did together," "What I learned," "What I miss most," "Special qualities," "What I will always remember." Assign each student or small group of students to design one of the pages of the book reflecting each category, as well as pages for general information (date of birth, death), pictures, mementos (birthday cards, notes). Reproduce these pages for each student and assemble into a booklet. Students can save these booklets to use at an appropriate time or complete them and share with the class.

8. Tombstone rubbings are often used as an important resource for learning about the past. Arrange for the class to visit a Jewish cemetery, if possible one with older headstones. Demon-

strate how a rubbing is made. Use newsprint, butcher paper, or other large sheets of paper. Place the paper over the stone; tape it down or have someone hold it still. Use the long side of artist's charcoal and rub across the face of the stone. When the rubbing is completed, spray a fixative on the paper to preserve the image. In small groups students should then make rubbings of some of the stones. After returning to the classroom, discuss what information is learned from the inscriptions on the stones. How might such information be useful to a historian?

9. Obtain a burial shroud from a *Chevra Kaddisha* or Jewish funeral home and bring it to class. Display it to the students, explaining that it is the traditional burial garment called *tachrichim* — a shroud. Ask students to examine it and to describe its characteristics. Write these on the board as the students say them. Discuss these characteristics, being sure to emphasize that the shroud has no pockets (to indicate that one does not take anything with them to the grave) and that it is a plain garment (to show that all are equal in death).

10. Complete the mini-course *Death, Burial & Mourning in the Jewish Tradition* by Audrey Friedman Marcus, Sherry Bissell, and Karen S. Lipschutz.

11. Complete the instant lesson *The Red in My Father's Beard* by Alan Kay, which is about a young boy dealing with the death of his grandfather.

12. Complete the instant lesson *Pebbles on a Stone* by Alan Kay, which focuses on the end of the mourning period and the unveiling of the grandfather's headstone.

13. Complete the instant lesson *The Empty Drawer* by Naomi Bromberg Bar-Yam, about children dealing with a relative's death.

Secondary

1. With the students, read Job 1:13-21, which describes Job's reactions to learning of the death of his children. Discuss the similarity (rending one's garments) and difference (Job cuts his hair, whereas today one does not cut one's hair) between his response and modern mourning customs. Also discuss Job's response in verse 21: "*Adonai* gives, *Adonai* takes, blessed be the name of *Adonai*." Is this the type of response you would expect from someone who has just lost his/her children? Why does Job (and later Jewish tradition) use this response? What does it mean to say "*Adonai* gives" and "*Adonai* takes?" In what way does God give and take lives?

2. To introduce students to the significance of the *hesped* (eulogy) in the Jewish funeral, have each student write a *hesped* for a famous Jew of the past. After choosing the individual, each student should research basic information about the person, accomplishments, personal characteristics, contribution to Judaism and/or the world, etc. Explain to the class the purpose of a *hesped* in Jewish tradition (see Overview, p. 104). Each student should then write the *hesped*, using imagination to fill in details if necessary. Each student in turn should then deliver the *hesped* before the class.

3. Teach students how to find the traditional Hebrew date in order to observe the *Yahrzeit* of a relative. Ask each student to bring to class the date of death of a relative, according to the Gregorian calendar, as well as the time of day the person died. Show the students how to use a perpetual Jewish calendar to find the corresponding Hebrew date of death. Students should then look up the Hebrew date of death corresponding to the Gregorian date. Once they know the Hebrew date, they can look up the Gregorian date on which it will fall during the next ten years, and make a chart to serve as a reminder.
Resource: *The Standard Guide to the Jewish and Civil Calendar* by Fred Reiss.

4. Older students may have already had the experience of making a condolence call, or should at least begin thinking about how to do it. Have students research suggested guidelines for making a condolence call. Role play students making condolence calls in a variety of situations, such as the death of a friend's parent, the death of a friend, the death a teacher. Students should have the opportunity to take the roles of both mourner and comforter. After each role play, evaluate how the condolence call was carried out. What did the comforter do to help comfort the mourner? What could he or she have done differently? Each student should then create a list of guidelines for his/her own practice of comforting the mourner.
Resources: *A Time to Mourn, A Time to Comfort* by Ron Wolfson; *A Guide to Life* by Tzvi Rabinowicz; *The Second How-To Handbook for Jewish Living* by Ronald H. Isaacs and Kerry M. Olitzky.

5. Jews espouse a number of differing beliefs about life after death. With the students, create a survey which asks people about their personal beliefs on this subject. In order to write the survey, the students will need to know about some of Judaism's teachings regarding life after death. Summarize the material in the Overview (see p. 108) or from another source. Students should then brainstorm questions to include, such as: What do you believe happens to a person's soul after death? Do the souls go somewhere? Do they reunite with other souls of family members or friends? Do you think the souls are rewarded or punished? Do you believe that the body will be resurrected at some time and be reunited with the soul? Do you believe in reincarnation? Create the survey and ask each student to give it to about five Jewish teenagers or adults. Compile the results of the completed surveys and discuss. To extend the activity, have the students give the survey to non-Jews and compare the results with those of the previous survey.

6. Invite clergy of different religious traditions (including a Rabbi) to participate in a panel discussion. Each representative should have the opportunity to make a brief presentation about beliefs and practices pertaining to death, burial, mourning, and life after death. Leave time for questions. At a subsequent session, create a chart comparing the beliefs and practices of each religion.

7. Create a *Yizkor* service with the class. Gather a variety of prayer books which contain a *Yizkor* service. Each student or small group of students receives one prayer book and composes an outline of the *Yizkor* service. The outline should list each component of the service: prayers, Psalms, readings, etc. Each group should write its outline on the board. Students then spend a few minutes examining each of the outlines, noting similarities and differences. Based on these observations, discuss with the students which prayers and readings are usually included in a *Yizkor* service. Which are optional? Now create the *Yizkor* service. The class may choose a theme such as: Holocaust Remembrance, Yom HaZikaron (Israeli Memorial Day), American/Canadian Memorial Day, or a general *Yizkor* service. Students may write their own poetry, choose songs or readings, and intersperse this material with the traditional parts of the *Yizkor* service. Hold the service at the appropriate time.

8. Organ donation is an important contemporary biomedical issue. Anyone 18 years and older may choose to donate any needed organs or tissue for medical transplantation. It is common to indicate on one's driver's licence that one is a donor. Obtain from the Department of Motor Vehicles information about organ donation and forms that are distributed to drivers in your state. Review this material with the students and discuss how one should go about deciding whether or not to be an organ donor. Share with your students *Responsa* and other material from Jewish sources pertaining to this topic. Each student should write a statement about

whether he or she would choose to be an organ donor and why or why not. These statements may be shared orally or displayed on a bulletin board.
Resources: *Modern Medicine and Jewish Ethics* by Fred Rosner, pp. 255-275; *Contemporary American Reform Responsa* by Walter Jacob, pp. 128-132.

9. Do the dramatic reading "The Death of Moses" based on *midrashim* about Moses' death for your class (see Appendix 1, p. 131). Invite a Rabbi, psychologist, or grief counselor to the class to lead a discussion about how Moses faces his death in relationship to the stages that modern psychology identifies.

Hebrew

1. Do an activity with your students to teach or review the following words which are related to death and mourning rituals. For example: provide students with the definitions to these words and ask them to match the definitions to the terms, make a crossword puzzle, do a word search.

   Shivah/שִׁבְעָה
   Sh'loshim/שְׁלוֹשִׁים
   Kaddish/קַדִּישׁ
   K'riah/קְרִיעָה
   Chevra Kaddisha/חֶבְרָה קְדִישָׁא
   Yizkor/יִזְכֹּר
   Yahrzeit/יאָרצייט
   Tahara/טָהֳרָה
   Tachrichim/תַּכְרִיכִים

2. Teach your students the traditional phrase (see Overview, p. 105 above) spoken by the community to mourners as they leave the graveside after the funeral (and when they enter the synagogue during *Kabbalat* Shabbat). Discuss the *mitzvah* of comforting the mourners and how this phrase plays a role in that process.

3. Teach your students the following phrases, which are sometimes used after mentioning the name of a person who has died:

זִכְרוֹנוֹ לִבְרָכָה/*Zichrono l'Vrachah*

May his memory be for a blessing

זִכְרוֹנָהּ לִבְרָכָה/*Zichronah l'Vrachah*

May her memory be for a blessing

זֵכֶר צָדִּיק לִבְרָכָה/*Zaycher Tzaddik l'Vrachah*

May the memory of the righteous be for a blessing.

Ask students why one might use these phrases. Tell students to look and listen for these phrases during the week and report back to the class at another session.

4. Write the following terms on the board:

   בֵּית עוֹלָם/*Bayt Olam* (House of Eternity)

   בֵּית חַיִּים/*Bayt Chayim* (House of the Living)

   בֵּית שָׁלוֹם/*Bayt Shalom* (House of Peace)

   Translate the phrases with the students and ask what these phrases might be used to describe. Explain that each term is a euphemism used to refer to a Jewish cemetery. Discuss why these phrases might be used, as opposed to phrases such as "House of the Dead."

5. Teach the class the Mourner's *Kaddish* and the various traditions concerning who recites it (see Overview, pp. 106-7). Point out that most of the *Kaddish* is written in Aramaic, the common language of the Jews during the Rabbinic period.

6. For advanced Hebrew students, invite the Cantor to teach the students to chant the "*Ayl Malay Rachamim*" prayer. Discuss the meaning of the prayer and the occasions on which it is chanted. The class (or a member of the congregation) could chant it at a *Yizkor* service.

Adult

1. Read together Job 2:11-13, which describes how Job's three friends consoled him after the death of his children. Consider these questions for discussion: What did Job's friends do? How do their actions demonstrate their compassion for Job? How do their actions compare to contemporary death and mourning rituals? What is the significance of their silence? How can silence be comforting?

2. Consider establishing a *Chevra Kaddisha* or a Bereavement Committee in your congregation. Begin with a panel discussion including a Rabbi, bereavement counselor, member of a *Chevra Kaddisha*, funeral home director, or other individuals. After the presentation, discuss what aspects of the preparation for the funeral and bereavement process the group wishes to undertake. Create a mission statement and a set of objectives for implementing this project. Recruit additional members and publicize the services that the group will offer.

3. Set up a program to explore and learn about three different types of wills: will of inheritance, ethical will, and living will. Invite experts in each of these areas to make a presentation and provide material for participants to begin preparing these types of wills. Divide participants into three groups, and rotate between each speaker. Resources: *Ethical Wills: Handing Down Our Jewish Heritage* by Barbara Binder Kadden and Bruce Kadden; *So That Your Values Live On: Ethical Wills and How to Prepare Them* edited by Jack Riemer and Nathaniel Stampfer.

4. View and discuss the video *The Corridor: Death*. This film uses the story of a car accident in Israel as a means to explore important issues relating to death and life after death. (Older students might also be invited to the showing.)

5. Dealing with death and loss is an important process. To help adults begin this journey, view the video *When Bad Things Happen to Good People*, which is based on Rabbi Harold Kush-ner's book of the same name. Invite participants to share their own stories of loss and what they did to begin the healing process. This program may form the basis of an ongoing bereavement group.

6. Hold an adult education class about ethical wills utilizing *Ethical Wills: Handing Down Our Jewish Heritage* by Barbara Binder Kadden and Bruce Kadden.

Family

1. It is traditional to hold a study session to commemorate the *Yahrzeit* of a Jewish scholar. Based on this tradition, hold a family program of study which honors the memory of a famous Jew. All families should gather at the beginning of the program to hear a short presentation about the person's life and contributions to Judaism.

   Families then rotate among a number of stations to learn more about the person. Among the stations might be: (1) view a short video, (2) create an illustration based on a quotation from or about the person, (3) interview someone role playing the person, (4) write a poem about the person, (5) write an obituary or eulogy about the person, (6) create a headstone for the person's grave. Conclude with a memorial service. Suggested individuals: Moses, Miriam, Deborah, King David, Hillel, Maimonides, Glückel of Hameln, Theodor Herzl, Henrietta Szold, Golda Meir, Yitzchak Rabin.

2. Arrange a day to help clean up and renovate a Jewish cemetery. In order to locate an appropriate cemetery, contact a synagogue administrator, a (Jewish) historical society, the Jewish Federation, or a community leader. Arrange a meeting to plan the event, including: transportation, needed gardening tools and supplies, food and drinks. A few people may need to visit the cemetery first in order to determine what needs to be done. Be sure to take pictures before, during, and after the work, and publicize the group's effort in the local Jewish and general press.

3. Organize a program for families to make a "remembering quilt" for a loved one who has died. Families should be told to bring with them decorative fabric, pictures, pieces of clothing or buttons from clothing of the person, and/or small mementos such as medals or ribbons which can be attached to the quilt (also portable sewing machines if possible). Provide for each family five to ten 6½" squares of 100 percent cotton muslin fabric, batting (padding which goes between the decorated quilt front and the backing fabric), backing fabric (any cotton fabric), and fabric markers. Find an experienced quilter to help with the activity. Each family is given the white muslin squares. Leaving a ¼" minimum seam allowance all around, embellish the squares with stories, anecdotes, memories, and information about the person. The decorated squares can be sewn adjoining each other, interspersed with 6½" squares of a decorative fabric, or can be joined with sashing (strips of fabric placed around the squares like a frame). Attach the front of the quilt to the batting and backing, basting to hold all three layers in place. Machine or hand quilt all three layers together. Then add the mementos and finish off with a quilted binding.

All-School

1. Divide the students into groups of mixed grade level, assigning a teacher to each group. Utilizing the Rabbinic material in the Sources from the Tradition section above, create illustrated murals to display. Each group should begin by discussing the particular source to be sure that students understand it. Ask for suggestions about how to illustrate the teaching. Suggested media: tempera paints, markers, chalk, or crayons. Use butcher paper and include the teaching on the mural or on a separate piece of paper.

2. To help students learn about the customs and rituals related to burial and mourning, set up a series of stations, each focusing on a particular aspect of this process. Divide students into groups (with a teacher or other resource person as leader) to rotate through the stations. Each group is considered a *Chevra Kaddisha*, and should begin by discussing the significance of this communal institution. Suggested stations:

Tachrichim (shrouds) – provide a shroud for the students to examine. Explain how it used and why it has no pockets.

Aron (casket) – Using popsicle sticks, students make a miniature casket. Explain that it is traditional that the casket be made entirely of wood.

Who Is a Mourner? – Give students a pre-test which lists a variety of family relationships and asks who one is required to mourn. After the pre-test, provide students with this information.

K'riah – Provide a black ribbon for each student. Explain how and why it is used. Have each student pin it on and do the ritual cutting.

Burial – Explain the ritual of participating in filling in the grave. Act out this ritual, with a hole in the ground and a pile of dirt (or using sand in a box or other container).

Shivah – Set up a corner like a *shivah* house, with a pitcher of water, a basin, and a towel at the entrance, low benches or chairs, covered mirrors, a *shivah* candle, and a table with hard-boiled eggs, *kipot*, and *shivah* prayer books. Utilize material from the Overview to provide students with explanations appropriate to each station. Conclude the program with a game, with each group competing to answer questions about the material they have learned.

3. Show the students the scene of Tevye's dream (the return of Fruma Sarah) from *Fiddler on the Roof*. Divide students into groups which will perform "Paper Bag Dramatics." Provide each group with a paper bag that contains diverse items to be used as props. Each group writes a script based on the idea of someone returning from the dead in order to share his or her message with the living. Groups perform their skits for each other.

GLOSSARY

Aninut – Period from the moment one learns about the death of a loved one until burial. A person in this situation is called an *onen* (m.) or *onenet* (f).

Aron – Casket

Ayl Malay Rachamim – Traditional memorial prayer

Chevra Kaddisha – Burial society.

Gosays – Person who is close to death.

Kaddish – Prayer recited by mourners.

K'riah – Tearing of a garment as a sign of mourning.

Seudat Havra'ah – Meal of condolence served to mourners following the funeral.

Shivah – Seven day mourning period following burial.

Sh'loshim – Thirty day mourning period following burial.

Shomer – Guardian; a person who stays with the body from death until burial.

Tachrichim – Shrouds; traditional burial garment.

Taharah – Ritual cleansing of the body following death.

Tzidduk HaDin – Prayer said at time of burial proclaiming the righteousness of God's judgment.

Vidui – Confessional prayer recited by or on behalfo f one who is dying.

Yahrzeit – Anniversary of death

Yizkor – Memorial prayer or service held on Yom Kippur, Shemini Atzeret, the last day of Pesach and Shavuot.

RESOURCES

For the Teacher

Bleich, J. David. *Judaism and Healing: Halakhic Perspectives*. Hoboken, NJ: KTAV Publishing House, Inc., 1981.

Brener, Anne. *Mourning & Mitzvah: A Guided Journal for Walking the Mourner's Path through Grief to Healing*. Woodstock, VT: Jewish Lights Publishing, 1993.

Elkins, Dov Peretz. *Jewish Guided Imagery: A How-To Book for Rabbis, Educators and Group Leaders*. Princeton, NJ: Growth Associates, 1996.

Goodman, Arnold M. *A Plain Pine Box: A Return to Simple Jewish Funerals and Eternal Traditions*. Hoboken: NJ: KTAV Publishing House, Inc., 1981.

Isaacs, Ronald H., and Kerry M. Olitzky. *A Jewish Mourner's Handbook*. Hoboken, NJ: KTAV Publishing House, Inc., 1991.

————. *The Second How To Handbook for Jewish Living*. Hoboken, NJ: KTAV Publishing House, Inc., 1996.

Jacob, Walter. *Contemporary American Reform Responsa*. New York: Central Conference of American Rabbis, 1987.

Kolatch, Alfred. *The Jewish Mourner's Book of Why*. Middle Village, NY: Jonathan David Publishers, Inc., 1991.

Lamm, Maurice. *The Jewish Way in Death and Mourning*. New York: Jonathan David Publishers, 1969.

Rabinowicz, Tzvi. *A Guide to Life: Jewish Laws and Customs of Mourning*. Northvale, NJ: Jason Aronson Inc., 1994.

Reiss, Fred. *The Standard Guide to the Jewish and Civil Calendar*. West Orange, NJ: Behrman House, Inc., 1986.

Riemer, Jack, and Nathaniel Stampfer, eds. *So That Your Values Live On: Ethical Wills and How to Prepare Them*. Woodstock, VT: Jewish Lights Publishing, 1993.

Rosner, Fred. *Modern Medicine and Jewish Ethics*. Hoboken, NJ: KTAV Publishing House, Inc. and New York: Yeshiva University Press, 1986.

Sonsino, Rifat, and Daniel B. Syme. *What Happens After I Die? Jewish Views of Life after Death*. New York: UAHC Press, 1990.

Wolfson, Ron. *A Time to Mourn, A Time to Comfort*. New York: The Federation of Jewish Men's Clubs, 1993.

For the Students

Bar-Yam, Naomi Bromberg. *The Empty Drawer*. Los Angeles: Torah Aura Productions, 1996.

Buscaglia, Leo. *The Fall of Freddie the Leaf: A Story of Life for All Ages*. Thorofare, NJ: Charles B. Slack, Inc., 1982.

Kadden, Barbara Binder, and Bruce Kadden. *Ethical Wills: Handing Down Our Jewish Heritage*. Denver: A.R.E. Publishing, Inc., 1990.

Kay, Alan. *Pebbles on a Stone*. Los Angeles: Torah Aura Productions, 1992.

————. *The Red in My Father's Beard*. Los Angeles: Torah Aura Productions, 1992.

Lanton, Sandy. *Daddy's Chair*. Rockville, MD: Kar-Ben Copies, Inc., 1991.

Marcus, Audrey Friedman; Sherry Bissell; and Karen S. Lipschutz. *Death, Burial & Mourning in the Jewish Tradition*. Denver: A.R.E. Publishing, Inc., 1976.

Polacco, Patricia. *Mrs. Katz and Tush*. New York: Dell Publishing, 1994.

Techner, David, and Judith Hirt-Manheimer. *A Candle for Grandpa: A Guide to the Jewish Funeral for Children and Parents*. New York: UAHC Press, 1993.

Audiovisual

The Corridor: Death. Ergo Media Inc. Videocassette.

Fiddler on the Roof. Videocassette. Available at video stores.

Friedman, Debbie. *And the Youth Shall See Visions*. A.R.E. Publishing, Inc. Audiocassette.

Kol B'seder. *The Bridge*. A.R.E. Publishing, Inc. Audiocassette.

When Bad Things Happen to Good People. Yale Roe Films, Ltd. Videocassette.

STRANGER IN THE LAND: THE STORY OF RUTH
By Elaine Rembrandt

PRODUCTION NOTES

This play was written to accommodate a large group. The narration is spoken by a chorus, although parts may be assigned for various lines or verses to add variety to the delivery. It should be given at an exciting, fast paced clip.

The play can be as elaborate as desired and performed on any type of stage, including the pulpit, using no scenery and only a few props to suggest the various scenes. Group the chorus facing the audience on stairs or risers which lead to the pulpit. They may stand to recite and sit when the scene on the pulpit begins to play.

CAST OF CHARACTERS

Ruth
Orpah
Naomi
Boaz
Man in the Field
Man at the Gate
Chorus
Woman 1
Woman 2
Woman 3
Woman 4

PROLOGUE

Chorus: We've a story to tell and we can't wait
    to say it,
    It's a story of love and the courage to
    obey it,
    It's the tale of the power of loyalty and
    truth,
    It's the story of a stranger,
    It's the story of Ruth.
    With an ending that's happy and a
    moral, too,

You'll find out for yourself when we're all
    through.

Now our story takes place a long time
    ago,
About eleven hundred fifty before the
    common era,
That's way before the kings of Israel
    lived,
But a long time after Moses and
    Pharaoh.
There was a drought in the land of
    Judah then,
It hadn't rained for years.
And the crops dried up and the people
    were hungry,
Filled with doubts and fears.

But Elimelech said, "To heck with all
    this,
We'll starve if we stay much longer.
I'll take my sons and Naomi, my wife,
We'll go to Moab and we'll grow
    stronger."

Now that took courage 'cause it wasn't
    exactly
Like driving from Cleveland to L.A.
They'd be outsiders and the people
    weren't friendly,
They were mean and war-like, some way.

But people are people, wherever they
    live,
And Elimelech knew this was true.
So he took his family and opened a
    business,
And he prospered and both his sons
    grew.

But then — oh, dear (sniff), Elimelech
    died,
And the boys married girls who weren't
    Jewish.
But what else could they do living in a
    strange land,
Their own kind were very fewish.

As if this wasn't enough trouble and
    grief,
You could cry when you hear what
    comes next,
Both her sons died, leaving childless
    widows,
And Naomi was bereaved and perplexed.

Where should she go — what should
    she do?
Hers was a desperate plight.
With no sons to inherit — she'd lost
    everything,
For a woman alone had no rights.

At a time like this, she needed a family,
Some relatives to stand behind her.
So she decided to go back to the land of
    Judah,
And this is where we now find her . . . .

SCENE 1: On the Trail

Naomi: *(Carrying sacks of belongings.)* Ruth — Orpah — you have come far enough with me — you have seen me more than halfway back to Judah — to my city of Bethlehem — now you must return to your own people. May God keep faith with you and may God grant each of you security in the home of a new husband.

Orpah: Oh, no, mother Naomi, we will return with you to your people.

Naomi: Orpah — what can you be thinking? You are a Moabitess. Surely you know it would not be easy for you — you will be outcasts — strangers in my land — as I was in yours.

Ruth: We know, my Mother, but we love you. We have shared much with you, including our grief — we do not wish to leave you now.

Naomi: My daughters, my love for you is as great as if you were my own. That is why I am urging you to return to your own land. You are still young — you can marry again — have children — have sons to care for you in your old age — a woman alone is despised.

Orpah: We will find husbands in your land.

Naomi: My people do not like to marry outsiders. Yours will be a difficult lot. Don't you see — with me, your future is so unsure. You must return to the people who know you and worship your own gods.

Orpah: Yes, I can see you are right. Ruth, I am afraid for my future, both our futures. She is right — we must return to Moab.

Ruth: You must do what is right for you — but as for me — I must stay with Naomi. She is my family. Good-bye, Orpah.

Orpah: Good-bye — good-bye, Naomi.

Naomi: Good-bye, my daughter. Ruth, you must go with her, back to your people and the worship of your gods.

Ruth: Please do not urge me to desert you and go back. Where you go, I will go and where you stay, I will stay. Your people shall be my people and your God, my God. Where you die, I will die and there I will be buried. I swear a solemn oath before God: Nothing but death shall divide us.

Chorus: On they walked to Bethlehem city,
In need of charity, not wanting pity.
With downcast eyes, Ruth walked beside,

Her doubts and fears she tried to hide.

As they entered into the market square,
Naomi's friends spied her walking there.
She was surprised they even recognized
her,
For the years of sorrow had all but
disguised her.

Her friends all helped situate the two,
But they couldn't hang around,
they had so much to do.
Everyone was busy and with good
reason,
'Cause in Bethlehem it was harvest
season.

SCENE II: At the Market

(Several women of the chorus ascend to the stage and play the scene.)

Woman 1: Oh, Naomi — we're so happy you've come back.

Woman 2: It's been so long — we want to hear all about Moab — we've heard stories . . .

Woman 3: They are supposed to be barbarians there — I'd be so afraid.

Woman 4: No one knew if you were alive or dead — I mean, living in that place . . .

Naomi: I'll tell you all about my years in Moab — and of how God has seen fit to bring disaster on me. But first, I must secure a place to stay for me and my daughter-in-law Ruth.

Woman 1: We will help you, Naomi — you are one of us. We are happy to have you back.

Woman 2: And we will bring you food, too — until you have become established.

Woman 3: Thanks to the Almighty — we have

had plentiful harvests. Things have gone well with us the last several years here in Judah. We will help you. *(women return to chorus.)*

CHORUS: But they couldn't expect help forever,
They had to survive by their own
endeavor.
So Ruth went off to the fields to glean,
And while she was there — by Boaz
was seen.

SCENE III: In the Fields

(Boaz and a man enter from the audience and begin speaking as they are walking onto the stage.)

Boaz: Who is that dark haired young girl out there working so hard? I have not seen her before.

Man: She is a Moabitess who has just come back with Naomi. She even asked permission if she might glean in your fields, Boaz — and she has been on her feet with hardly a moment's rest from daybreak to now.

Boaz: Ah — I have heard the story of this young girl, who wishes herself an uncertain fate in a strange land rather than abandon her mother-in-law. Bring her over to me. *(The man brings Ruth over.)* Listen to me, my daughter, do not fear — you are welcome here. Do not go to any other field to glean. You may come here and gather all you can, and if you are thirsty, drink from the jars the men have filled.

Chorus: Assured was she of a safe surrounding,
With gratitude her heart was pounding.
And when she told Naomi where she
had been,
She learned that Boaz was her next of
kin.

SCENE IV: At Home

(Ruth and Naomi are stirring something in wooden bowls or looking otherwise occupied.)

Ruth: And he treated me so kindly — at first I was afraid, but he assured me that no one would harm me — and that I should return.

Naomi: I have been wondering why Boaz has not called on us to see if he could help us. I suppose he has been busy — but now I know the stories of his greatness and his generosity are true.

Ruth: The other girls speak of how rich he is, that he is practically the head of the whole city! He doesn't have to be so kind — and yet he is. *(They freeze in position as the chorus speaks.)*

CHORUS: Now ideas were rushing through Naomi's head,
Ruth needn't go gleaning — she could marry instead.
For she had the right as the law then read,
To ask her kin to take her to wed.
And ensure by a child that *Kaddish* is said,
For the husband she mourned — who lay in Moab — dead.

SCENE V: At Home

Naomi: Tonight after the harvest is finished, there will be a great party — eating and drinking and dancing — for everyone who worked. I want you to put on your best dress, fix your hair, and perfume yourself — then go to the party.

Ruth: Why? What do you want me to do? I will do anything you ask — but I do not understand.

Naomi: Because Boaz is next of kin, you have the right to ask him to do what the law requires. I must sell my parcel of land since I cannot work it — and I need the money to live — and you need a husband to care for you — to give you a child.

Ruth: But Boaz? I don't know . . . he is so important. Why should he do this for me?

Naomi: I have seen the way he looks at you — and I have heard the way he speaks of you — he thinks you are special. I don't think he will mind at all.

Ruth: He is the kindest man I know — but how far will his kindness reach? After all, if we have a son, it really will not be his, but will belong to your son, my first husband — to carry on his name among our people — as you have told me.

Chorus: So Ruth went off as she was told,
Feeling nervous and somewhat bold.
And when Boaz awoke during the night,
His eyes beheld a surprising sight.
Afraid to disturb him and being discreet,
Ruth was waiting silently at his feet.

He was greatly flattered at her request,
For of all the women — he thought her the best.
But someone was standing between Ruth and him,
Another relative who was closer in kin.
Boaz thought of a plan — told Ruth to wait,
And approached the man at the city gate.

SCENE VI: At the Gate

Boaz: Here — come here — it is I, your kinsman, Boaz! I must speak with you.

Man: Hello, Boaz. How are you? I hope your harvest was plentiful. What can I do for you?

Boaz: I have some business to discuss — I would like the elders of the city to stay and listen and bear witness. *(As Boaz says this in the direction of the chorus, they all come up onto the stage and gather around, reacting to the scene.)* Do you remember the field that belonged to our kinsman Elimelech?

Man: Yes — yes — a fine piece of land.

Boaz: Well, his widow Naomi wishes to sell. As the next of kin, it is your duty to buy the land. If you don't want it, then I will help Naomi out and buy it.

Man: Oh — no — no — it is a good piece of land. Ahem. I mean, I should do what is right — after all, as the next of kin . . .

Boaz: Of course, you know, along with the property comes the daughter-in-law — the Moabitess, Ruth. She is in need of a husband — and a child to carry on the name of her poor dead husband.

Man: Oh — well — I don't know — spend my money on the land — and then it won't really even be mine — but will belong to the sons of Ruth! I — uh — I don't think so — no — I cannot do this! I take off my shoe — *chalitzah* — *chalitzah!*

BOAZ: Don't worry, my friend — I will act as next of kin! You have all heard this — and are witnesses to it. I, Boaz, have accepted the duty of next of kin to Ruth, daughter-in-law of Naomi.

Chorus: Well, there was a wedding — and joy of joys,
Ruth and Boaz had a baby boy.
He brought great happiness and when he grew,
He married and had a boy child, too.

And this child, Jesse, also had a son,
and he grew up to be number one.
And of this great-grandson of Ruth we sing,
His name was David — a mighty king!

(Reprinted with permission of A.R.E. Publishing, Inc. from *Heroes, Heroines and Holidays* by Elaine Rembrandt.)

HALL OF JEWISH ADULTHOOD
Stan J. Beiner

CAST OF CHARACTERS
Guide
Assistant
Mr. Cohen
Mrs. Levin
Mr. Schwartz
Sammy
Molly
Docent
Contestant 1
Contestant 2
Contestant 3
Waitress

Guide: Right this way — watch your tootsies. Welcome to our tour of the Jewish Hall of Life. Today you will journey through the exotic world of the Jewish life cycle.

Assistant: Bask in the warmth of the baby naming . . . gasp at the drama of the *Brit Milah* . . . laugh with joy at the Bar and Bat Mitzvah ceremony . . . cry loving tears at the wedding . . . cry mournful tears at the divorce . . . and grab a tissue for the funeral.

Guide: Please be careful entering the gondolas. We sail down this canal to the birth ceremonies exhibit.

Mr. Cohen: Pardon me, Mr. Guide, but where are all those people going?

Assistant: Oh, they're not signed up for this tour.

Mr. Cohen: But they're so excited. Where are they going?

Guide: They're off to see our new exhibit.

It's called "Jewish Adulthood: The Emerging Frontier."

Mrs. Levin: Stop this gondola! I want to go there. I want to see the new exhibit.

Mr. Schwartz: Me, too. Brit Milah . . . been there, done that. I don't need to experience *that* again!

Sammy: Ah, Dad, come on. Adulthood is so lame. I want to go see a mohel at work.

Mr. Cohen: Bar Mitzvah . . . our son just went through that. Still paying off the caterer.

Mrs. Levin: Wedding . . . been there, done that . . . twice.

Molly: Mom, come on, let's go on this tour. I want to look at Bat Mitzvah dresses.

Assistant: Well, since most of the group wants to see the new exhibit — so be it.

Mrs. Cohen: Here we are. Hey, don't rock the gondola!

Mr.Schwartz: Look at this, they're raffling off a free night away from the kids.

Mrs. Cohen: I'll take 10 tickets.

Guide: Let's start our tour in this room. Welcome to "Jewish Adulthood: The Emerging Future."

Mrs. Cohen: What is this room?

Docent: This is the "Create Your Own Ceremony" room. As you know, the world today is quite complex, and Judaism has always been a responsive religion. In this room, we review all the new requests that come in and decide whether they will make the cut. Contestant number one, create your own ceremony.

Contestant 1: I call this the *Simchat Hochmah* Ceremony, and it was created to mark the milestone of reaching sixty years of age and having attained wisdom through my experiences. Part of the ritual includes wearing a shroud to symbolize coming to terms with mortality.

Mrs. Cohen: That's a cheerful celebration. What kind of food goes along with that kind of ceremony?

Molly: Probably prune juice, calcium, and lots of fiber.

Sammy: Don't forget the pills for lactose intolerance. And some tranquilizers.

Mrs. Cohen: That's another problem of adulthood. No respect.

Docent: Kids, respect your elders. *Kavod, kavod*— honor your parent.

Molly & Sammy: Yeah, right.

Docent: Our policy is to confiscate all CD players and walkmen from children who do not behave in the Hall of Jewish Adulthood.

Molly & Sammy: We're sorry, Mrs. Cohen. We didn't mean to be disrespectful.

Contestant 1: As I was saying, the *Simchat Hochmah* Ceremony is a liberating experience in which the title of "wise person" is bestowed upon the participant.

Docent: The judges vote "yes," and accept it. Next!

Contestant 2: I wrote a ceremony for paying off the mortgage on your house and having your kid get a full college scholarship. It's entitled *Simchat Oy I'm Glad That Monkey Is Off My Back.*

Docent: I'm sorry, but the judges say it's not a worthy ceremony. Although, *mazal tov* on your *mazal.* Next!

Contestant 3: I call this the Adult B'nai Mitzvah ceremony. It's for people who didn't have the ceremony as a child for one reason or another.

Docent: We approved that ceremony years ago. Lots of congregations are doing them.

Contestant 3: Mine's different. You have to learn the blessings in Hebrew.

Docent: Yes, I know. That ceremony already exists.

Contestant 3: Not only in Hebrew, also in Swahili.

Docent: Next!

Contestant 3: And Mandarin Chinese?

Docent: Next! Next!

Contestant 3: Can I at least get a consolation prize?

Guide: Perhaps it is time to move on. As

you can see, Jews are creatively involved in new rituals to commemorate important milestone events.

Contestant 3: How about an adult Confirmation class? A women's Rosh Chodesh group that meets at the start of the new Jewish month? A golden anniversary celebration?

Docent: Good ideas, but we already have these ceremonies. All right, here's a consolation prize, a year's supply of *kasha varnishkes.*

Assistant: Our next stop in the Hall of Jewish Adulthood will be the snack shop.

Sammy: Finally, a normal place in the grown-up village.

Molly: I know. This place is kind of creepy. If I hear one more parent whining about how expensive it is to raise a child, I'm going to freak.

Mr. Schwartz: *(to the waitress.)* What's good today?

Waitress: It depends on your life situation. I've got a sandwich special for adults who are parenting their parents and their kids. That's very popular.

Mrs. Cohen: What's this omelet using single slices of cheese.

Waitress: That's especially recommended for the large number of single Jewish adults. You put the cheese and eggs on two pieces of toast and hope they stick together.

Mr. Schwartz: I think I'll just have some coffee.

Waitress: With regular milk or half and half?

Mr. Schwartz: What's the difference?

Waitress: Regular is for the settled adult. Half and half is for those adults who are intermarried and trying to decide how to raise their children.

Sammy: Don't you have something normal . . . like pizza?

Waitress: Sure. It's our blended pizza. It's for the blended family that's trying to combine lots of different elements — children from the mom, children from the dad, half brothers, half sisters, step parents, step grandparents.

Molly: Actually, we were hoping for some pizza with extra cheese and veggies.

Guide: Thanks for the food for thought. Seeing how diverse the needs of Jewish adults are makes you realize that in the Jewish life cycle, you can't just jump from wedding to death.

Sammy: This place is bizarre.

Mrs. Cohen: Has anyone seen my dentures?

Sammy: Let's run for the nearest exit. This is scary.

Molly & Sammy: Aahhhhhhh.

Assistant: The Hall of Jewish Adulthood is now open. Feel free to wander around here. Be sure to try our gravity free room where you can feel what it's like to be isolated, without your family, and living in a brand new community.

Mr. Levin: I'm feeling a bit bewildered and overwhelmed.

Guide: Exactly! Welcome to the Hall of Jewish Adulthood!

THE DEATH OF MOSES – A DRAMATIC READING

By Rabbi Bruce Kadden, Based on the Midrash

Introduction

Sooner or later each of us must confront death. As much as we would like to avoid it, each time we read of death, each time we know someone who dies, we are confronted with our own mortality. And it is scary, in part because we do not know what awaits us following our life-long journey.

But we can learn about death and how to respond to it from our tradition. We can learn from what the Bible and Midrash teach us about the most dramatic death in Jewish history: the death of Moses.

Imagine that you are an Israelite who has journeyed through the wilderness, and are now at the edge of the Promised Land. Moses, your leader, has just left to ascend Mt. Nebo, where he is to die. As you watch him walk slowly up the mountain, you wonder what is going through his mind and what he is feeling. It might have been something like this:

★ ★ ★

(Slowly raising head from chest to heaven, with outstretched hands) Ribono Shel Olam, Sovereign of the Universe, it has been almost forty years since you decreed that I will not lead this people into the Promised Land. I have led the people and repented during this long journey. Leading the people has been my repentance.

During these forty years, how often did Israel sin? Yet, whenever I prayed for them, You withheld the punishment. Now I pray to You on my behalf: accept my prayer, grant me life, permit me to lead Israel into the land. I will draw a circle, and stand inside *(Goes through the motions.)*, and I won't move from here until You suspend Your decree and let me live. O Lord of the world, I suffered when Israel suffered. Don't I have the right to take part in her rejoicing? I shared in my people's pain; why can't I share in its good fortune?

I know that I sometimes disappointed You: when I questioned whether I was capable of leading My people out of Egypt; when Pharaoh made us work harder, I blamed You; when at times I doubted Your power; when I insulted Your people Israel, calling them rebels when they gave me a bad time.

Yes, all of this I did. But how often did Israel sin before You? You split the Reed Sea and they doubted You. You provided water in the desert and they doubted You. You fed them with manna, and still they doubted You. You answered my prayers, forgiving them of all these sins. What are my sins compared to theirs? And yet You refuse to forgive me?

Sovereign of the World: I don't want to die. What good am I dead? Alive, I lead your people. Alive, I praise you. Alive, I bear witness to You and Your words. I beseech You, grant me life that I may praise You to all the inhabitants of the earth. Who will tell them that You divided the Sea of Reeds? Who will tell them that You gave the Torah to Israel? Who will tell them that You led Israel for 40 years in the desert and brought them into the Promised Land?

I know what You are thinking. No one has ever received such honor and distinction as I have. That should be enough. But it isn't. All of that is meaningless in the face of death. I would give up all the honor, all the privileges, all the prestige. I would give it all up for the gift of life.

You are a God of justice and a God of mercy. Allow your mercy to respond to my prayer. Didn't You hearken to my prayer when Israel committed the terrible sin of worshiping the golden calf? You said, "Let Me alone so I may destroy them."

If the prayer of one man can save the community, can't the prayer of the community save one man? Hear my cry, O God . . .

Remember when you told me to save Israel from the hands of the Egyptians? I said that I couldn't do it because I had promised Jethro, my father-in-law, that I wouldn't leave him. You released me from that vow. Wouldn't it be just as easy for You to break *Your* vow and allow me to enter the land of Israel? And if You don't want me to enter Israel as the leader of my people, let me at least enter as a common citizen. And if You don't want me to go with this people, permit me to go on my own. And if I must die here, at least allow my bones to be carried across the Jordan to be buried in the Promised Land.

Could that really be such a problem? Would it change the destiny of nations if I lived?

I know. I know what you said to Adam. You gave him a simple commandment — don't eat fruit from the tree of knowledge of good and evil. Such a simple request, and yet he disobeyed. I have not transgressed any of Your commandments, even the most difficult to keep, and yet I, too, must suffer the same fate as Adam. I could understand it if I had transgressed or disobeyed, but I have not.

I want to believe that You are a just God, that you have mercy upon all Your creations. You forgive a person who sins once, twice, even three times, but You won't even forgive a single sin of mine? Is this justice?

Yes, You gave me more honor than I could ever measure. The entire world knows that You are the one God, the only one, that there is none beside You, and none like You. You created everything, from the stars in the sky to the plants of the earth.

Don't tell me that it is better to die here than in the land of Israel. Don't tell me about all the honor awaiting me in the world to come. And don't tell me that though I will be gone, my memory will remain forever. I don't want to hear these promises. They mean nothing to me now. Understand me; I beg You, listen to my prayer.

And if You won't listen to my prayer, won't You at least listen to the prayers of some of your greatest creations?

Listen to the earth. *(Looking downward.)* O earth, I beg you: demand God's mercy for me. Perhaps for your sake God will take pity upon me and let me enter the land of Israel.

(Looking upward.) O heavens, ask God to deal mercifully with me. Maybe God will listen to you and permit me to cross the Jordan with my people.

(Pause.) O God, You won't listen to my prayers. Your first creations, the heaven and the earth, refuse to pray on my behalf. So, too, the sun and moon, the stars and planets, mountains and rivers. Won't anyone stand with me and challenge the Holy One of Israel. Doesn't anyone believe that death is wrong, and that I deserve to live?

Joshua, you showed your faith in God when you told us we should settle the land of Canaan. You said it was flowing with milk and honey, and you brought back fruit from its trees to prove it. Remember, Joshua, how I treated you day and night, teaching you laws and customs, arts and sciences.

Oh Joshua, it hurts me to see you weep bitterly. I'm sorry that I asked you to plead for me. I was wrong to expect you to oppose God's command. Oh, Joshua, I hope you understand . . .

I must face it. God has determined that I may not enter the land of Israel. The time has come for my disciple Joshua to step forward and lead the people into the land.

Hear ye, O people of Israel. Moses stands at Joshua's gate, and announces that whoever wishes to hear God's word should approach Joshua, for he now is the leader of Israel.

Joshua, I have come to serve you. Don't be ashamed that I, whom you once served, now serves you. Fear not; just as I was once your master, it is now only proper that you are my master. You must now precede me for all the people to see.

(Pointing outward.) Look, look at the sun come over the horizon. I never noticed it before. How astonishing! How beautiful. I shall never see it rise again, for today, the seventh of Adar, I shall die. God has already ordered the sun not to set as long as I remain alive. But I have much work ahead of me: thirteen scrolls of the Torah to write: one for each of the twelve tribes and one for the Holy Ark. I must also honor Joshua so the people of Israel will know that he is to succeed me.

(Pause.) What, can it be? The sun is already overhead. Only a half day remains. Sovereign of the Universe, listen, just once more, to my plea. I am more than willing to give up my role as leader of this people. I will be Joshua's student and he will be my teacher. Or if that's not acceptable, use Your power to make me into a fish. Transform my two arms to fins and my hair to scales so that I will be able to leap over the Jordan and see the land of Israel. If this is not possible, let me fly like a bird so that I may see the land of milk and honey. And if this is not possible, then cut me up limb by limb and throw me over the Jordan. Then revive me that

I might see the land. Certainly there must be some way I can catch a glimpse of the Holy Land?

(Lifting his head.) What's this? Has my prayer been granted? It is as if the land were before my eyes. Four hundred square miles and yet I can see it as if it were just a few feet away. Yet, if I reach to touch it . . . I grasp only air.

I see the valleys and hills, the streams and seas, I see all of Israel's history: the Judges and Kings and foreign rulers who will shape Israel's future. I see everything. Joshua destroying the walls of Jericho, Solomon's Temple, the last stand at Masada, even in the distant future a Jewish state again.

Oh, how you tempt me. If you won't allow me to enter the land, at least let me remain on this side of the river and witness Israel's history. Allow me to see the Temple being built and a Jewish state being founded.

Only two hours left to plea and avert the sentence of death. Almighty God, even if You don't let me enter the land, let me live and not die. This is all I request. Is it too much? Then let me live like the beasts of the field which feed on herbs and drink water, let me live and see the world: let me be as one of these.

But no, the decree is final. And now, as the remaining minutes pass, I must carry on the tradition of blessing my children, the people of Israel.

O God, bless the tribes of Israel: Reuben and Judah, Simeon and Levi, Benjamin, Joseph, and Zebulun, Issachar, Gad, Dan, Naphtali, and Asher. Happy are you, Israel! Who is like you, a people saved by God, the shield of your help?

And now that I have blessed you, O Israel, I cannot depart without asking your forgiveness. You have had much to bear from me in regard to the fulfillment of the Torah and its commandments, but please forgive me now, and please, when you enter the land of Israel, remember me.

Do not fear that you will not survive without me. God, who lives and endures to all eternity, will be with you. And if you have faith, God will perform your desires. Don't put your trust in princes or kings; put your trust in God, who created the world.

Dwell in peace, O Israel. We shall meet again.

And now, I see my time is at an end. I have begged, pleaded, and prayed . . . all in vain. Your will be done. My soul shall reluctantly depart from my body, but not . . until I say: *Sh'ma Yisrael Adonai Elohaynu, Adonai Echad.*

CREATING JEWISH RITUALS
Patricia Karlin-Neumann

Recent years have seen an explosion of new Jewish rituals. From mimeographed rituals to xeroxed rituals to desktop published rituals to rituals which have been performed but not recorded, the willingness to capture the large and small moments of our lives through ritual has become part of the landscape of Jewish life. Whereas once the creation of new ritual was both daring and rare, now the practice of creating new rituals with fragments of a tradition seems, if not commonplace, scarcely outrageous.

Why are so many Jews creating new rituals? Rabbi Laura Geller, one of the first women Rabbis, tells about her epiphany at Hebrew Union College when one of her teachers said, "There are no important moments in a Jew's life for which there is not a blessing," and, daydreaming, Laura started cataloguing all the moments in her life which had gone unmarked.

Rabbi Margaret Holub shares a story from the book *To Dance with God* by Gertrude Mueller Nelson about a two-year-old who had outgrown his crib. When he protested at the idea of giving it up, his mother devised a ritual for this transition. She made a special dinner; the whole family talked about his crib, how sad it would be to see it go, and how exciting it would be to move to the new stage of sleeping in a "big boy bed." They all lovingly took the crib apart, made the bed up with linens the boy had chosen, said his prayers, and tucked him in.

This description of a ritual moment, this acknowledgment of a moment of transition, touched Margaret deeply. "How different my childhood, indeed my adulthood would be, if people around me valued and marked the things that I think are important," she has written ("Ritual: The Next Phase," unpublished).

Rituals of the kitchen and bedroom variety and rituals of the religious variety are an integral part of human experience. For those who live in Jewish rhythms, the desire to mark those occasions of importance, of transition, with rituals which affirm both our individual and our communal life, has prompted us to invention.

Ritual and liturgy are analogous to sign language.

One who is deaf has as much desire to communicate as one who hears, but often needs sign language to do so. Similarly, ritual and liturgy become tools for communicating meaning. For the language of ritual to serve the purpose of communication, there must be those who share and can use its tools and those who receive and understand the messages.

In doing Jewish ritual, we are attempting to etch Jewish meanings into the lives and souls and bodies of Jews. Ritual both gives people access to Judaism, and shapes their sense of themselves as Jews. In the atomized modern world in which we live, rituals place the individual in community, in continuity. Rituals create a place.

Few people have taught the Jewish community as much about valuing ritual and story as Barbara Myerhoff, *zichronah livrachah,* author of *Number Our Days,* a sensitive and profound study of the elderly Jews of Venice. She once said, "Ritual is the enactment of a wish. It is the display of a state of mind. And above all, it is a performative enterprise. It is made up of symbols, almost always that deal with ambiguities or paradoxes. Something irresolvable. Change, chaos, disruption. It handles these chaotic elements by being sensory and very concrete, and also by being rhetorical . . . Ritual subverts, undermines the cognitive and critical faculties . . . and glosses the contradictions and paradoxes. In ritual, it is the doing that is the believing. And the doer, being your own body, is singularly persuasive, because it is your own experience which finally persuades you.

"Ritual makes things sacred. It sets them apart. It sanctifies them by announcing and calling attention to their specialness. Ritual is formalized, stylized, artificial" ("Sanctifying Women's Lives through Ritual," unpublished).

We create ritual, then, to ennoble the everyday. Doing ritual is, at base, a Jewish enterprise, complementing the tradition of praising God with one hundred *brachot* a day, of noticing and calling attention to what is around us. Yet, having lost so much of daily practice, and living in the contemporary world, it becomes necessary to reconstruct or invent.

How do we know when an occasion demands a ritual? Is every moment equally filled with possibility? If, as Barbara Myerhoff claims, rituals help us deal with chaos or change or ambiguities, any moment of liminality, of transition from one world to another, calls out to be marked. There are many ways to make this mark, to honor the transition. We might create a new ritual or use an old one in a new way. We might create a synagogue ceremony or a private meditation. We might write a new *brachah* or use traditional ones in ways they were not originally intended.

Modern rituals give us some sense of where people feel the blank spaces were in their lives: aging, marriage, separation, divorce, pregnancy, choices about childbirth, nursing, weaning, infertility, giving a baby up for adoption, pregnancy loss, menstruation, death, Rosh Chodesh, and holidays. Barbara Myerhoff suggests that rituals are necessary in those places where we usually suffer alone: surgery, menopause, retirement, empty nest, and loss. Esther Broner, author of *The Telling: A Weave of Women* and *Her Mothers,* and perhaps the most prolific creator of Jewish rituals, says that her best customers are people with broken hearts ("Sanctifying Women's Lives through Rituals" unpublished).

Rabbi Debra Orenstein adds to the list: completing a creative project, becoming a grandparent, forgiving yourself for a sin you have committed, celebrating a time of family closeness, first love, first sex, first apartment, planning a wedding, publishing a book, deciding to leave a lover, coming out as a lesbian or a gay man, acknowledging that someone you love is terminally ill, leaving a batterer, reconciling with someone from whom you have been estranged, making *aliyah,* recovering from an addiction, healing from sexual abuse, and cooking a special family dish with your bubbe's recipe *(Lifecycles: Jewish Women on Life Passages and Personal Milestones, Vol. 1).*

I offer this list because I am concerned that we sometimes limit creative rituals to the biological events, particularly in women's lives, which have not been marked. There is a paradox in women creating ritual for biological moments. Women bristle at being tied only to biology; yet, there is a need to sanctify in a Jewish way what our bodies experience. Rachel Adler cautions that "Creating religious metaphors solely out of our biological experience will tend to make us womanists rather than Jews" (*Face to Face,* Spring, 1981).

Women have been the primary initiators of creative ritual. As people who have felt, like Barbara Myerhoff, an inevitable sense of exclusion, women have found a connection back to the tradition in large measure, by invention. Because women have not traditionally lived our lives in the public Jewish sphere, women have honored the private realm by sharing it with others through ritual.

Yet, in contrast to T. S. Eliot who wrote, "Birth, copulation and death, that's all, that's all, that's all," not only those marginal, but those enfranchised also experience a great deal of contemporary life which the tradition does not address. As Rabbi Debra Orenstein suggests, "Women's perspectives will call attention to forgotten or neglected issues, broaden Jewish thinking and practice, re-open basic questions from a new vantage point. When we ask, 'What does it mean for a woman . . . to wrestle with aspects of the tradition from which she is alienated?,' we eventually apply the same quesiton to men, and then to Jews, and still further down the line we get to core questions about God and learning and a holy tradition that has been both shaped and muddled by human hands" ("Women and Jewish Lifecycle: Bridging 'Real Life,' Academics and Popular Literature," unpublished).

When my mother died, I began asking all my observant women friends, "How do Jewish women mourn their mothers?" I was answered with the silence of the tradition. Whatever rituals had been performed hadn't been passed down. My dear friend and teacher, playwright Merle Feld, told me to be idiosyncratic. She gave me permission to create a ritual for this moment of transition.

My mother was an expert knitter. Before she died, I brought knitting needles and yarn to her in the hospital so that she could knit a baby bunting for the child we had not yet conceived. She died unable to knit the bunting. I began to think about my mother's knitting, of her having taught me to knit — part of her Torah — and I decided to knit the baby bunting I had urged on her and say *"Kaddish D'Rabbanan,"* originally said following Torah study in someone's honor, each morning. As I knit with yarn, I knit memory, and during that year I came to make peace with who my mother was, and what her legacy is. I also came to know that life is finite, and realized that it was time to become a mother myself. At our daughter's *Brit*

Bat (Covenant of the Daughter ceremony) I gave her the completed bunting, a gift of the journey from death to life.

As a Jewish ritual, this was idiosyncratic, healing, innovative, and traditional. The form was determined by the tradition. The content was determined by the needs which the tradition didn't address.

I became a mother the same week I became an orphan. Being the link between the generation before me and the generation after me has had a profound impact on how I experience Judaism. It has given me an urgent desire that the stream which flows through and nourishes the next generation will be watered by previous ones. This makes me a conservative innovator. I want the Judaism which I share with my children to be recognizable to my parents.

Rituals which resonate with the tradition allow us to enter into a timeless stream. They invite us into the eternal. Sheryl Robbin wrote an essay entitled "Hands," in which she describes the considerable and solitary preparations she makes for Shabbat late Thursday night in her kitchen. While she makes dishes her foremothers would not have known and uses her Cuisinart to create them, she feels "an eternity beyond time as strong as the ageless communion we invoke when engrossed in prayer." She invites the women before her into her kitchen with her work, work which she understands as *avodah,* "the sacrifice that women have offered through the centuries" (*Tikkun,* July/August, 1991).

These kitchen rituals are also part of our repertoire, the rituals of placing ourselves in Jewish time, of living by Jewish rhythms, of using Jewish language to sanctify the experience of the moment. For ritual to be Jewish, it needs to partake of our rhythms, our language, to tie the participants more fully to a stream of tradition, to a community of memory, which belongs to all of us.

Esther Broner reminds us that "the words ritual and rite and rhythm and arithmetic all have the same root. And Jews always ask the same question regarding roots, 'Are they Jewish?'" ("Sanctifying Women's Lives through Ritual," unpublished). Rabbi Debra Orenstein insists on grappling with the tradition in creating Jewish rituals, and, even in the case of what I call "protest rituals," the very process ties one more fully to Judaism. "It is important to engage the tradition in a real dia-

logue . . . I would not want to see new rituals without also seeing a thorough and profound consideration of traditional sources, lacunae in those sources, new visions and understanding of the tradition, the process of struggling with the tradition, the use of old texts in new ways, the creation of new texts that is somehow in keeping with ancient themes and methods . . . It is crucial to develop an understanding of the tradition on its own terms. At the same time, it is vital to explicate and model the methods by which we may choose to interpret it anew and/or to transform it" ("Issues to Consider in the Creation of Effective and Convincing Ritual," unpublished).

For a ritual to work, it needs to resonate, to draw on, and allude to traditional texts, symbols, and stories, but, as Rabbi Orenstein cautions, it should not "explain itself to death." Good rituals tread a fine line between being particular and being general. Rituals should be grounded in the personal experience and thoughts of its creators, but should be meaningful to those outside the circle where they originated.

Anthropologists identity three stages of ritual: a stage of separation from one's previous status, a stage of transition, and a stage of re-embodiment and incorporation. A ritual which works creates a sense of this transformation. Effective rituals transform the community as well as the individual. As Rabbi Orenstein writes, "Lifecycle events and categories define both personal and communal status . . . What event is more private and more public than a funeral? Effective ritual should never ignore the communal in pursuing the personal. Convincing ritual asserts the integrity of individual and communal life by reflecting forward and backward. Thus we name children after relatives who have died, and at the same time pray for their arrival at the chuppah, and, implicitly, the arrival of still the next generation" ("Issues to Consider in the Creation of Effective and Convincing Ritual" unpublished). Convincing ritual draws on the senses, addresses a multiplicity of concerns, and grounds the participants in the sacred.

Many Rabbis have an instinctual sense of how to create ritual which works. So do many lay people, who are sometimes less encumbered by the do's and don'ts of Jewish tradition. They are sometimes able to bridge the personal and communal with less self consciousness than Rabbis. At times, it is the laity's very yearning to enter the stream of tradition which gives power to ritual.

However, we must always be aware that rituals can be discreet moments with fleeting transformations. While rituals are powerful, they take most fully when the participants are rooted in community, in a tradition of meaning. Creating a ritual is not as simple as following a recipe and taking the finished product out of the oven.

Barbara Myerhoff teaches that a "ritual is an occasion when one takes the chaos within the world and within oneself and pours it into a vessel that gives it shape and gives it order and power and form. A meaning-making activity. Ritual makes authoritative and sacred and axiomatic that which it treats . . ." ("Sanctifying Women's Lifes through Ritual," unpublished).

This can be a breathtaking power, literally the power to make Jews. We who are grounded in Judaism, who live with the power of its reach in our lives, who have the symbols, the texts, the language and the strength of the tradition in our marrow have a central place in the energy and excitement of Jews claiming Judaism for their own. May we celebrate our place and rejoice in our time.

THE SPIRITUALITY OF RITUAL

Rabbi Raymond A. Zwerin

Of all the behaviors available to us humans, religious ritual is certainly among our most spiritual acts. Ritual is an odd subject because, until very recently it was thought to be such a private matter — a topic for the home and the religious institution. Rarely was it a topic for public discussion, much less the subject of intellectual scrutiny. Those who engage in ritual behavior rarely give what they do much thought — they just do it. Those who do not engage in ritual behavior also rarely give it much thought — they just avoid doing it.

In a study published by the Center for Family Research of George Washington University, St. Louis, Steven Wolin and Linda Bennett made some interesting findings. They noted that families which use rituals of whatever kind as a means of passing on rules of behavior, expectations, and family history create children who are likely to be more resilient as adults.

They studied 240 students entering college and 70 of their parents and found that "the more meaningful that family rituals were thought to be, the more positive that student's sense of self, and the better able the freshman is at adapting to the stresses of college."

Incredibly, in families of alcoholics where there was some ongoing daily ritual as a family, the offspring were found to be less likely, by a dramatic margin, to become alcoholics.

And, in individuals, rituals viewed as being important are shown to lower levels of anxiety dramatically and to lessen chronic stress. Therefore, the researchers were quick to point out, how sad it is to see that such core family rituals as dinner together and bedtime reading and family outings are disappearing because of the time demands of jobs, the increase in single parent families where one parent hasn't the energy at day's end to fully engage the children, and, of course, the shrinking paycheck.

What is ritual; what do we mean by the term? That's not an easy question, because ritual is a fairly elusive concept. There is, of course, a great difference between *actual ritual* and merely *ritualized actions*. Ritualized actions are behavioral mannerism, tension relievers, or superstitious quirks which we all have — avoiding black cats and leaning ladders, or knocking on wood or saying *"kee ain eyin hara."* Ritualized actions are the sort of thing a baseball player does when coming to bat — a tug on the cap, knocking dirt out of cleats, or grabbing the bat at both ends and rolling it back over the head. Such mannerisms are transitory or they are habits much as lighting up after dinner or checking hair and lipstick in a mirror for the umpteenth time. Such ritualized actions neither elevate nor transcend; they neither mark a particularly memorable moment nor do they connect us with one another.

Actual rituals, however, have a certain power all their own. Authentic rituals communicate values. So, when before a ball game or a session of Congress or in a schoolroom or at a public meeting we stand for the "Pledge of Allegiance" or the "National Anthem" we are saying that the principles of our country are important to us.

Rituals also foster identity. So, when we look forward to fireworks or a picnic on the 4th of July, or when we share a Thanksgiving day turkey with family and friends, or when we plan a last few days of vacation together on Labor Day weekend, we say a lot about who we are in relation to the country in which we live.

Some rituals can promote health and healing. Physical exercise, a few moments of meditation, prayers before sleep and during difficult times in one's life . . . are certainly beneficial to body and mind.

Ritual can relieve tensions between people. Socially agreed upon behaviors — rituals — can take the guesswork out of what is expected and what is not acceptable. Proof, if such is needed, was the simple matter of the handshake in 1993 between Rabin and Arafat — old enemies standing side-by-side on the White House lawn. That ritual gesture was as important to the moment as the signing of the papers. Such ritualized proprieties can relieve social anxieties and serve as "safety valves" for potential flash points in interpersonal relationships. That's why people from different cultures can have such a difficult time relating to one another at first — they don't know each other's ritualized mores.

Some rituals can promote family and group bonds or even establish household traffic patterns. So, when family traditions develop around the celebration of birthdays and anniversaries, they serve to bond us. And perhaps less dramatic, but just as significant, is the morning "do-si-do" of family members scurrying from bed to bath to breakfast to bye-bye out the door. Then there is the controlled pandemonium of getting children ready for bedtime, or of getting everyone ready for an outing or a party or for company or for a holiday or a life cycle celebration — household members act and maneuver in a sort of expected and anticipated symphony . . . within defined patterns and behavioral parameters . . . which, in time, are set and, over time, are ritualized — rehearsed again and again.

Some rituals are merely symbolic — public expressions of life passages. We don't really benefit from graduation exercises; the diploma could more easily be sent by mail. But still, the ritual persists. International diplomacy is suffused with ritual and so are initiations into clubs, fraternities, or sororities. Being introduced to one another, testifying in court, and being inducted into military service or into public office are all well known and well rehearsed rituals. Even asking for one's hand in marriage is ritualized in the ideal — kneeling, asking, and presenting the ring.

The research shows that families and members of those families with a *low* commitment to meaningful and appropriate rituals have certain traits in common:
- they tend to be oriented solely in the present;
- they tend to have less precise generational boundaries so that the parent-child hierarchy is out of kilter;
- they tend to have less attachment to ethnic or religious or community groups;
- they tend to see their small nuclear family group as the sum total of what family is all about;
- they tend to feel that there is no power behind the few rituals they do share so that, in time, all their rituals fade away;
- and, perhaps even more revealing, individuals raised in such families tend to have a minimal sense of identity with their family group — especially if there are crises — then they tend to disconnect and simply go their separate ways.

Typical comments by such family members comes from a mother of five who said: "I don't think we've done anything together as a family except sleep under the same roof," and "I don't really even know these people." Therefore, families without ritual in their home tend to be if not dysfunctional, at least disconnected and isolated and dispassionate about one another.

The research done by Wolin and Bennett is truly ground breaking. Households without a sense of ritual . . . without shared activities that give structure to the values, the celebrations, and the routines of daily life tend, in time, to disintegrate! Families (including even two people households in which there are no children) without definite, structured, defined ritual tend to fall apart. In the context of what we see in society today, which families do survive intact, and which do not? Which families have a sense of inter-generational structure, and which do not? Astoundingly, the implication is, that even for a couple without children, a lack of meaningful ritual in their relationship tends to put the relationship at risk.

For thousands of years, the Jewish family has been the prototype, the model, the paradigm of what family is all about. Even in this day and age of fragmentation and family dissipation, non-Jews still express amazement at how close-knit Jewish families seem to be and how close-knit we are as a people. This positive stereotype, while a bit tarnished, is still true today in comparison to society in general. We Jews, of course, take it all for granted. We rationalize or we assume that our family stability is a result of centuries of persecution, or of ghettoization and/or of isolation, or of a guilt-producing gene found especially in Jewish mothers.

The more we reflect on what in the past has enabled Jews to create strong family bonds, the more reasonable it is to deduce that it has little to do with isolation and guilt and much to do with our commitment to Jewish ritual. I know of no other people, no other heritage, no other religion that puts such emphasis on rituals performed in the home. But not just ritual for the purpose of random activity — ritual that elevates and ennobles and teaches values along the way. And we Jews sort of take for granted what we have done as a matter of course for milenia.

But just because our tradition encourages and allows and proffers rituals in abundance . . . if we don't accept them and incorporate them into our lives, it is as if they never existed at all. For a lost treasure or an unappreciated treasure is, in reality, no treasure at all.

Jewish ritual has power — spiritual power. It feeds the subconscious mind and prepares us to meet the world with optimism. It connects us to this world and protects us against a sense of existential loneliness and uncertainty so prevalent in society today. It opens us to possibilities beyond the mundane, enabling us to see that there is more to life than buying and selling, working and playing. And Jewish ritual transmits the shared beliefs of family members across generational lines. It enables us to celebrate time and space — something that can't be done without ritual and, something that without doing, makes being a Jew somewhat irrelevant.

In general, observing rituals tends to put life in perspective; it slows us down; it enables us to appreciate life; it connects us to ourselves. Observing certain ritual behaviors, such as meditation or prayer tends to lower levels of anxiety. Studies conducted years ago showed that those who attended worship services regularly had fewer signs of stress, were less likely to suffer from severe headaches, and lived longer. The studies seem to show that ritual observances tend to evoke a sense of stability in life; they serve as a dependable anchor amidst a sea of change.

Now, at this point, I could simply affirm the message that ritual is good for all of us and encourage all to . . . go do it! But that would hardly satisfy the thrust of this paper. Instead, let me take the research a step further and apply it to Jewish life. If research shows that ritual is beneficial, then Jewish ritual "Al achat kamah v'chamah" — "is even more so!" And as if to emphasise the point, I would like to suggest that there are at least five

gifts that Jewish rituals bestow upon Jewish families and upon individual Jews who bring them into their homes and into their lives. And that the benefits derived from such rituals are spiritual in nature.

First of all, unlike any other forms of ritual, Jewish ritual serves as a bridge enabling us to connect our present . . . our here and now . . . to both the past and to the future of our people.

Think about it. When we sit with Haggadah in hand at the Seder table, we remember that we were once slaves in a strange land, and we were redeemed from that terrible time and place. As we rehearse that simple story and embellish it with song and blessings and readings, we cannot help but be transformed. At that moment, we become those Jews in Egypt departing for the Sinai Desert. And as our "now" and that "then" become one, we also realize that we will not be slaves again. That value has become a part of our collective psyche. That value informed us to get our people out of the former USSR and out of Ethiopia, and out of Syria, and Yemen, and Iran. Slaves no more to no one! The message of the Seder pulses in us because we have ritualized it — we have rehearsed it again and again in our homes and in our hearts.

Through Jewish ritual, present, and future unite. When grandparents of a Bar/Bat Mitzvah are called to the Torah they stand next to their grandchild and recite words of blessing — it is a moment of poignant transcendence. And when the Sandak holds his eight day old grandson at the *brit milah* while his son, the new father, recites the blessing, it is not just three generations present, but dozens and hundreds of generations standing together in that place at that moment.

Jewish ritual opens us to possibilities we could not otherwise experience. For implied at the *Brit Milah* ceremony, as he is at each Seder, is Elijah the Prophet with his hidden whisper-promise that this new infant could redeem humankind. No other people has as its prime religious goal a world of peace for all humanity. But, we Jews take that for granted, as if it is a little thing . . . nothing really, just a commonplace thought — the redemption of all peoples everywhere. But we should not be so casual — it is not to be taken for granted.

That the welfare of men and women everywhere is in our prayers and in our hearts . . . that is the stuff of grandeur and nobility. That is what makes our heritage unique and uniquely spiritual.

Second, Jewish ritual enables us to celebrate time.

Celebrate time — that's what we are commanded to do. We are enjoined to put time into perspective — to distinguish between time which is for work, *mundane time*, and time which is significant, *time made holy*.

Jewish life is all about time. To be a Jew is to make time sacred. That's what we do when we celebrate Rosh HaShanah or Yom Kippur or the first and last days of the Festivals or each and every Shabbat — we sanctify that time. Sacred time is time without tools, time without labor, time for re-creating the mind and the spirit, time without enslavement, time in which ritual becomes preeminent. No other religion does this. It is a concept totally foreign to others. For non-Jews, a holiday might begin or end in a house of worship, but the after-worship hours are no different from any other hours in the year. Aside from its religious content, Christmas has the same holiness as a birthday or as Labor Day or as Martin Luther King day. It's a national observance, a paid holiday, but it is not sacred time.

Non-Jewish holidays have with rare exception no observance strictures. Like any other day, non-Jewish holidays are an opportunity to drive, play football, smoke, carry on in any and every way just as if it was any other time of the year — except for whatever worship one may participate in, of course.

To many of our non-Jewish neighbors, a holiday, *as a period of time*, is simply a day off; it is not sacred time. It's vacation, not vocation. And that's why non-Jews can be understandably insensitive to Jewish holidays — it's not a matter of anti-Semitism so much as it is unintelligible to them. They simply have no parallel in their religion. They have no way of understanding the basic concept of sacred time. So what if soccer tournaments or high school proms are held on Friday nights, or exams or airport dedications are scheduled on Yom Kippur!

Time without boundaries is like a train without stations — a journey without markings along the way. Without boundaries we cannot fully appreciate the journey — we cannot put time in perspective. If we cannot appreciate time, we cannot live fully in it, nor reverence it, nor celebrate it. Jewish ritual helps us to establish the boundaries. To forget to make times sacred is to give up one of the principal spiritual gifts of our tradition. Judaism offers us the sacredness of time. It is ours alone to enjoy and to savor . . . holy days and Sabbaths . . . whole periods of time . . . entire days . . . to make special . . . to turn into spiritual moments.

Third, Jewish ritual connects us to our place in the world. It teaches us to make space holy.

One cannot read the prayer book or study Torah without knowing beyond a shadow of a doubt that we belong in this world! In Torah, we are taught 39 times, be kind to the stranger because you were once strangers in Egypt. Once upon a time, yes . . . but no longer . . . not now you aren't strangers . . . no longer will you be strangers . . . never again will you be strangers . . . no siree. We are not strangers . . . others are. We are the ultimate non-strangers in this world of ours! We of all peoples belong here.

Every blessing we recite reinforces the fact that a Jew belongs to this world. Before reading Torah we say: ". . . Blessed are You, *Adonai* our God, who has called us from among all other peoples and has given us Your Torah . . ." We are *mitzvah* doers. No one else, just Jews, because we are the only people to accept Torah as the basis of ethical and religious laws. Without Torah there are no *mitzvot*. Do not misunderstand. A non-Jew can be a wonderful, kind, caring, even saintly-type person without Torah. A non-Jew can do wonderful, noble, caring, generous things without Torah. But, by definition, a non-Jew cannot not be a doer of *mitzvot* because he or she did not receive Torah, therefore, he or she was not elected to be . . . was not commanded to be . . . a *mitzvah* doer.

We belong here because we're the *mitzvah* people. Regardless of how many of us or how few of us there are in this world of ours, we're absolutely necessary to this world. In fact, the world can't exist without us. A government that gets rid of its Jews, dies. It's as simple as that. It's a historical fact. It has happened to each and every country in history. And a country which is open to Jews prospers. Don't ask me why; ask God. Read the history books; maybe it's because of our rituals . . . and the doing of *mitzvot*?! Torah implies it; the prophets say it directly; the Talmud doesn't doubt it. So, who am I to argue?

We Jews tend to take Jewish rituals, even simple rituals, such as blessing food for granted. And yet simple blessings tell us again and again how much we belong here: "Blessed are You, *Adonai* our God . . . who brings forth bread for us to eat . . . wine for us to drink . . . light for us to enjoy . . ." Even in the simple blessings the message is clear — this is God's world and ours . . . and we are to enjoy it and partake of its bounty . . . and we absolutely belong here.

Even our doorposts bear the symbol of God's presence in our homes. So each time we enter or leave our homes, to kiss the *mezuzah* is to reaffirm that we as a people are . . . as if . . . God's *mezuzah* on the doorposts of the world. And one need not read too far in Torah before coming upon the divine promise to give us a land flowing with milk and honey . . . it shall be yours forever so long as you keep and renew my Covenant . . . it is your eternal inheritance, regardless of who shares it with you. Another affirmation of our place in the world. Can you imagine how much mental illness could be avoided if all peoples everywhere knew without a doubt that they belonged in this world of ours . . . that they were necessary to this world?

To be a Jew is to celebrate space. That is our faith statement. We believe in sanctifying space. Think about it for a moment. Most churches are faith oriented. Yes, they may for sure have a social action agenda . . . a good works component . . . but, by and large, for most, *belief* is their path to divine rewards. Their path to heaven is in the mind. And if that is what they choose to espouse, that's fine with me. I would be the last to tell non-Jews how to think, feel, or pray. But within the context of Judaism that concept simply makes no sense. Why should God care a wit what one believes or what one thinks? People have little control over many of the thoughts that blink in and out. Are we to be morally responsible for every random mental synapse? And if belief and thought were the keys to the kingdom, so to speak, why create the body altogether? For what do we need hands and feet and senses if belief and

thought were all that mattered? Just create us as minds perched on plastic poles — "brainsicles" — and wait to see what we think and believe!?

Instead, we Jews are a deed oriented people; we maintain that we are judged by our acts not our thoughts. In the context of Jewish thought, one can not sin in the mind. We can't even begin to understand what Jimmy Carter meant when he confessed to "lusting in his heart." That is a foreign concept . . . out of the realm of Jewish thought. But we can be judged remiss if we act improperly or if . . . even worse, we don't act at all. And that is supremely, uniquely Jewish. We are enjoined not to stand idly by the blood of our neighbor. We are not a folded arms people. In fact, folded arms are immoral. We aren't even allowed to walk by an animal in pain, much less a person. Even if the animal belongs to our worst enemy, we are enjoined to help it to its feet . . . even if it means removing its load and then packing it again.

And so we create spaces in which to celebrate what we are about . . . to celebrate what we cherish . . . to celebrate the seasons of the year and the times of our life. And so a *sukkah* . . . to remind us not to take the harvest for granted — or the ecosystem . . . or our personal successes . . . or, whatever we might mean by the metaphor we call harvest — because our harvests are as fragile as the *sukkah,* as delicate as the temporary space in which it is celebrated; and so a *chupah* . . . to remind us that marriage is a special, sacred relationship confined to just these two people under this *tallit,* this *chupah,* and that it can be a beautiful and solid relationship of the mind and the soul or it can be as ephemeral as this canopy; and so the *Aron HaKodesh* . . . to remind us that what we value must be prominent and foremost in our thoughts and in our sight; and so Jerusalem . . . *Ir HaKodesh,* the city which can be holy, the ideal, the dream, the city of cities, place of places, center of our focus, core of our hopes for the future. Each space is an ideal made holy and sacred for a moment of transcendence . . . so that we, in turn, may transcend the moment in our thoughts and through our deeds!

Fourth, while rituals in general tend to foster personal identity and identification with family or group, Jewish rituals are at the core of a sound Jewish identity.

One who is born to a U.S. citizen can be registered as a U.S. citizen. And no matter where in the world he/she was born or resides, so long as a passport is renewed in timely fashion, that citizenship is lifelong. One needn't make a commitment to the country or have primary residence here or swear allegiance or speak English or know the Constitution or have any knowledge of our customs or mores and, yet, by definition, that person is still a U.S. citizen.

Likewise, one who is born a Jew is always a Jew. That's what the world calls you; that's what your people call you. The act or accident of birth makes one a Jew. But a Jew who does not live the part, who does not participate, who does not celebrate, who undertakes no Jewish ritual . . . is like a citizen who stays away! We count him or her in the census, but with little enthusiasm.

Now, one who is born a Jew, regardless of how tenuous the connection, probably has that identity encrypted on the subconscious. Somewhere, perhaps in the recesses of the mind, there is a claim check for his or her identity. And someday, perhaps, he or she will find it and reclaim the heritage.

But for one who is not born a Jew, there is no such subconscious claim check, there is no subliminal identity. For the Jew who is new to Judaism, ritual is not an optional activity; it is a vital, crucial, necessary aspect of being a Jew. For the Jew-by-Choice, religious identity is validated again and again through ritual . . . and not annual ritual, not once a year ritual, but monthly, weekly, daily ritual, great, heaping, helpings of ritual . . . holiday ritual, blessings ritual, worship ritual . . . supplemented, of course, by Jewish cultural opportunities and study and Jewish communal activities.

And, likewise, for newly constituted and blended families, Jewish ritual can set the tone for a new household and enable smoother transitions from one house to another. It can even act as a comforting constant for children who spend time in several different parenting situations.

But ritual needs to have integrity . . . otherwise, it's hollow. We have all attended the Bar/Bat Mitzvah service of a child who has little if any connection with the synagogue. The family never attends and never brings the child to services. For that child, a Bar/Bat Mitzvah ceremony could be a very empty ritual. Empty because the purpose of Bar/Bat Mitzvah is for a child to show that he/she is ready to take his or her place as an adult in the congregation — ready to conduct and participate in the worship service. But if he/she never comes to the synagogue to worship and to participate along with the community . . . what's the point of becoming a Bar/BatMitzvah? Ritual without integrity is empty, meaningless, emotionally bankrupt, hardly worth the effort.

Likewise, Jewish ritual needs to be Jewishly authentic. It's just fine to invent new customs, but unless they are invested with history and connected to traditions that transcend the present, from a Jewish perspective, they are just nice, cute, funky, fun, and little more. Just because a Jew does it doesn't mean it's authentic — doesn't mean it's Jewish.

When Jewish ritual connects us to the greater family of Jews around the world, to *Klal Yisrael*, it's authentic. A few years ago, I had the incredible experience of conducting worship services in Barcelona for about 125 Jews. Now, my Spanish is barely better than my nonexistent knowledge of Catalan — which is the language of Barcelona, so how, pray tell, did I manage to conduct services?

It was easy because Jewish ritual connects us with Jews all over the world. The president of this new liberal congregation was fluent in Catalan and Spanish and he understood English, but couldn't speak it very well. However, since he had spent many years in Israel, his Hebrew was excellent. So, I led the Hebrew parts of the service and everyone there joined with me in the readings; he led the responsive readings in Catalan, and he led the singing because the melodies were unusual; and I gave a sermon in English and *un poco de Español*. My English he translated into Catalan. When he didn't understand a word or phrase, I translated it into Hebrew for him. My Spanish, he translated into English much to the amusement of everyone.

There were 20 children present that night. They all came up to sing Kiddush. They knew the service intimately and participated from beginning to end with such love and such joy it brought tears to my eyes. I was a Rabbi from America, but for them the accent was on Rabbi. That was all they cared about. I was Rabbi and we were all Jews, and together we prayed as our ancestors had. Through ritual we were united. That was a spiritual experience.

And I will say with no fear whatsoever of contradiction, that the tens of thousands of Russian Jews who have found their way to these shores of late will never become part of this Jewish community or of any Jewish community except through Jewish ritual and except through Jewish worship. And we could assign volunteers and we could overwhelm them with social workers and we could buy them apartments and cars and find them jobs, but they will never be a part of us, never connect with this Jewish community, until and unless they connect through ritual and worship. And language is no barrier — Russian, Spanish, English, Hebrew, Catalan — unless we or they choose to make it so.

Rabbi Wayne Dosick tells the story of a woman in an airport with a three-year-old child by her side. A policeman approached the lady and said," I know it may seem strange to you, but we have a report of a missing child — about the age description of this child. Can you prove that this is your daughter?"

"Preposterous," the woman exclaimed!

"Even so, Madam, I'll need to ask the child some questions. Tell me, dear, what is your name?"

"Melissa."

"What's your last name?" Silence.

"Well, where do you live?"

"At home."

"Do you know the name of your city?"

"Nope."

"What's your daddy's name?"

"Daddy."

"What does he do?"

"He goes to work."

Since the officer wasn't getting anywhere, he turned back to the woman. "Do you have any pictures of this child or of your husband that the child might recognize?"

"I didn't bring any pictures with me."

"Well, let me see your plane tickets."

"We don't have any tickets, yet. We're on standby."

"Mommy, Mommy, what does the man want from us?" the child cried. Hearing that, the officer, smiled, tipped his hat, and walked away.

A bit frightening, isn't it? So how would you prove that the child was yours, the Rabbi asks? And he answers: "I would have turned to my two-year-old and said, tell the officer what we say before we eat. And he would have recited *HaMotzi*. And I would have turned to my four-year-old and said: Tell the officer what we say before going to sleep. And he would have recited the *Shema*. And the officer would have darn well known that these were my children. [1]

But perhaps the most wonderful story having to do with ritual and identity comes from my congregation. When Sophia Singer was just an infant, her mother Stacy brought her to Temple quite often. The entire staff dropped everything to play with Sophia; we enjoyed her immensely. The baby smiled constantly. In fact for many weeks, we never saw her unhappy or even on the verge of tears. Then one day . . . as we were gooing and gaaing together . . . a pout . . . a brief *kretz* . . . and then tears galore — great lungs!

"Oh, she's hungry, it's lunchtime," said Mother. And with that Stacy held her daughter straight in front of her . . . eyes to eyes . . . and began to sing softly: "*Baruch Atah Adonai . . .*" The tears stopped; "*Elohaynu Melech HaOlam . . .*" The baby's feet begin to kick; "*HaMotzi Lechem . . .*" Sophia's face is now a smile from ear to ear; "*Min HaAretz . . .*" The baby is now kicking and smiling, she's giggling aloud, her tongue is darting in and out, and she's beginning to make swallowing sounds; "*Ah-ah-men.*" And in this lovely way a little child already associates a mother's love and compassion and joy and food and blessing and Judaism and identity . . . months and months before she's ready to walk or talk. That's the power of authentic Jewish ritual.

Fifth, while the function of most Jewish ritual is to connect us to our heritage, to our people here and abroad, and to authenticate and actuate our own Jewish identities, Jewish ritual can also connect us to a spiritual dimension.

Spirituality is a strange expression because it usually comes with no precise definition. Ask a group of people what it means and all sorts of answers pour forth. It's the feeling you get when you hear a great piece of music or see great art. It's how you feel when you see a beautiful sunset or when you're in the mountains or on the sea. It's like when you survive a dangerous moment; it's like love; it's like being one with the universe.

For a Roman Catholic, a spiritual moment might be seeing the Pope or standing in St. Peter's Cathedral in Rome. For a Muslim, it might be walking around the Ka'abah — the black stone in Mecca — and becoming a Hajji. For Jews, a spiritual moment might be the first time one stands before the Western Wall in Jerusalem. Each of those moments are spiritual because they connect a person with the core of his or her oldest traditions.

Judaism is a non-sacramental religion. We don't have sacraments that must be administered by priests. Even our rites of passage can be conducted by any learned Jew; Rabbis are not a necessity in the practice of Judaism. Since we don't have to rely on the administration of rites by those in power or authority, it is up to each Jew to become knowledgeable enough to come to terms with the potential inherent in Judaism. To learn and to teach and to celebrate — that's what we as a religious heritage are all about.

Our holidays are all value laden — by celebrating we connect with our values. A people blesses what it believes to be eternal. Ritual, therefore, connects us with what we as a people believe to be lasting, everlasting, of profound significance, at the root and core of being. Implied in every Jewish celebration are rituals . . . and implied in every ritual act is a connection with that which transcends us.

It's easy to be Jewish. It's like a feeling. I feel Jewish — see how easy that is?! Unfortunately, that is about as valuable as saying that seeing a beautiful sunset is a spiritual moment. That kind of spirituality takes no effort at all — it's poignant entertainment.

A musician can have a spiritual moment through music; an artist can have a spiritual moment through art; a mountain climber can have a spiritual moment on a jagged cliff . . . a Jew has a spiritual moment within the context of performing a Jewish act. And only acts count — for Jews, acts alone define us. But every act that celebrates life, every act that acknowledges our place in this universe, every act that affirms our identity as a Jew, every act that strengthens our bonds to family and community, every act that sanctifies time, every act that implies a connectedness to that which urges us toward *mitzvot* . . . toward blessings . . . *is a ritual*. And within every Jewish ritual lies the seed, the potential, for achieving renewal . . . and wholeness — which, in the final analysis, is what spirituality is all about.

[1] From *Moments of Transcendence* by Dov Peretz Elkins. Jason Aronson Inc., Northvale, NJ, 1992, pp. 124ff.

*General books about the Jewish life cycle.

For the Teacher

Abrams, Judith Z., and Steven A. Abrams. *Jewish Parenting: Rabbinic Insights.* Northvale, NJ: Jason Aronson Inc., 1994.

A Rabbi and a physician look at parenting in Jewish tradition.

Adelman, Penina V. *Miriam's Well: Rituals for Jewish Women around the Year.* 2d. ed. New York: Biblio Press, 1990.

Collection of creative women's rituals for life cycle and other celebrations.

Aiken, Lisa. *Beyond Bashert: A Guide to Dating and Marriage Enrichment.* Northvale, NJ: Jason Aronson Inc., 1996.

Examination of dating and marriage from a traditional Jewish perspective.

Barth, Lewis M., ed. *Berit Mila in the Reform Context.* Los Angeles: Berit Mila Board of Reform Judaism, 1990.

Collection of essays about *Brit Milah* from the persepective of Reform Judaism.

Belin, David. *Why Choose Judaism: New Dimensions of Jewish Outreach.* New York: UAHC Press, 1985.

Booklet which explains Reform Judaism's outreach efforts to attract Jews-by-Choice.

Bell, Roselyn, ed. *The Hadassah Magazine Jewish Parenting Book.* New York: The Free Press, 1989.

Collection of articles about Jewish parenting.

Berkowitz, Allan L., and Patti Moskovitz, eds. *Embracing the Covenant: Converts to Judaism Talk About Why & How.* Woodstock, VT: Jewish Lights Publishing, 1996.

Collection of essays written by those who have become Jewish about the reasons for their conversion.

Bleich, J. David. *Judaism and Healing: Halakhic Perspectives.* New York: KTAV Publishing House, Inc., 1981.

Essays about the positions of Jewish law on contemporary biomedical issues.

Brener, Anne. *Mourning & Mitzvah: A Guided Journal for Walking the Mourner's Path through Grief to Healing.* Woodstock, VT: Jewish Lights Publishing, 1993.

Explanation of the traditional Jewish mourning process with guided writing exercises to help the mourning process.

Bulka, Reuven. *Jewish Divorce Ethics: The Right Way to Say Goodbye.* Ogdensburg, New York: Ivy League Press, 1992.

Guide to divorce according to Jewish law.

———. *Jewish Marriage: A Halakhic Ethic.* Rev. ed. Hoboken, NJ: KTAV Publishing House, Inc., 1986.

Traditional guide to Jewish marriage.

———. *Judaism on Pleasure.* Northvale, NJ: Jason Aronson Inc., 1995.

Judaism's view of pleasure from an Orthodox perspective.

Cardozo, Arlene Rossen. *Jewish Family Celebrations: The Sabbath, Festivals, and Ceremonies.* New York: St. Martin's Press, 1982.

Guide to celebrating Jewish holidays, Shabbat, and life cycle rituals.

Carmel, Abraham. *So Strange My Path: A Spiritual Pilgrimage.* New York: Bloch Publishing Company, 1993.

Autobiography of a Catholic priest who converted to Judaism.

Cohen, Debra Nussbaum. "The Plight of the Agunah." In *The Jewish Monthly,* January-February 1996.

Article about Jewish women whose husbands refuse to give them a *get.*

Cohen, Eugene J. *Guide to Ritual Circumcision and Redemption of the First-Born Son.* Hoboken, NJ: KTAV Publishing House, Inc., 1984, o.p.

Traditional guide to the background and practice of *Brit Milah* and *Pidyon HaBen.*

Cohen, Jack S. *Intermarriage and Conversion: A Halakhic Solution.* Hoboken, NJ: KTAV Publishing House, Inc., n.d.

Traditional response to the challenge of intermarriage.

Cowan, Paul. *An Orphan in History: Retrieving a Jewish Legacy.* Garden City, NY: William Morrow & Co. Inc., 1996.

Autobiographical account of the author's journey from assimilation to an active Jewish life.

Cowan, Paul, with Rachel Cowan. *Mixed Blessings: Overcoming the Stumbling Blocks in an Interfaith Marriage.* New York: Penguin Books, 1987.

Comprehensive guide to issues relating to intermarriage.

Danan, Julie Hilton. *The Jewish Parents' Almanac.* Northvale, NJ: Jason Aronson Inc., 1993.

Comprehensive guide to Jewish parenting.

Diamant, Anita. *Choosing a Jewish Life: A Handbook for the New Jewish Convert.* New York: Schocken Books, 1997.

Guidance for the convert to Judaism.

———. *The New Jewish Baby Book: Names, Ceremonies & Customs, A Guide for Today's Families.* Woodstock, Vt.: Jewish Lights Publishing, 1993.

Contemporary resource on Jewish rituals and practices related to birth.

———. *The New Jewish Wedding.* New York: Summit Books, 1985.

A contemporary guide to planning a Jewish wedding.

Diamant, Anita, and Howard Cooper. *Living a Jewish Life: A Guide for Starting, Learning, Celebrating, and Parenting.* New York: HarperCollins Publishers, 1991.

Presents an overview of Jewish rituals for the family.

Diamond, Barbara. *Bat Mitzvah: A Jewish Girl's Coming of Age.* New York: Viking Press, 1995.

Examination of the Bat Mitzvah experience.

Divre Gerut: Guidelines Concerning Proselytism. New York: Central Conference of American Rabbis, 1983.

Reform Judaism's official document about conversion.

Donin, Hayim. *To Raise a Jewish Child: A Guide for Parents.* New York: Basic Books, Inc., 1977.

Orthodox guide to raising a Jewish child.

Dosick, Wayne. *Golden Rules: The Ten Ethical Values Parents Need to Teach Their Children.* San Francisco: HarperCollins Publishers, 1995.

Theoretical and practical guide to teaching basic values to children in the modern world.

Eichhorn, David Max, ed. *Conversion to Judaism: A History and Analysis.* Hoboken, NJ: KTAV Publishing House, Inc., 1966.

Overview of Judaism's attitude toward conversion throughout history and information about prominent converts.

Elkins, Dov Peretz. *Jewish Guided Imagery: A How-To Book for Rabbis, Educators and Group Leaders.* Princeton, NJ: Growth Associates, 1996.

Explains how, when, and why to use guided imagery and offers guided imagery scripts on all aspects of Jewish life.

Encyclopaedia Judaica. Jerusalem: Keter Publishing House Jerusalem Ltd., 1972.

Sixteen-volume reference work on Judaism. (Now available on CD-ROM from Davka Corporation.)

Epstein, Lawrence J. *Conversion to Judaism: A Guidebook.* Northvale, NJ: Jason Aronson Inc., 1997.

Resource guide to conversion.

———, ed. *Readings on Conversion to Judaism.* Northvale, NJ: Jason Aronson Inc., 1995.

Feldman, David M. *Marital Relations, Birth Control and Abortion in Jewish Law.* New York: Schocken Books, 1974, o.p.

Classic guide to Jewish tradition's viewpoint about issues relating to marriage and birth.

Feldman, David M., and Fred Rosner, eds. *Compendium on Medical Ethics: Jewish Moral, Ethical and Religious Principles in Medical Practice.* New York: Federation of Jewish Philanthropies of New York, Inc., 1984, o.p.

Presents traditional Judaism's attitude toward a variety of biomedical issues.

Fine, Irene. *Midlife, A Rite of Passage and The Wise Woman, A Celebration.* San Diego, CA: Woman's Institute for Continuing Jewish Education, 1988.

Presents a variety of modern creative rituals for midlife.

Friedman, Debbie. *The Best of Debbie Friedman.* Cedarhurst, NY: Tara Publications, 1987.

Songbook with music to the songwriter's most popular songs.

* Geffen, Rela M., ed. *Celebration & Renewal: Rites of Passage in Judaism.* Philadelphia: Jewish Publication Society, 1993.

Essays about the Jewish life cycle.

Gillman, Neil. *The Death of Death: Resurrection and Immortality in Jewish Thought.* Woodstock, VT: Jewish Lights Publishing, 1997.

Examination of the themes of immortality and resurrection in Judaism.

Gold, Michael. *and Hannah wept: Infertility, Adoption, and the Jewish Couple.* Philadelphia: Jewish Publication Society, 1988.

Comprehensive overview of Judaism's attitude toward infertility and adoption.

———. *Does God Belong in the Bedroom?* Philadelphia: Jewish Publication Society, 1992.

Addresses Judaism's position on a variety of sexual issues.

Goodman, Arnold M. *A Plain Pine Box: A Return to Simple Jewish Funerals and Eternal Traditions.* Hoboken, NJ: KTAV Publishing House, Inc., 1981.

Advocates traditional Jewish burial rituals and explains how to create a *Chevra Kaddisha* to enact them.

*Gordis, David, and David Bamberger. *Teaching Guide for When a Jew Celebrates.* West Orange, NJ: Behrman House, Inc., 1971.

Teacher's guide to *When a Jew Celebrates.*

Greenberg, Sidney, and Jonathan D. Levine, eds. *Mahzor Hadash: The Mahzor for Rosh Hashanah and Yom Kippur.* Bridgeport, CT: The Prayer Book Press, 1978.

A High Holy Day prayer book with some interesting and different readings.

HaLevi, Aaron. *Sefer haHinnuch: The Book of [Mitzvah] Education,* vol. 1. New York: Feldheim Publishers, 1978.

Translation of the classic Jewish work which lists and explains each *mitzvah* in the Torah by *parashah.*

Huberman, Steven. *New Jews: The Dynamics of Religious Conversion.* New York: UAHC Press, 1979.

Isaacs, Ronald H. *The Bride and Groom Handbook.* West Orange, NJ: Behrman House, Inc., 1989.

Brief guide to the Jewish wedding.

*———. *Rites of Passage: A Guide to the Jewish Life Cycle.* Hoboken, NJ: KTAV Publishing House, Inc., 1992.

Concise overview of the Jewish life cycle.

Isaacs, Ronald H., and Kerry M. Olitzky. *A Jewish Mourner's Handbook.* Hoboken, NJ: KTAV Publishing House, Inc., 1991.

A brief guide to Jewish mourning practices.

*———. *Sacred Moments: Tales from the Jewish Life Cycle.* Northvale, NJ: Jason Aronson Inc., 1995.

Collection of texts and stories from Jewish tradition about the life cycle.

———. *The Second How-To Handbook for Jewish Living.* Hoboken, NJ: KTAV Publishing House, Inc., 1996.

Step-by-step explanation of many Jewish rituals.

Jacob, Walter, ed. *American Reform Responsa.* New York: Central Conference of American Rabbis, 1983.

Collection of *Responsa* written by Reform Rabbis covering a wide variety of issues.

Jacob, Walter. *Contemporary American Reform Responsa.* New York: Central Conference of American Rabbis, 1987.

Further collection of Reform *Responsa.*

Kadden, Barbara Binder, and Bruce Kadden. *Teaching Mitzvot: Concepts, Values, and Activities.* Denver: A.R.E. Publishing. Inc., 1988.

Resource for teachers about *mitzvot.*

Kaufman, Michael. *Love, Marriage, and Family in Jewish Law and Tradition.* Northvale NJ: Jason Aronson Inc., 1992.

Examines what Jewish law teaches about marriage, family, and relationships.

Keeping Posted. Vol. XVIII, No. 1, October 1972.

Issue about names in Judaism.

Kessler, Eve Jacobson. "Jewish Magic: New Age Jews and Chasidim Discover Ancient Charms in Segullas and Amulets." In *Forward,* September 9, 1994, p. 11.

Article about how modern Jews have discovered ancient Jewish amulets and charms.

——— "New Afterbirth Ritual Takes Root in Berkeley." In *Forward,* October 22, 1993, p. 12.

Article about the creation of a ritual for burying the afterbirth.

Kimmel, Eric A. *Bar Mitzvah: A Jewish Boy's Coming of Age.* New York: Penguin Books USA Inc., 1995.

The significance of the Bar Mitzvah in the life of a Jewish boy.

Klein, Isaac. *A Guide to Jewish Religious Practice.* New York: The Jewish Theological Seminary of America, 1979.

Comprehensive guide to Jewish practice from a Conservative perspective.

Kohn, Ingrid; and Perry-Lynn Moffit; with Isabelle A. Wilkins. *A Silent Sorrow: Pregnancy Loss: Guidance and Support for You and Your Family.* New York: Dell Publishing Co. Inc., 1993.

Suggestions for dealing with miscarriage and stillbirth.

Kolatch, Alfred J. *The Complete Dictionary of English and Hebrew First Names.* New York: Jonathan David Publishers, Inc., 1984.

Comprehensive list of first names and their meanings.

———. *The Jewish Book of Why.* Middle Village, NY: Jonathan David Publishers, Inc., 1981.

Questions and answers about a wide range of Jewish topics including marriage, divorce, death, and mourning.

———. *The Jewish Mourner's Book of Why.* Middle Village, NY: Jonathan David Publishers, Inc., 1991.

Question and answer guide to burial and mourning customs.

———. *The Second Jewish Book of Why.* Middle Village, NY: Jonathan David Publishers, Inc., 1985.

More questions and answers about a wide range of Jewish topics, including marriage and death and dying.

———. *This Is the Torah.* Middle Village, NY: Jonathan David Publishers, Inc., 1988.

Everything you want to know about the Torah.

Kukoff, Lydia. *Choosing Judaism.* New York: UAHC Press, 1981.

Practical guide to conversion, written by a Jew-by-choice.

Lamm, Maurice. *Becoming a Jew.* Middle Village, NY: Jonathan David Publishers, Inc., 1991.

Orthodox guide to conversion.

————. *The Jewish Way in Death and Mourning.* Rev. ed. Middle Village, NY: Jonathan David Publishers, Inc., 1972.

Comprehensive guide to Jewish rituals of burial and mourning from a traditional point of view.

————. *The Jewish Way in Love & Marriage.* San Francisco: Harper & Row, 1980.

Traditional guide to the Jewish wedding.

Leneman, Helen, ed. *Bar/Bat Mitzvah Basics: A Practical Family Guide to Coming of Age Together.* Woodstock, VT: Jewish Lights Publishing, 1996.

A book to help families think about and plan a Bar or Bat Mitzvah.

————. *Bar/Bat Mitzvah Education: A Sourcebook.* Denver: A.R.E. Publishing, Inc., 1993.

Collection of articles on all aspects of Bar/Bat Mitzvah training and education.

Lester, Julius. *Lovesong: Becoming a Jew.* New York: Henry Holt and Company, 1988.

Autobiographical account of a Black man's conversion to Judaism.

Levine, Elizabeth Resnick, ed. *A Ceremonies Sampler: New Rites, Celebrations, and Observances of Jewish Women.* San Diego: Woman's Institute for Continuing Jewish Education, 1991.

Collection of contemporary rituals for Jewish women.

Lewittees, Mendell. *Jewish Marriage: Rabbinic Law, Legend, & Custom.* Northvale, NJ: Jason Aronson Inc., 1994.

A variety of material from Jewish sources about marriage.

Lieberman, Dale. *Witness to the Covenant of Circumcision: Bris Milah.* Northvale, NJ: Jason Aronson Inc., 1997.

Presents the essence of *Brit Milah* through photographs and words.

Lilith. No. 21, Fall, 1988.

Contains articles about creative life cycle rituals.

Lilith. Vol. 16, No. 4, Fall, 1991.

Contains articles about creative life cycle rituals.

Lilith. Vol. 20, No. 3, Fall, 1995.

Contains articles about creative life cycle rituals.

Maslin, Simeon J., ed. *Gates of Mitzvah: A Guide to the Jewish Life Cycle.* New York: Central Conference of American Rabbis, 1979.

Reform Judaism's statement about *mitzvot* that Jews should do in observing life cycle events.

Mason, Ruth. "Adult Bat Mitzvah: A Revolution for Women and Synagogues." In *Lilith,* Vol. 14, No. 4, Fall 1989.

Discusses the spiritual significance of Adult Bat Mitzvah.

Mayer, Egon. *Love & Tradition: Marriage Between Jews & Christians.* New York: Plenum Press, 1985.

A sociologist examines the challenges of intermarriage.

Metzker, Isaac. *A Bintel Brief*. New York: Schocken Books, 1990.

Selection of questions and answers from the advice column of the Yiddish daily, *The Forward*.

Myrowitz, Catherine Hall. *Finding a Home for the Soul: Interviews with Converts to Judaism*. Northvale, NJ: Jason Aronson Inc., 1995.

Jews-by-choice explain the reasons for their conversions.

Olitzky, Kerry M.; Steven M. Rosman; and David P. Kasakove. *When Your Jewish Child Asks Why: Answers for Tough Questions*. Hoboken, NJ: KTAV Publishing House, Inc., 1993.

Offers answers to theological and practical questions asked by children (and adults).

* Orenstein, Rabbi Debra, ed. *Lifecycles: Jewish Women on Life Passages and Personal Milestones,* vol. 1. Woodstock, Vermont: Jewish Lights Publishing, 1994.

Collection of essays and rituals by Jewish women pertaining to the life cycle, from birth through death.

Pasternak, Velvel, ed. *From the Song of Songs*. Cedarhurst, NY: Tara Publications, 1988.

Music for wedding songs from this biblical text.

————. *Mazel Tov! Music For a Jewish Wedding and Other Joyous Occasions*. Cedarhurst, NY: Tara Publications, 1992.

Music for Jewish wedding songs.

Patera, Meridith Shaw. *Kings and Things: 20 Jewish Plays for Kids 8 to 18*. Denver: A.R.E. Publishing, Inc., 1996.

Plays about holidays, Bible stories, Israel, and other Jewish topics.

Plotkin, Janis; Caroline Libresco; and Josh Feiger, eds. *Independent Jewish Film: A Resource Guide*. 3d ed. San Francisco: The San Francisco Jewish Film Festival, 1996.

Brief summary of hundreds of Jewish films and sources for renting and buying them.

Porter, Jack Nusan, ed., *Women in Chains: A Sourcebook on the Agunah*. Northvale, NJ: Jason Aronson Inc., 1996.

Collection of articles about the problem of Jewish women whose husbands won't grant their wives a divorce.

Prusan, Peretz. *A Guide to Hebrew Lettering*. New York: UAHC Press, 1981.

Resource for teaching Hebrew calligraphy.

Rabinowicz, Tzvi. *A Guide to Life: Jewish Laws and Customs of Mourning*. Northvale, NJ: Jason Aronson Inc., 1989.

Traditional guide to burial and mourning customs and laws.

Reiss, Fred. *The Standard Guide to the Jewish and Civil Calendar*. West Orange, NJ: Behrman House, Inc., 1986.

Calendars for finding Jewish and civil dates for the years 1899-2050.

Richards, Stephen, ed. *Manginot: 201 Songs for Jewish Schools*. New York: Transcontinental Music Publications and New Jewish Music Press, 1992.

Musical arrangements of Jewish songs from liturgy, folk tradition, and Israel.

Riemer, Jack, ed. *Jewish Insights on Death & Mourning*. New York: Schocken Books, Inc., 1996.

Collection of essays about Judaism's view of death and mourning.

Riemer, Jack, and Nathaniel Stampfer, eds. *So That Your Values Live On: Ethical Wills and How to Prepare Them*. Woodstock, VT: Jewish Lights Publishing, 1993.

Collection of ethical wills and a guide to preparing them.

Romanoff, Lena, with Lisa Hostein. *Your People, My People: Finding Acceptance and Fulfillment as a Jew by Choice*. Philadelphia: Jewish Publication Society, 1990.

Comprehensive guide to conversion to Judaism.

Rosenbloom, Joseph R. *Conversion to Judaism: From the Biblical Period to the Present*. Cincinnati: Hebrew Union College Press, 1978, o.p. (Available from Books on Demand, 300 N. Zeeb Rd., Ann Arbor, MI 48106)

Historical overview of Judaism's attitude toward conversion.

Rosenkrantz, Linda, and Pamela Satran. *Beyond Sarah & Sam: An Enlightened Guide to Jewish Baby Naming*. New York: St. Martin's Press, 1992.

Guide to choosing a Jewish name for your child.

Rosner, Fred. *Modern Medicine & Jewish Ethics*. Hoboken NJ: KTAV Publishing House, Inc. and New York: Yeshiva University Press, 1986.

The Jewish perspective on a variety of bioethical issues.

Rosner, Fred, and J. David Bleich, eds. *Jewish Bioethics*. Brooklyn, NY: Hebrew Publishing Company, 1979, o.p.

Articles about *halachah* pertaining to biomedical issues.

Rossel, Seymour. *A Spiritual Journey: Bar Mitzvah and Bat Mitzvah Handbook*. West Orange, NJ: Behrman House, Inc., 1993.

Brief guide to the observance of Bar and Bat Mitzvah.

Salkin, Jeffrey K. *Putting God on the Guest List: How to Reclaim the Spiritual Meaning of Your Child's Bar or Bat Mitzvah*. Woodstock, VT: Jewish Lights Publishing, 1992.

How to make the Bar or Bat Mitzvah experience meaningful for the child and family.

Scalamonti, John David. *Ordained to Be a Jew*. Hoboken, NJ: KTAV Publishing House, Inc., 1992.

A Catholic priest's journey to Judaism.

Schachter-Shalomi, Zalman, and Ronald S. Miller. *From Age-ing to Sag-ing: A Profound New Vision of Growing Older*. New York: Warner Books, 1995.

A new approach to appreciating and honoring the elderly.

Schulweis, Harold M. "Seek Converts!" In *Moment*, April 1997/Nissan 5757, pp. 43-45.

Article urging Jews actively to seek converts.

*Shekel, Michal. *Teacher's Guide to The Jewish Lifecycle Book*. Hoboken, NJ: KTAV Publishing House, Inc., 1989.

Offers ideas for discussion and activities on the Jewish life cycle.

Sher, Nina Streisand, and Margaret A. Feldman. *100+ Jewish Art Projects for Children.* Denver: A.R.E. Publishing, Inc., 1996.

Contains many creative projects for children of all ages.

Siegel, Richard; Michael Strassfeld; and Sharon Strassfeld. *The First Jewish Catalog.* Philadelphia: Jewish Publication Society, 1973.

A how-to guide to Judaism with chapters on weddings and death and burial.

Sonsino, Rifat, and Daniel B. Syme. *What Happens After I Die? Jewish Views of Life after Death.* New York: UAHC Press, 1990.

Presents a variety of Jewish ideas about what happens after we die.

Starkman, Elaine M. *Learning to Sit in Silence: A Journal of Caretaking.* Watsonville, CA: Papier Mache Press, 1993.

Guide for those who must care for older family members.

Stern, Chaim, ed. *On the Doorposts of Your House: Prayers and Ceremonies for the Jewish Home.* New York: Central Conference of American Rabbis, 1994.

Reform Judaism's prayer book for the home.

Stopler, Pinchas. *Jewish Alternatives in Love, Dating and Marriage.* New York: National Conference of Synagogue Youth and University Press of America, Inc., 1984.

Traditional guide to Jewish relationships and marriage.

Strassfeld, Sharon, and Michael Strassfeld, eds. *The Second Jewish Catalog: Sources and Resources.* Philadelphia: Jewish Publication Society, 1976.

Collection of articles on a variety of Jewish topics, including a chapter on rituals pertaining to birth.

Telushkin, Joseph. *Jewish Literacy: The Most Important Things to Know About the Jewish Religion, Its People, and Its History.* New York: William Morrow & Company, Inc., 1991.

Short articles on hundreds of Jewish topics.

———. *Jewish Wisdom: Ethical, Spiritual, and Historical Lessons from the Great Works and Thinkers.* New York: William Morrow & Company, Inc., 1994.

Collection of quotations about a wide variety of Jewish issues.

Tucker, JoAnne. *Creative Movement for a Song: Activities for Young Children.* Denver: A.R.E. Publishing, Inc., 1993.

Simple activities on Jewish themes that involve movement.

Tucker, JoAnne, and Susan Freeman. *Torah in Motion: Creating Dance Midrash.* Denver: A.R.E. Publishing, Inc., 1990.

Guide for teachers to use dance to interpret more than 100 passages from the Torah.

Twersky, Isadore, ed. *A Maimonides Reader.* West Orange, NJ: Behrman House, Inc., 1972.

Collection of the most important works of Maimonides.

Warshawsky, Gale Solotar. *Creative Puppetry for Jewish Kids.* Denver: A.R.E. Publishing, Inc., 1985.

Directions for making puppets and using them to teach a variety of Jewish subjects.

Wertheimer, Jack; Charles S. Liebman; and Steven M. Cohen. "How to Save American Jews." In *Commentary,* vol. 101, no. 1, January 1996, pp. 47-51.

Article challenging Judaism's emphasis on outreach.

Wolfson, Ron. *A Time to Mourn, A Time to Comfort.* New York: the Federation of Jewish Men's Clubs, 1993.

Jewish mourning rituals and how it has affected those who observed them.

For Students

Albert, Eleanor. *Jewish Story Theater.* Los Angeles: Torah Aura Productions, 1989.

Collection of short skits on Jewish themes.

Bar-Yam, Naomi Bromberg. *The Empty Drawer.* Los Angeles: Torah Aura Productions, 1996.

Instant lesson for intermediate students about children dealing with the death of their aunt.

Beiner, Stan J. Class Acts: *Plays & Skits for Jewish Settings.* Denver: A.R.E. Publishing, Inc., 1992.

Thirty Jewish plays for preschool through high school students.

Benson, Paulette, and Joanne Altschuler. *The Jewish Family: Past, Present and Future.* Denver: A.R.E. Publishing, Inc., 1979.

Minicourse which teaches about the Jewish family.

Blume, Judy. *Are You There God? It's Me, Margaret.* New York: Bradbury Press, 1990.

An 11-year-old girl comes to terms with her religious identity.

Buscaglia, Leo. *The Fall of Freddie the Leaf: A Story of Life for All Ages.* Thorofare, NJ: Charles B. Slack, Inc., 1982.

Introduces children to the idea of death by telling the story of a leaf falling from a tree.

Bush, Lawrence. *Emma Ansky-Levine and Her Mitzvah Machine.* New York: UAHC Press, 1991.

Twelve-year-old Emma has a *mitzvah* machine which helps her to learn important Jewish values and what it means to be a Bat Mitzvah.

Curtis, Sandra. *Gabriel's Ark.* Los Angeles: Torah Aura Productions, 1996.

Instant lesson about the Bar Mitzvah of a child with special needs.

Feigenson, Emily. *Changes Recognized, Changes Achieved: Bat Mitzvah.* Los Angeles: Torah Aura Productions, 1993.

An instant lesson relating Bat Mitzvah to achieving Jewish womanhood.

Feigenson, Emily, and Joel Lurie Grishaver. *Coming of Mitzvah: What the Jewish Tradition Has to Say About Coming of Age.* Los Angeles: Torah Aura Productions, 1993.

An instant lesson introducing Bar/Bat Mitzvah as a rite of passage relating to maturity and legal responsibility.

Foreman, Michael. *Grandfather's Pencil and the Room of Stories.* New York: Harcourt, Brace & Company, 1994.

A magic pencil connects a boy and his grandfather.

Gallant, Janet. *My Brother's Bar Mitzvah.* Rockville, MD: Kar-Ben Copies, Inc., 1990.

A young girl experiences the Bar Mitzvah of her older brother.

*Gersh, Harry. *When a Jew Celebrates*. West Orange, NJ: Behrman House, Inc., 1971.

Text for teaching the life cycle to the intermediate grades.

Gordon, Sol. *When Living Hurts*. Rev. ed. New York: UAHC Press, 1994.

A guide for dealing with depression and suicide for teenagers and adults.

*Grishaver, Joel Lurie. *The Life Cycle Workbook*. Denver: A.R.E. Publishing Inc., 1983.

Workbook for teaching the life cycle to intermediate grades.

———. *A Lifetime of Torah*. Los Angeles: Torah Aura Productions, 1991.

Instant lesson for young children about the study of Torah and the life cycle.

———. *Maseket Bar/Bat Mitzvah*. Los Angeles: Torah Aura Productions, 1996.

An instant lesson which enables students to create their own section of the Talmud about Bar or Bat Mitzvah.

———. *The True Story of Bar Mitzvah*. Los Angeles: Torah Aura Productions, 1993.

An instant lesson introducing the history and background of Bar Mitzvah.

Grode, Phyllis Agins. *Sophie's Name*. Kar-Ben Copies, Inc., 1990.

Picture book for elementary students about a Jewish girl who does not like her name until she learns who she is named after.

Harlow, Jules, ed. *Lessons from Our Living Past*. West Orange, NJ: Behrman House, Inc., 1972.

Stories from Jewish tradition for elementary students.

Hest, Amy. *The Crack-of-Dawn Walkers*. New York: Macmillan Publishing Company, 1984.

A young girl and her grandfather share a special walk.

Hirshman, Fran. *Mikvah and the Jewish Laws of Sex and Marriage*. Los Angeles: Torah Aura Productions, 1996.

Instant lesson for secondary students about *mikvah* and its relationship to sexual intercourse and marriage.

Kadden. Barbara Binder, and Bruce Kadden. *Ethical Wills: Handing Down Our Jewish Heritage*. Denver: A.R.E. Publishing, Inc., 1990.

Minicourse which gives an overview of this Jewish tradition and helps one write an ethical will.

Karkowsky, Nancy. *Grandma's Soup*. Rockville, MD: Kar-Ben Copies, Inc., 1989.

Story of a young girl and her relationship to her grandmother whose memory is slipping.

Kay, Alan. *Pebbles on a Stone*. Los Angeles: Torah Aura Productions, 1992.

Instant lesson for intermediate grades and up focusing on the unveiling of a grandfather's tombstone.

———. *The Red in My Father's Beard*. Los Angeles: Torah Aura Productions, 1992.

Instant lesson for intermediate grades and up about a boy experiencing the death of his father.

Keeping Posted. November, 1975.

Magazine for secondary students focusing on the issue of whether Judaism should actively seek converts.

Lanton, Sandy. *Daddy's Chair.* Rockville, MD: Kar-Ben Copies, Inc., 1991.

A child comes to terms with his father's death with the help of the father's special chair.

Levinson, Riki. *Watch the Stars Come Out.* New York: E.P. Dutton, 1985.

A young girl hears the story of how her ancestors came to America.

Lifton, Betty Jean. *Tell Me a Real Adoption Story.* New York: Alfred A. Knopf, 1993.

Story introducing adoption to elementary students.

Marcus, Audrey Friedman, et. al. *Bar and Bat Mitzvah: A Family Education Unit.* Denver: A.R.E. Publishing, Inc., 1983.

Minicourse for junior high students and their families to explore the background and meaning of Bar or Bat Mitzvah.

Marcus, Audrey Friedman; Sherry Bissell; and Karen S. Lipschutz. *Death, Burial & Mourning in the Jewish Tradition.* Denver: A.R.E. Publishing, Inc., 1976.

Minicourse introducing students in grades 4 to 8 to Jewish traditions related to death, burial, and mourning.

Miller, Kathryn Ann. *Did My First Mother Love Me? A Story for an Adopted Child.* Buena Park, CA: Morning Glory Press, 1994.

Sensitive story about adoption for young children.

Mirel, Barbara, and Jeff Mirel. *Relationships: A Jewish View.* Denver: A.R.E. Publishing, Inc., 1981.

Minicourse for secondary students about the Jewish view of love and relationships.

Moskowitz, Nachama Skolnik. *The Bar/Bat Mitzvah Game.* Los Angeles: Torah Aura Productions, 1986.

A values clarification game for class groups and/or families to confront important issues relating to Bar or Bat Mitzvah.

*———. *The Jewish Life Cycle Game.* Denver: A.R.E. Publishing, Inc., 1984.

Teaches facts, concepts, and values related to the Jewish life cycle.

Musleah, Rahel. *Journey of a Lifetime: The Jewish Life Cycle Book.* West Orange, NJ: Behrman House, Inc., 1997.

This text and activity book for Grades 4 and 5 takes students on a tour of Jewish life cycle events. Teacher's Guide with family education material available.

*Olitzky, Kerry M. *The Life Cycle Workbook Leader Guide.* Denver: A.R.E. Publishing, Inc., 1983.

Leader Guide for *The Life Cycle Workbook* by Joel Lurie Grishaver.

Olitzky, Kerry M., and Lee H. Olitzky. *Aging and Judaism.* Denver: A.R.E. Publishing, Inc., 1980.

Minicourse about Judaism's attitude toward the elderly.

Pasachoff, Naomi. *Basic Judaism for Young People: God.* West Orange, NJ: Behrman House, Inc., 1987.

Textbook about Jewish theological concepts, including chapter on *Brit* and *Brit Milah*.

Polacco, Patricia. *The Keeping Quilt.* New York: Simon & Schuster, Inc., 1988.

Story of a special quilt used for a variety of purposes, including as a *chupah*.

———. *Mrs. Katz and Tush.* New York: Dell Publishing, 1994.

An African-American child befriends an elderly Jewish widow.

Pomerantz, Barbara. *Who Will Lead Kiddish?* New York: UAHC Press, 1985.

A mother and daughter continue their Shabbat rituals after a divorce.

Portnoy, Mindy. *Mommy Never Went To Hebrew School.* Rockville, MD: Kar-Ben Copies, Inc., 1989.

Children's book about a woman who converted to Judaism.

Prevention Is a Mitzvah. Los Angeles: Torah Aura Productions, 1992.

Instant lesson for grades six and above which addresses the issue of whether schools should provide students with condoms and information about safer sex.

Rose, Shirley. *Let's Discover the Bible.* West Orange, NJ: Behrman House, Inc., 1992.

Retelling of biblical stories for elementary age classes.

Rossel, Seymour. *Lessons from the Prophets and Writings.* West Orange, NJ: Behrman House, Inc., 1989.

Retells stories from the second and third parts of the Jewish Bible.

Rothenberg, Joan. *Inside-Out Grandma: A Hanukkah Story.* New York: Hyperion Books for Children, 1995.

A grandmother shares stories about her family with her granddaughter as they prepare for Chanukah.

Samuels, Ruth. *Prophets, Writings and You.* Hoboken, NJ: KTAV Publishing House, Inc., 1989.

Variety of stories from the later biblical tradition.

Schnur, Steven. *The Narrowest Bar Mitzvah.* New York: UAHC Press, 1986.

When disaster strikes, a Bar Mitzvah must be relocated to the unusual home of the boy's grandparents.

———. *The Return of Morris Schumsky.* New York: UAHC Press, 1987.

Tale about a Jewish wedding which teaches important lessons about the Jewish family and caring for the elderly.

*Shekel, Michal. *The Jewish Lifecycle Book.* Hoboken, NJ: KTAV Publishing House, Inc., 1989.

Textbook about Jewish life cycle events.

*———. *Skill Text for The Jewish Lifecycle Book.* Hoboken, NJ: KTAV Publishing House, Inc., 1989.

Student activity book to be used with *The Jewish Lifecycle Book* by Michal Shekel.

Siegel, Danny. *Munbaz II and Other Mitzvah Heroes.* Spring Valley, NY: The Town House Press, 1991.

Stories about people who do amazing work in serving others.

Stevenson, James. *No Friends.* New York: Green-willow Books, 1986.

> Story of a brother and sister who have moved to a new neighborhood.

Seuss, Dr. *Horton Hatches the Egg.* New York: Random Books, 1966.

> Story of an elephant that helps a bird to hatch its egg.

* Sugarman, Morris J. *Student Activity Book for When a Jew Celebrates.* West Orange, NJ: Behrman House, Inc., 1986.

> Contains activities to be used with *When a Jew Celebrates* by Harry Gersh.

Taylor, Sydney. *More All-of-a-Kind Family.* New York: Taylor Productions, Ltd., 1988.

> Five girls have interesting adventures on New York's Lower East Side in the early twentieth century.

Techner, David, and Judith Hirt-Manheimer. *A Candle for Grandpa: A Guide to the Jewish Funeral for Children and Parents.* New York: UAHC Press, 1993.

> Introduces Jewish burial and mourning customs to children and their parents.

Turner, Ann. *Through Moon and Stars and Night Skies.* New York: HarperCollins Publishers, 1990.

> Book about adoption for primary grades.

What Must Parents Do? What Must Children Do? Los Angeles: Torah Aura Productions, 1990.

> Instant lesson for secondary students and their parents that enables them to discuss their expectations of each other.

Wise, Ira J. *LifeChoices: An Instant Lesson on Abortion.* Los Angeles: Torah Aura Productions, 1993.

> Instant lesson for secondary students which examines abortion from a Jewish perspective.

Wolff, Ferida. *Pink Slippers, Bat Mitzvah Blues.* Philadelphia: Jewish Publication Society, 1994.

> An eighth grade girl struggles to understand her Jewish identity.

Wolfson, Havi. *What Should the Bird Tell the Fish?* Los Angeles: Torah Aura Productions, 1995.

> Instant Lesson for secondary students about a girl who considers and rejects a prom date with a non-Jew.

Zwerin, Raymond A., and Audrey Friedman Marcus. *Marriage in Jewish Life and Tradition.* Denver: A.R.E. Publishing, Inc., 1978.

> Minicourse for secondary students about Jewish marriage.

Zwerin, Raymond A.; Audrey Friedman Marcus; and Leonard Kramish. *Circumcision.* Denver: A.R.E. Publishing, Inc., 1983.

> Minicourse designed for the intermediate grades introducing students to the ritual of *Brit Milah.*

Audiovisual

Bar Mitzvah in Israel. Ergo Media Inc. Video.

> An American boy and his Israeli cousin tour Israel and celebrate the American boy's Bar Mitzvah at the Wall in Jerusalem. (37 minutes)

Beged Kefet. *Beged Kefet: The First Album*. Sounds Write Productions, Inc. Audiocassette/CD.

A variety of contemporary Jewish songs.

Bloomers. Brooks-Antonio. 16mm film.

The relationship between a mother and her daughter. (30 minutes)

Brighton Beach. Arthur Cantor Films. Video.

Portrait of this Brooklyn neighborhood focusing on its elderly Jewish residents. (55 minutes)

Chicks in White Satin. Elaine Holliman. Video.

1994 Academy Award Nominee for Best Short Documentary about two lesbians preparing for and celebrating their marriage. (20 minutes)

Choosing Judaism: Some Personal Perspectives. UAHC TV & Film Institute. Available from Direct Cinema Ltd. Video.

Panel discussion about conversion to Judaism, followed by an explanation of outreach. (30 minutes)

Close Harmony. Cornell University Audio-Visual Resource Center. Video.

Story of the development of an intergenerational choir. (30 minutes)

Cohen, Myrna. *Lullabies & Quiet Time*. Sounds Write Productions, Inc. Audiocassette.

Recording of a variety of Jewish lullabies.

Complaints of a Dutiful Daughter. Women Make Movies. 16mm film.

A daughter chronicles her mother's struggle with Alzheimer's disease and her own response to the illness. (44 minutes)

The Corridor: Death. Ergo Media Inc. Video.

A car accident involving two young Americans visiting Israel triggers a debate about the meaning of death and afterlife in Judaism. (25 minutes)

Crossing Delancey. Swank Motion Pictures (or available at video stores). Video.

A single Jewish woman confronts tradition when her grandmother hires a matchmaker to find her a marriage partner. (97 minutes)

The Discovery (Bar Mitzvah). Ergo Media Inc. Video.

A 12-year-old boy struggles with his Jewish identity as he prepares for his Bar Mitzvah. (58 minutes)

The Eighth Day: Circumcision/Hanukah. Ergo Media Inc. Video.

Historical drama, set in the time of the Maccabees, focusing on a family that must decide whether to circumcise their son. (25 minutes).

Enemies: A Love Story. Facets Multimedia, Inc. Video.

A Holocaust survivor finds himself married to three women in 1949 New York. Based on an Isaac Bashevis Singer novel. (119 minutes)

Fiddler on the Roof. Video available at video stores.

Classic film about a Jewish family's struggles with love and tradition in a *shtetl*.

Fiddler on the Roof. RCA Cassette #OK-1005; CD #RCDI-7060. Audiocassette.

Music from the hit Broadway play.

Friedman, Debbie. *And the Youth Shall See Visions.* A.R.E. Publishing, Inc. Audiocassette.

Contemporary Jewish songs based on the liturgy and biblical passages.

———. *Ani Ma-amin.* A.R.E. Publishing, Inc. Audiocassette.

Contemporary Jewish songs, many of them based on passages from Song of Songs.

———. *Renewal of Spirit.* A.R.E. Publishing, Inc. Audiocassette.

Songs for healing.

I Love You, Rosa. Facets Multimedia, Inc. Video.

Story about a widow who falls in love with her husband's younger brother, who she must release from marrying her by the ceremony of *chalitzah.* (90 minutes; Hebrew with English subtitles)

The Imported Bridegroom. Ergo Media Inc. Video.

An American father wants his daughter to marry a brilliant student from the old country, but his daughter has other ideas. (93 minutes)

Interlove Story. Anne Flatte. Video.

Reflective film about the marriage between the filmmaker's Catholic mother and Jewish father. (9 minutes)

Intermarriage: When Love Meets Tradition. Direct Cinema Ltd. Video.

Interfaith couples discuss relations with parents, raising of children, and other issues. (28 minutes)

Intimate Story. Ergo Media Inc. Video.

A *kibbutz* couple's struggle with childlessness. (95 minutes; Hebrew with English subtitles)

The Journey: Bar Mitzvah/Jewish Identity. Ergo Media Inc. Video.
In 1939, an assimilated American Jew is faced with helping a Russian Jewish youth prepare for his Bar Mitzvah. (35 minutes)

Kol B'seder. *The Bridge.* A.R.E. Publishing, Inc. Audiocassette.

Variety of contemporary Jewish songs in folk, jazz, and rock styles.

———. *Sparks of Torah.* A.R.E. Publishing, Inc. Audiocassette.

Collection of contemporary Jewish songs for children and adults.

The Last & Only Survivor of Flora. Lee Hirsch. 16mm film.

Portrait of 93-year old poet and Wall Street courier Nathan Solomon. (11 minutes)

Lies My Father Told Me. Modern Sound Pictures, Inc. Video.

Moving film about the relationship between a young Jewish boy, his assimilated father, and his traditional grandfather. (102 minutes)

Losing Isaiah. Video available at video stores.

Story of an abandoned African-American crack baby and his adoption by a white family. When the birth mother attempts to regain custody of the child, a court battle ensues. (108 minutes)

Mazel Tov! Music for a Jewish Wedding and Other Joyous Occasions. Tara Publications. Audio-cassette/ CD.

Collection of Jewish wedding music.

Mikva, Marriage and Mazel Tov. Alden Films. Video.

Explains the ritual of the *mikvah* as it pertains to marriage. (10 minutes)

The Miracle of Intervale Avenue. Ergo Media Inc. Video.

Jews, African-Americans, and Puerto Ricans work and live together in the South Bronx. (65 minutes)

The Mitzvah Machine. United Synagogue Book Service. Video.

Bored with his Bar Mitzvah preparation, a boy builds a robot to take his place at the ceremony. (10 minutes)

The Mountain. Jarmaq Productions. Video.

A Palestinian woman defies tradition and marries the man she wants. (30 minutes, Arabic with English subtitles)

Number Our Days. Direct Cinema Ltd. Video.

Based on the book by Barbara Myerhoff, this film portrays the elderly Jews of Venice, California. (29 minutes)

Polonaise. Polygram Beneluk. Video.

The marriage of a couple who, as children, were hidden during the Holocaust brings back painful memories of the war. (90 minutes, Dutch with English subtitles)

A Private Life. Museum of Modern Art Circulating Film Library. Video.

Two elderly immigrants share memories and develop a relationship. (30 minutes)

A Question of Authority. Ergo Media Inc. Video.

Dramatic story of a pregnant woman who is declared brain dead after a fall. Focuses on what is to be done with the fetus, which may have suffered brain damage. (25 minutes)

Reuven, Steve. *Especially Wonderful Days: Sing Along Jewish Holiday Songs for the Primary Grades*. A.R.E. Publishing, Inc. Audiocassette.

Songs for young children which teach about the Jewish holidays and other topics.

Seal Upon Thy Heart. Ergo Media Inc. Video.

Portrait of a couple's traditional Jewish wedding. (30 minutes)

The Shidduch. U.S.C. Film School. Video.

An Orthodox woman struggles between tradition and her own inclinations. (5 minutes)

Simchat Chochmah. Sounds Write Productions, Inc. Video.

Documentary about a ceremony created to celebrate a Jewish woman's 60th birthday. (30 minutes)

Sleep My Child: A Collection of Jewish Lullabies Sung in Yiddish, Hebrew, Ladino and English. Sounds Write Productions, Inc. Audiocassette/CD.

A collection of Jewish lullabies.

Solnik, Tanja. *A Legacy of Lullabies*. Sounds Write Productions, Inc. Audiocassette/CD.

A collection of Jewish lullabies.

———. *Lullabies and Love Songs.* Sounds Write Productions, Inc. Audiocassette/CD.

A collection of Jewish lullabies.

Tell Me a Riddle. The Saul Zaentz Center. Video.

An elderly couple rediscovers their love for each other through relationships with others. (90 minutes)

Uncle Moses. Facets Multimedia Inc. Video.

Love and romance in pre-World War I Lower East Side New York. (90 minutes, Yiddish with English subtitles)

When Bad things Happen to Good People. Yale Roe Films, Ltd. Video.

Six persons share the loss they suffered and how they dealt with it. (40 minutes)

Young at Hearts. Outsider Enterprises. Video.

Eight elderly Jewish women discuss life, death, and other issues at their regular card games. (85 minutes)

Alden Films
Box 449
Clarksburg, NY 08510

A.R.E. Publishing, Inc.
3945 South Oneida St.
Denver, CO 80237

Arthur Cantor Films
1501 Broadway #403
New York, NY 10036

Brooks-Antonio
315½ North Sycamore
Los Angeles, CA 90036

Cornell University Audio-Visual
Resource Center
8 Business Technology Park
Ithaca, NY 14850

Davka Corporation
7074 N. Western Ave.
Chicago, IL 60645

Direct Cinema Ltd.
Box 10003
Santa Monica, CA 90410

Ergo Media Inc.
Box 2037
Teaneck, NJ 07666

Facets Multimedia, Inc.
1517 West Fullerton Avenue
Chicago, IL 60614

Anne Flatte
3426 22nd Street
San Francisco, CA 94110

Lee Hirsch
139 West 69th Street
New York, NY 10023

Elaine Holliman
2247 28th Street, Apt. #A
Santa Monica, CA 90405

Jarmaq Productions
8033 Sunset Boulevard, Suite 224
Los Angeles, CA 90046

Modern Sound Pictures, Inc.
Box 710
East Lansing, MI 48826

Museum of Modern Art
Circulating Film/Video Library
11 West 53rd Street
New York, NY 10019

Outsider Enterprises
2940 16th Street, Suite 200-1
San Francisco, CA 94103

Polygram Beneluk
Mozartlaen 27
1217 CM Hilvenswan
The Netherlands

The Saul Zaentz Center
2600 Tenth Street
Berkeley, CA 94710

Sounds Write Productions, Inc.
6685 Norman Lane
San Diego, CA 92120

Swank Motion Pictures
201 South Jefferson
St. Louis, MO 63103

Tara Publications
P.O. Box 707
Owings Mill, MD 21117

UAHC TV & Film Institute
838 Fifth Avenue
New York, NY 10021

United Synagogue Book Service
155 Fifth Avenue
New York, NY 10010

U.S.C. Film School
850 West 34th Street, GT 100
Los Angeles, CA 90089

Women Make Movies
462 Broadway, 5th Floor
New York, NY 10013

Yale Roe Films, Ltd.
90 Park Avenue
New York, NY 10016